MAKERS OF MODERN SOCIAL SCIENCE

KARL MARX

EDITED BY
TOM BOTTOMORE

A SPECTRUM BOOK
Prentice-Hall, Inc.
Englewood Cliffs, New Jersey

Library of Congress Cataloging in Publication Data

BOTTOMORE, T. B.   comp.
    Karl Marx.

    (Makers of modern social science) (A Spectrum Book)
    CONTENTS: Bottomore, T. Karl Marx.—Schumpeter,
J. A. Marx the sociologist.—Berlin, I. Historical
materialism. [etc.]
        1. Marx, Karl, 1818–1883—Addresses, essays, lectures.
2. Dialectical materialism—Addresses, essays, lectures.
I. Series.

HX39.5.B62   335.4′092′4 [B]   73–5887
ISBN 0–13–559716–1
ISBN 0–13–559708–0 (pbk.)

10 9 8 7 6 5 4 3 2 1

PRENTICE-HALL INTERNATIONAL, INC. (*London*)
PRENTICE-HALL OF AUSTRALIA, PTY. LTD. (*Sydney*)
PRENTICE-HALL OF CANADA, LTD. (*Toronto*)
PRENTICE-HALL OF INDIA PRIVATE LIMITED (*New Delhi*)
PRENTICE-HALL OF JAPAN, INC. (*Tokyo*)

CONTENTS

INTRODUCTION

Karl Marx, *Tom Bottomore*   **1**

The Sources of Marx's Thought, 4
The Structure of Capitalist Society, 11
The Theory of Classes, 19
Social Movements and Ideologies, 27
General View of Marxist Sociology, 34
A Note on the Selections, 41

SELECTED ESSAYS ON KARL MARX

ONE	Marx the Sociologist, *J. A. Schumpeter*	43
TWO	Historical Materialism, *Isaiah Berlin*	56
THREE	Concerning the Limitation of the Materialistic Theory of History, *Benedetto Croce*	69
FOUR	The Marxian Synthesis, *Stanislaw Ossowski*	79
FIVE	Class Consciousness, *Georg Lukács*	92
SIX	The Proletariat, *Shlomo Avineri*	102
SEVEN	Ideology, *H. B. Acton*	113
EIGHT	Ideology and Theory, *Leszek Kolakowski*	119
NINE	The Economic and Social Functions of the Legal Institutions, *Karl Renner*	123
TEN	Marx and the State, *Ralph Miliband*	128
ELEVEN	Marx and the "Asiatic Mode of Production," *George Lichtheim*	151
TWELVE	Karl Marx's "Enquête Ouvrière," *Hilde Weiss*	172

SELECTED BIBLIOGRAPHY   185

CONTRIBUTORS   187

INTRODUCTION

MARX'S SOCIAL THEORY was one of the great intellectual achievements of the nineteenth century, comparable—and often compared—with Darwin's theory of evolution. Its remarkable synthesis of ideas from philosophy, history, and the nascent social sciences, the originality of the conceptions which it expressed, were unrivaled in the work of any other contemporary thinker. The theory was unique, moreover, in its close relationship with the political movements of the time. Marx set out to change the world, as well as to interpret it; and his theoretical analysis of the course of social development, especially in the modern capitalist societies, was also intended to have a practical effect by helping to form the consciousness of the industrial working class—the class, in Marx's words, "to which the future belongs."

Yet the very breadth of Marx's synthesis, which he was far from elaborating in all its aspects, and the problems posed by the connections between Marxist theory and Marxist practice through a century of profound social changes have given rise to diverse formulations of the Marxist theory itself. These different, often conflicting, interpretations have been affected both by changing political circumstances and by the piecemeal discovery and publication of some of Marx's manuscripts, which have raised new questions about the development of his thought.[1]

Thus, the *Economic and Philosophical Manuscripts* of 1844, first published in 1932,[2] but not extensively discussed until two decades later,[3] have often been treated as marking a point of transition be-

---

[1] It is a notorious scandal that there does not yet exist a critical, scholarly edition of the complete works of Marx and Engels. Such an edition—*Karl Marx/Friedrich Engels. Historisch–Kritische Gesamtausgabe (MEGA)*—was planned and begun in the 1920s by David Riazanov, the founder and director of the Marx-Engels Institute in Moscow; but Riazanov's dismissal and subsequent disappearance, as one of the early victims of Stalinism, brought the enterprise to an end when only twelve of the projected forty-two volumes had been published.

[2] In an incomplete version in S. Landshut and J. P. Mayer, *Karl Marx. Der historische Materialismus. Die Frühschriften*, and fully in *MEGA*, I/3.

[3] Some scholars recognized their importance at the time, but no general discussion took place. For example, Henry de Man published (in the journal of

tween the "young Marx" and the "mature Marx"—the former a humanist philosopher, the latter the author of a deterministic social theory known as "historical materialism." In the discussion of these manuscripts since the mid-1950s, two main issues have been raised: first, whether the transition does represent a total break in Marx's thought—the replacement of one theoretical scheme by another— or whether there is an underlying continuity of ideas; and second, the nature of the relation in Marx's theory between philosophy and social science, or in a narrower sense, between his socialist aspirations and his analysis of the historical development of the working-class movement in capitalist society.[4]

The widespread discussion of Marx's early writings reflects political as well as intellectual interests. Those who have emphasized most strongly Marx's "humanism" have been engaged in a struggle (which has evolved in many different forms since the crisis marked by the Polish and Hungarian revolts of 1956) against the Stalinist version of Marxism and its expression in political movements and institutions. They have sought deliberately to revise the interpretation of Marx's thought that prevailed from the 1930s to the 1950s by calling attention to other themes in his work, above all his conception of human nature and its needs, and the implicit moral doctrine of human liberation for which it provides a basis; and in so doing they have drawn upon ideas derived from currents of thought outside Marxism—from phenomenology and existentialism or from sociology.

The revision, which is also in part a revival, of Marxist thought has been given a new impetus by the still more recent publication and discussion of Marx's preliminary drafts of *Capital*, published in Moscow from 1939 to 1941 under the title *Grundrisse der Kritik*

---

the Austro-Marxists, *Der Kampf* [1932] an essay entitled "The Newly Discovered Marx," in which he argued that these manuscripts showed ". . . more clearly than any other work the ethical-humanist themes which lie behind Marx's socialist convictions and behind . . . his whole scientific work." In England, H. P. Adams, in *Karl Marx in his Earlier Writings* (London: George Allen & Unwin Ltd, 1940), published an interesting analysis of the manuscripts and other early writings, making use of the *MEGA* edition, but his work was ignored at the time. In the last decade many of Marx's early writings have become available in English translation: see especially T. B. Bottomore, ed., *Karl Marx: Early Writings* (New York: McGraw-Hill, 1963); L. Easton and K. Guddat, eds., *Writings of the Young Marx on Philosophy and Society* (New York: Anchor Books, 1967); D. McLellan, ed., *Karl Marx: The Early Texts* (Oxford: Basil Blackwell, 1971).

[4] For a useful collection of essays and bibliographical references on Marx's early writings, see *Annali*, VII (1964–65).

der politischen Oekonomie (Rohentwurf).[5] This text was first discussed comprehensively, in English, in an essay by Martin Nicolaus,
"The Unknown Marx." [6] Nicolaus argued, first, that the *Grundrisse*
shows a direct line of continuity with the *Economic and Philosophical Manuscripts* insofar as it develops the notion of alienation, and
the analysis of money as a social bond (so that a rigorous separation
of the "young" from the "mature" Marx becomes implausible),[7]
and second, that it formulates, more explicitly than is done in
Capital, Marx's newly gained insight into the fundamental contradiction of capitalist society and the conditions of its breakdown.
On this view, the *Grundrisse* is of crucial importance in providing
the starting point for a comprehensive analysis of the development
of capitalism—such as Marx himself was unable to complete—that
would take account of the social and political factors, as well as
the economic processes, affecting the capacity of capitalism to survive and of socialism to come into existence as a new form of
society.

The controversies over the interpretation of Marx's thought will
not arise in the future, as they have done in the recent past, from
the revelation of new texts; but they are unlikely to subside quickly,
for they are continually reanimated by cultural changes and by the
rise and decline of political movements. Nevertheless, the present
circumstances seem particularly favorable for attempting to assess
the structure and development of Marx's social theory in a more
comprehensive, more dispassionate way. The diverse interpretations
have taken shape in more or less distinct "schools," and they can
now be viewed in the light of our knowledge of the whole corpus of
Marx's major writings. At the same time, many of Marx's conceptions have been absorbed into the general intellectual stock of the

[5] The *Grundrisse* did not attract much attention until a new edition was published after the war by Dietz Verlag (Berlin, 1953). Excerpts were published in
English in T. B. Bottomore and Maximilien Rubel eds., *Karl Marx: Selected
Writings in Sociology and Social Philosophy* (New York: McGraw-Hill, 1964),
where the importance of the manuscripts as outlining a comprehensive study
of modern capitalism, going far beyond an economic analysis, is stressed. Since
then, an English translation of one complete section of the *Grundrisse*, dealing
with precapitalist societies, has been published, with a valuable introduction by
Eric Hobsbawm, under the title *Pre-Capitalist Economic Formations* (New York:
International Publishers, 1964); and a more extensive selection has appeared,
edited by David McLellan, *Marx's Grundrisse* (1971).

[6] *New Left Review*, XLVIII (March–April, 1968).

[7] David McLellan, in the introduction to his selections, advances this as the
principal reason for considering the *Grundrisse* "the centerpiece of Marx's
thought."

social sciences, while Marxism (in any of its versions) as an all-embracing theory of man and society is increasingly questioned, and in varying degrees abandoned, even by those thinkers whose work has been mainly inspired by this tradition, but who now find the Marxist system inadequate especially for understanding the main trends of social development in the late twentieth century.[8]

In the passionate debates of recent years about the proper scope and methods of the social sciences, Marxism has been one of the chief sources of critical and politically radical ideas. But as a theoretical system, it is itself an object of criticism. After a century of turbulent economic and political changes, and in the face of entirely new problems, we have to ask what is still living and what is dead in Marx's theory. I propose to explore this question by looking first at those ideas and preoccupations of Marx's own time that helped to shape his thought; then tracing the stages in the formation of his theory, and examining some of its distinctive elements; and finally considering those aspects of it which remained undeveloped, or which seem questionable in the light of historical experience and of later social thought about that experience.

THE SOURCES OF MARX'S THOUGHT

The earliest intellectual influences upon Marx came from the French Enlightenment and the Revolution.[9] The Rhineland where Marx was born, at Trier in 1818, had been strongly affected by French ideas and became a center of liberal, and even socialist, doctrines in the 1820s and 1830s. Marx's father—described by his granddaughter Eleanor as a "true eighteenth-century Frenchman" who "knew his Voltaire and Rousseau by heart"—was a moderate liberal; and so too was the principal of the high school which Marx attended. His future father-in-law, Ludwig von Westphalen, was

---

[8] See the discussion in Norman Birnbaum's essay, "The Crisis in Marxist Sociology," included in his book *Toward a Critical Sociology* (New York: Oxford University Press, 1971), pp. 94–129; and also the earlier criticisms of Marxism in C. Wright Mills, *The Marxists* (New York: Dell Publishing Co., 1962).

[9] A good short account of Marx's life which gives particular attention to his early environment is that by Werner Blumenberg, *Karl Marx* (1962: English translation, London: New Left Books, 1972). The most comprehensive biography of Marx and Engels is Auguste Cornu, *Karl Marx et Friedrich Engels*, of which four volumes have so far been published (Paris: Presses Universitaires de France, 1955–70).

more radical and had embraced the Saint-Simonian doctrines that were circulating widely in the Rhineland; it was he who introduced Marx to Saint-Simon's writings.

Later at the University of Berlin, another Saint-Simonian, Eduard Gans, the professor of law, had a strong influence upon Marx. In 1836 Gans published a book[10] in which he expounded the ideas of the Saint-Simonians, using phrases which foreshadow those of the *Communist Manifesto*: ". . . amidst all this intellectual confusion the Saint-Simonians have said something of importance, and have put their finger on a public scandal of the day. They have correctly observed that slavery has not really disappeared; though it has been formally prohibited, in practice it still exists in the fullest form. Once there was the opposition between master and slave, then between patrician and plebeian, and later still between feudal lord and vassal; now we have the idle rich and the worker. . . . It will be more necessary now for future history to speak of the struggle of the proletariat against the middle classes." [11]

Marx himself did not become a Saint-Simonian, and he remained sceptical about all the new socialist and communist doctrines until 1843; but the social ethic of the Saint-Simonians—above all their concern with the future of the "poorest and most numerous class" —entered deeply into his outlook, animated his critical attitude toward Hegel's philosophy, and eventually led him into the socialist movement. The extent to which Marx's moral views derived from the humanism and rationalism of the Enlightenment and from the development of Enlightenment ideas in the thought of the early socialists is suggested by a passage in *The Holy Family* (1845) where he observes: "When one studies the materialist theories of the original goodness of man, the equality of intellectual endowment among men, the omnipotence of education, experience, and habit, the influence of external circumstances upon man, the great importance of industry, the value of pleasure, etc., there is no need for extraordinary penetration to discover what necessarily connects them with communism and socialism." [12]

Marx's reservations about the socialist and communist doctrines as he encountered them at the beginning of the 1840s arose mainly

[10] E. Gans, *Rückblicke auf Personen und Zustände* (Berlin, 1836).

[11] Quoted in Blumenberg, *op. cit.*, pp. 45–46.

[12] See, for the whole passage, T. B. Bottomore and M. Rubel, eds., *op. cit.*, p. 243.

from his judgment that while they expressed a new world view they did not connect their moral aspirations with a philosophical or theoretical conception of reality.[13] In his philosophical studies in Berlin Marx had been preoccupied with the problem of the conflict between what is and what ought to be; and in describing the development of his views in a letter to his father[14] he notes that, setting out from the idealism of Kant, Fichte, and Schelling, he had "hit upon seeking the Idea in the real itself" and had arrived at Hegel's system. At this time Marx joined a Hegelian discussion group, the Doctors' Club, in which some of Hegel's disciples, inspired by the ideas of the French Revolution, were attempting to develop his philosophy in a more radical fashion. From these discussions, and from the writings of Feuerbach and other Young Hegelians,[15] several themes emerged which assumed importance in the development of Marx's own thought. One of these was the notion of "praxis," expounded by August von Cieszkowski; in a short book published in 1838 [16] he argued that philosophy should ". . . become a practical philosophy or rather a philosophy of practical activity, of 'praxis,' exercising a direct influence on social life and developing the future in the realm of concrete activity." Far more significant in Marx's development, however, was the work of Ludwig Feuerbach, not only for its exposition of a radical naturalism and humanism, which reinforced Marx's own orientation,[17] but still more for its approach to the criticism of Hegel's philosophy.

[13] As editor of the liberal *Rheinische Zeitung*, Marx replied to an accusation by the *Augsburger Allgemeine Zeitung* that the paper had communist sympathies by declaring: "The *Rheinische Zeitung* does not even concede *theoretical validity* to communist ideas in their present form, let alone desires their practical realization, which it anyway finds impossible, and will subject these ideas to a fundamental criticism."

[14] November 10, 1837. The letter is translated in L. Easton and K. Guddat, eds., *Writings of the Young Marx on Philosophy and Society* (New York: Anchor Books, 1967), pp. 40–50.

[15] For a general account of the milieu and ideas of the Young Hegelians, see David McLellan, *The Young Hegelians and Karl Marx* (London: Macmillan & Co. Ltd., 1969).

[16] August von Cieszkowski, *Prolegomena zur Historiosophie* (Berlin, 1838). See David McLellan, *op. cit.*, pp. 9–11.

[17] Though Marx had some reservations; in a letter to Arnold Ruge, after Feuerbach's essay, "Vorläufige Thesen zur Reformation der Philosophie" was published early in 1843 in the *Anekdota* (edited by Ruge), he commented: "I approve of Feuerbach's aphorisms, except for one point: he directs himself too much to nature and too little to politics. But it is politics which happens to be the only link through which contemporary philosophy can become true."

It was Feuerbach who first "inverted" Hegel's system, transforming
the subject of idealist philosophy (thought) into a predicate, and
the predicate (man) into a subject,[18] a real individual from whose
practical existence philosophical inquiry should begin. Marx went
on to apply this method in his criticism of Hegel's political philosophy.

The crucial period in the formation of Marx's own social theory
is that between March, 1843 (when he resigned as editor of the
Rheinische Zeitung), and the autumn of 1844. During this time
Marx wrote a long critique of Hegel's philosophy of the state,[19]
published his two essays—"On the Jewish Question" and "Contribution to the Critique of Hegel's Philosophy of Right: Introduction"—in the *Deutsch-Französische Jahrbücher*, and composed the
Economic and Philosophical Manuscripts. The most significant aspects of this intellectual development are, first, the formulation of
Marx's conception of the proletariat, and second, the beginning of
his critique of political economy.

A number of writers in France and Germany had already discussed the situation of the proletariat in modern society,[20] but the
most systematic account of this new class was given by Lorenz von
Stein in his book *Der Sozialismus und Kommunismus des heutigen
Frankreich*.[21] There has been much controversy about the extent of
Marx's indebtedness to Stein;[22] it seems likely that he read Stein's
book soon after it was published in 1842, and although this was by
no means his first acquaintance with the ideas of the French socialist
thinkers, Stein's sociological interpretation of the role of the proletariat in industrial society was probably an important influence

[18] See the discussion in Shlomo Avineri, *The Social and Political Thought of
Karl Marx* (Cambridge: Cambridge University Press, 1968), pp. 10–12.
[19] The manuscript was first published in *MEGA*, I, 1/1 (1927), under the title
Kritik des hegelschen Staatsrechts. An English translation has recently been published, edited by Joseph O'Malley, *Karl Marx: Critique of Hegel's 'Philosophy of
Right'* (Cambridge: Cambridge University Press, 1971).
[20] Gans, as I noted earlier, had written of the class struggle of the proletariat;
and there were many other references to this phenomenon, as Avineri shows in
the selection included in this volume (see pp. 102–12 below).
[21] First published in 1842, a second revised and enlarged edition appeared in
1848, and the final version, under the title *Geschichte der sozialen Bewegung in
Frankreich von 1789 bis auf unsere Tage*, in 1850. There is an English translation of major sections of Stein's book, edited with an introduction by Kaethe
Mengelberg, *The History of the Social Movement in France, 1789–1850* (Totowa,
N.J.: Bedminster Press, 1964).
[22] See the discussion by Kaethe Mengelberg, *op. cit.*, pp. 25–31.

in clarifying his own views. At all events the conception of the proletariat as a new political force engaged in a struggle for emancipation had an immense significance, for here Marx at last discovered
the "idea in the real itself." The working-class movement, a new and
striking phenomenon in the political life of modern society, was also
the source of the new social doctrines of socialism and communism.
So Marx could conclude his essay on Hegel's philosophy of right by
proclaiming that the mission of the proletariat as a "universal class"
was to dissolve existing society and bring about a general human
emancipation; he could also express in a more precise way the
philosophy of "praxis": ". . . as philosophy finds its *material* weapons in the proletariat, so the proletariat finds its *intellectual* weapons in philosophy."

But the proletariat, as Marx noted, was a product of the industrial movement; and in order to fully understand its social situation
and role, it would be necessary to study the economic structure of
modern societies and the process of its development. Marx embarked on these new studies all the more willingly since as editor
of the *Rheinische Zeitung* he had been "embarrassed at first . . . in
discussions concerning so-called material interests"; and he was
encouraged, and initially guided, by the work which Engels had
already done in political economy, and had published in an essay,
"Umrisse zu einer Kritik der Nationalökonomie," in the *Deutsch–
Französiche Jahrbücher* (1844). Thus from October, 1843, when he
moved to Paris, until the end of 1844, Marx read voraciously in the
works of the economists—among others J. B. Say, James Mill, List,
Ricardo, and Adam Smith—and filled a series of notebooks with
excerpts from, and critical comments on, their writings.[23]

The first fruits of these studies were the *Economic and Philosophical Manuscripts,* in which Marx embarked on a critique of political economy that was to occupy him for the rest of his life. These
manuscripts mark the transition in Marx's thought from philosophical criticism to a critical social theory—the transformation of philosophical ideas into social concepts. Marx's argument develops two
main themes. First, the Hegelian conception of the spiritual self-
creation of man is reinterpreted in the language of political economy, according to which labor is the source of all wealth. But at
the same time the significance of human labor is more broadly

[23] Published in *MEGA*, I/3, 411–583.

conceived; through his labor man not only creates wealth, but develops his human qualities and a whole form of social life: "It is just in his work upon the objective world that man really proves himself as a *species-being*. This production is his active species-life. By means of it nature appears as *his* work and his reality. The object of labour is, therefore, the *objectification of man's species-life*; for he no longer reproduces himself merely intellectually, as in consciousness, but actively and in a real sense, and he sees his own reflection in a world which he has constructed." [24]

Second, Marx uses the notion of alienation, which Feuerbach had employed to criticize religion, in order to describe a condition of society in which, although the process of labor *should* involve the development of man's human potentialities and the creation of a world of human enjoyment, it actually produced, through private property, acquisitiveness, exchange, and competition, a devaluation and dehumanization of the worker: "We shall begin from a *contemporary* economic fact. The worker becomes poorer the more wealth he produces and the more his production increases in power and extent. The worker becomes an ever cheaper commodity the more goods he creates. The *devaluation* of the human world increases in direct relation with the *increase in value* of the world of things. Labour does not only create goods; it also produces itself and the worker as a *commodity*, and indeed in the same proportion as it produces goods. This fact simply implies that the object produced by labour, its product, now stands opposed to it as an *alien being*, as a *power independent* of the producer. . . . The performance of work appears in the sphere of political economy as a *vitiation* of the worker, objectification as a *loss* and as *servitude to the object*, and appropriation as *alienation*." [25]

All the elements of Marx's theory of society were now present—the moral commitment to a humanist doctrine of progress and human self-realization, which assumed the precise form of a commitment to the socialist movement, the idea of the proletariat as the embodiment of an ideal in the real world, the conception of labor and the system of economic production as generating the forms of society, the notion of private property and alienation as the sources of social antagonisms—and after an interlude in which he wrote, with Engels, a long and rather tedious critique of his former associates among the Young Hegelians,[26] who had remained immured in the sphere of "critical philosophy," Marx began to formulate a positive outline of the general view at which he had arrived. This view was expressed first in *The German Ideology* (1845–46): "This conception of history, therefore, rests on the exposition of the real process of production, starting out from the simple material production of life, and on the comprehension of the form of intercourse connected with and created by this mode of production, i.e. of civil society in its various stages as the basis of all history, and also in its action as the State. From this starting point, it explains all the different theoretical productions and forms of consciousness, religion, philosophy, ethics, etc., and traces their origins and growth, by which means the matter can of course be displayed as a whole (and consequently, also the reciprocal action of these various sides on one another)." [27] Similarly, in a letter written in December, 1846, to P. V. Annenkov, commenting on Proudhon's book *Philosophie de la misère,* Marx set forth succinctly his own outlook: "What is society, regardless of its particular form? The product of men's interaction. Are men free to choose this or that social form? Not at all. Assume a certain stage of development of men's productive powers and you will have a particular form of commerce and consumption. Assume certain levels of development of production, commerce, and consumption, and you will have a particular type of social constitution, a particular organization of the family, of ranks or classes; in short a particular form of civil society. Assume a determinate form of civil society and you will have a particular type of political regime, which is only the official expression of civil society." [28]

The next stage for Marx was to analyze in detail the system of production and to depict its interrelations with the other aspects of social life, especially in the modern capitalist societies; in fact, to carry out the program announced in the preface of the *Economic and Philosophical Manuscripts* where, after completing his study of political economy, Marx proposed to publish his "critique of law, morals, politics, etc. . . . and finally, to present the inter-

[26] *The Holy Family* (1845). English translation by R. Dixon (Moscow: Foreign Languages Publishing House, 1956).
[27] Bottomore and Rubel, eds., *op. cit.*, p. 54.
[28] Marx and Engels, *Ausgewählte Briefe* (Berlin: Dietz Verlag, 1953).

connected whole, to show the relationships between the parts, and to provide a critique of the speculative treatment of this material." [29]

THE STRUCTURE OF CAPITALIST SOCIETY

However, Marx was unable to carry out his youthful plans. The critiques of "law, morals, politics, etc." were never written, except in the form of occasional pieces on current political events,[30] or as fragmentary discussions in manuscripts, notably the *Grundrisse*. Even Marx's analysis of the economic structure of society remained unfinished. After sketching the outlines of his theory of history in *The German Ideology*, and beginning the major work which he referred to as his *Economics*, Marx was then diverted from his studies for the next decade by an active involvement in politics in the revolutions of 1848, and by the journalism in which he had to engage in order to support himself.

Only in 1857 did Marx resume his economic studies seriously; and he then drafted a new plan for his work on political economy, and wrote large sections of it in the thousand-page manuscript of the *Grundrisse*. His plan envisaged a work in six parts, preceded by a methodological introduction in which he established a distinction between "production in general" and the historical forms of production; and in the light of this, examined the categories of political economy—production, consumption, distribution, exchange: "Whenever we speak of production, therefore, we always refer to production at a certain stage of social development, to production by social individuals. Hence, it might appear that in order to speak of production at all we must either trace the historical process of development through its various phases, or else make clear at the outset that we are dealing with a specific historical period, for example, with modern bourgeois production, which is in fact the real theme of this work. But all stages of production have certain features and determining factors in common. *Production in general* is

---

[29] Bottomore and Rubel, eds., *op. cit.*, p. 63.

[30] Especially his articles in the *Neue Rheinische Zeitung* (1848–49), and in the *New York Daily Tribune* (from 1851 to 1862); his Address, on behalf of the General Council of the International Working Men's Association, on the Paris Commune (1871); and his notes on the Gotha Program of the German workers' party (1875).

an abstraction, but a rational abstraction in so far as it highlights
and establishes the common features, thus saving us repetition.
These *general* aspects or common features discovered by comparison
are themselves very complex, and their constituent elements develop
along different lines. Some of these elements belong to all epochs,
others are common to a few. Some are common to the most modern
and to the most ancient epochs. . . . The conditions which regulate production in general must be distinguished in order not to
lose sight of the essential differences within the uniformity which
arises from the fact that the subject—mankind—and the object—
nature—remain the same." [31]

Indeed, Marx devoted a long section of the *Grundrisse* to an
analysis—the most systematic that he ever wrote—of the different
stages of production and the process of economic evolution.[32] But
the main theme, as Marx noted, was modern bourgeois production;
and he proposed to deal with this in six books concerned with capital, landed property, wage labor, the state, foreign trade and the
international relations of production, the world market, and crises.[33]
Only the first of these books was written (even then, not in its complete and final version) and published as *Capital,* although it contained references to many problems that would have been discussed fully in the other books.[34] The *Grundrisse* deals in a preliminary fashion with some of these problems, and reveals more
clearly than does *Capital* the scope of Marx's work, as a study of the
social system of capitalist production rather than a narrowly economic analysis. But this does not exhaust the significance of the
text. It constitutes, as many commentators have pointed out, an
essential link between Marx's early and late writings, revealing the
way in which philosophical ideas were transformed into economic
and sociological concepts; and it provides a much more detailed
account of the trend of capitalist development, the contradictions
that will lead to a breakdown of capitalism, and the conditions for

[31] *Grundrisse,* pp. 6–7. Unless noted otherwise, all translations from the
Grundrisse were made by the editor.

[32] *Grundrisse,* pp. 375–413. English translation in Hobsbawm, ed., *op. cit.,* pp.
67–120.

[33] See Bottomore and Rubel, eds., *op. cit.,* pp. 16–18.

[34] It is evident, for example, that the fragment on social classes which Engels
published as the final chapter of *Capital,* Vol. III, is the draft of an analysis of
classes which was meant to come at the end of the three books dealing with the
"main constituent elements" of bourgeois society—capital, landed property, and
wage labor.

a transition to socialism, than is to be found in the volumes of *Capital*.

Use-Value and Exchange Value

The *Grundrisse* develops in a new way, and through a much more profound critique of political economy, the central concern of the *Economic and Philosophical Manuscripts* with the problem of alienated labor by elaborating the distinction between use-value and exchange value, and by introducing the concepts of "labor power" and "surplus value." Marx characterizes capitalism, in the first place, as a society based upon exchange and the market, in which exchange value predominates over use-value, or to express the same idea in another way (which relates the phenomenon to the system of production): "the product becomes a commodity." Capitalism is a form of society in which money is the social bond: "The universal reciprocal dependence of individuals who remain indifferent to one another constitutes their social bond. This social bond is expressed in *exchange value*. . . . [The individual] has to produce a general product—*exchange value*—or, in its isolated, individualized form—*money*. On the other side, the power that each individual exercises over the activity of others, or over social wealth, is based upon his possession of exchange values, money. He carries his social power and his bond with society in his pocket." [35] The predominance of exchange value, and the power of money, constitutes an alienated form of social life: "The social character of activity, and the social form of the product, as well as the participation of the individual in production, appear here as alien, material things in opposition to the individual; not in their behaviour to each other, but in their subordination to relations which exist independently of them and arise out of the collisions between indifferent individuals. The universal exchange of activities and products, which has become a condition of life for each individual, and the bond between individuals, appears to them as something alien and independent, like a thing." [36]

[35] *Grundrisse*, pp. 74–75.
[36] *Ibid.*, p. 75. The affinity of these passages with the discussion of money in the *Economic and Philosophical Manuscripts* is unmistakable; see Bottomore, ed., *op. cit.*, pp. 189–94. See also Marx's critique of utilitarianism in *The German Ideology*, where he wrote that: "The apparent absurdity which transforms all the various interrelationships of men into the single relationship of utility, an

Marx's analysis of capitalist society as one in which the social bond assumed the impersonal character of a relationship between *things* provided one of the major themes of sociological thought in Germany in the late nineteenth century, although at that time his influence could arise only from the brief references in the essays in the *Deutsch-Französische Jahrbücher,* the *Communist Manifesto,* the criticism of Proudhon in *Misère de la philosophie,* and *Capital* —not from the more extensive discussion in the manuscripts which have subsequently been published. Tönnies' distinction between two types of society, *Gemeinschaft* (community), characterized by direct personal relationships, and *Gesellschaft* (society), characterized by impersonal, especially economic, relationships, was inspired directly by Marx's thought.[37] Similarly, the major study of social relationships in a money economy, Simmel's *Philosophie des Geldes,*[38] was greatly influenced by reflection upon Marx's work. In his study Simmel deals not only with the impersonal character of social life in a developed money economy and the effects of the division of labor in restricting the individual's sphere of life, but also with the positive aspects of modern society—the growth of rationality exemplified by the development of an increasingly abstract measure of value, and the increase of social differentiation with all its possibilities for greater individual freedom. These ideas, however, were not entirely discordant with Marx's view, for he too regarded capitalism as a stage—the most significant stage—in the progress of human reason, and he recognized that it created more favorable conditions for the emergence of individuality: "Relations of personal dependence (at first completely natural and spontaneous [*naturwüchsig*]) are the first forms of society, in which human productivity develops only to a limited extent and at isolated points. Personal independence, based upon dependence on *things,* is the second great form, in which for the first time a system of general social exchange, universal relationships, universal needs, and universal capacities, is established. Free individuality, based upon the

---

apparently metaphysical abstraction, follows from the fact that in modern civil society all relationships are in practice subordinated to the single abstract relationship of money and speculation" (Bottomore and Rubel, eds., *op. cit.,* p. 161).

[37] Ferdinand Tönnies, *Gemeinschaft und Gesellschaft* (1887; English translation, edited by Charles P. Loomis, 1955). Tönnies' relation to Marx can be seen clearly from the study of Marx which he published later, *Marx: Leben und Lehre* (Jena: Lichtenstein, 1921).

[38] Georg Simmel, *Philosophie des Geldes* (Leipzig: Duncker and Humblot, 1900).

universal development of individuals, and the subordination of their communal, social productivity as their own social powers, is the third stage. The second stage creates the conditions for the third." [39]

Labor Power and Surplus Value

The second aspect of alienated labor is analyzed by Marx with the aid of the newly developed concepts of "labor power" and "surplus value." In capitalist society, in which all products and activities are converted into exchange values, labor power itself becomes an exchange value—i.e., a commodity. But it is a commodity very different from others in two ways. First, labor (the realization of labor power) is, as Marx describes it in the *Grundrisse,* "living, purposeful activity," or as he says in the *Economic and Philosophical Manuscripts,* it is "life activity, productive life . . . free, conscious activity," which is the characteristic of man as a species-being. The transformation of labor power into a commodity is an alienation of man's nature that deforms and cripples him.

Second, labor power as the capacity for productive activity has the unique characteristic of being able to create more value than is given in exchange for it. It creates "surplus value," and since this labor power has been acquired by the capitalist through an act of exchange, the surplus value which it produces becomes the property of the capitalist. Thus, Marx concludes, ". . . all the progress of civilization, or in other words every increase in the *social powers of production,* if you want, in the *productive powers of labor itself* —as it results from science, inventions, the division and organization of labor, improved means of communication, the creation of a world market, machinery, etc.—does not enrich the worker, but capital;

---

[39] *Grundrisse,* pp. 75–76. See also the discussion in *The German Ideology*: "But in the course of historical development, and precisely as a result of the assumption of independence by social relationships, which is the inevitable outcome of the division of labour, there emerges a distinction between the personal life of the individual and his life as it is determined by some branch of labour and the conditions pertaining to it. . . . In a system of estates (and still more in the tribe) this is still concealed: for instance, a nobleman always remains a nobleman, a commoner always a commoner, irrespective of his other relationships, a quality inseparable from his individuality. The distinction between the personal and the class individual, the accidental nature of conditions of life for the individual, appears only with the emergence of class, which itself is a product of the bourgeoisie" (Bottomore and Rubel, eds., *op. cit.,* pp. 249–50).

consequently it enhances still more the power which dominates labor, and only increases the productive capacity of capital." [40]

Marx's analysis of labor power as a commodity is intended to show that in capitalist society, in spite of the appearance of equal exchange, surplus value is created and is appropriated by a particular class. In a slave society, or a feudal society, the production and appropriation of surplus value is obvious; the slave works for the slave-owner, the serf works for a part of the year on his lord's demesne. In capitalist society this process takes place in a concealed form, but it still constitutes the basis of the whole social system. As Marx later formulated his general proposition: "The specific economic form in which unpaid surplus labour is pumped out of the direct producers determines the relation of domination and servitude, as it emerges directly out of production itself and in its turn reacts upon production. Upon this basis, however, is founded the entire structure of the economic community, which grows up out of the conditions of production itself, and consequently its specific political form. It is always the direct relation between the masters of the conditions of production and the direct producers which reveals the innermost secret, the hidden foundation of the entire social edifice and therefore also of the political form of the relation between sovereignty and dependence, in short, of the particular form of the State." [41]

It is plain from this analysis that the fundamental opposition in capitalist society, as in previous forms of society, is that between the "masters of production" and the "direct producers." But what is the course of development through which this opposition will reach a point of crisis; what are the conditions in which a social transformation can occur; and what factors will determine the form of a new society? Marx gives diverse answers to these questions. In *Capital* he emphasizes the periodic economic crises which will become increasingly destructive; and it was along these lines that Marxists in the 1930s analyzed what they termed the "general crisis of capitalism." From this standpoint Marx conceived an eventual struggle between the bourgeoisie and a proletariat reduced to a condition of extreme misery. As he expressed it in a well-known passage of *Capital*: "Along with the constantly diminishing number of the magnates of capital . . . grows the mass of misery, oppression,

[40] *Grundrisse*, p. 215.
[41] *Capital*, Vol. III; in Bottomore and Rubel, eds., *op. cit.*, p. 99.

slavery, degradation, and exploitation; but with this too grows the revolt of the working class. . . ." [42]

But in the *Grundrisse* Marx lays stress rather on the development of the *social character* of production within the capitalist system, through the advance of science and technology; and he refers in much vaguer terms to the supersession of capitalism as the process of material production is "divested of its impoverished and antagonistic form," and the conditions of social life are "subjected to the control of the general intellect":

> To the extent that large-scale industry develops, the creation of real wealth comes to depend less upon labor time and the quantity of labor expended, than upon the power of the instruments which are set in motion during labor time, whose powerful effectiveness is likewise unrelated to the labor time directly involved in their production, but depends rather upon the general state of science and the progress of technology, or the application of this science to production. . . . Labor no longer appears as an integral part of the process of production; instead, man acts as the supervisor and regulator of this process. . . . With this transformation, what appears as the mainstay of production and wealth is neither the labor which man directly expends, nor the time he spends at work, but his appropriation of his own general productive powers, his understanding and mastery of nature; in short, the development of the social individual. The *theft of other men's labor time, upon which present-day wealth depends,* appears a miserable basis compared with this new one which large-scale industry has created. As soon as labor in its direct form has ceased to be the great wellspring of wealth, labor time ceases, and must cease, to be its measure, and consequently exchange value must cease to be the measure of use-value. The *surplus labor of the masses* has ceased to be a condition for the development of wealth in general; just as the *nonlabor of the few* has ceased to be a condition for the development of the general powers of the human mind. Production based upon exchange value then collapses, and the process of direct material production is divested of its impoverished and antagonistic form. Individuals can then develop freely . . . and the reduction of necessary social labor to a minimum is accompanied by the development of education in the arts, sciences, etc. for all individuals, through the free time and means which have become available. Capital is itself a contradiction in action, for it strives to reduce labor time to a minimum, while at the same time it posits labor time as the only measure and source of wealth. Thus it reduces labor time in its necessary form in order to augment it in its superfluous form. . . . On one side it brings to life all the powers of science and nature, of social organization and intercourse, in order to make the creation

---

[42] *Capital,* Vol. I; in Bottomore and Rubel, eds., *op. cit.,* p. 141.

of wealth (relatively) independent of the labor time expended on it; but on the other side it wants to use labor time as a measure for the gigantic social powers thus created, and to confine them within the limits which are required in order to maintain already created values as values. Productive forces and social relations—which are different aspects of the development of the social individual—appear to capital only as a means, and are only a means, to produce on its own restricted basis. But in fact they are the material conditions to blow up this basis. . . . The development of fixed capital indicates the extent to which general social knowledge has become a *direct productive force*, and thus the extent to which the conditions of the social life process have themselves been brought under the control of the general intellect and reconstructed in accordance with it.[43]

It can be argued from this exposition in the *Grundrisse,* as Nicolaus has done in his essay "The Unknown Marx," that Marx, far from envisaging the breakdown of capitalism in terms of a revolt by starving, degraded, and oppressed proletarians in the midst of a profound economic crisis, conceived it as a much longer-term process in which, ultimately, the immense productive forces based upon advanced science and technology and directed by educated, technically competent workers, would prove incompatible with the capitalist system, and would, in some manner, "divest" themselves of this social framework.[44] But this conception poses some difficult problems. It is no longer clear how the transition from capitalism to socialism will be made, for the working class, as Marx conceived it in his earlier writings, seems to be progressively eliminated from any important role in the system of production; and thus the principal agent of social transformation vanishes from the scene.

There are two interpretations of social and political evolution that might be derived from Marx's discussion here. One is that the development of technology and the consequent changes in the economic system bring into existence a new class—distinct from the bourgeoisie and the proletariat—composed of the highly qualified technicians and administrators who pass from the domination of the system of production to a struggle for general social power. This would resemble the process in which the bourgeoisie emerged

---

[43] *Grundrisse,* pp. 592–94.

[44] This view has also been formulated positively in the argument that production based upon advanced science and technology is *more* compatible with a socialist form of society, especially in the work by Radovan Richta and his associates, *Civilization at the Crossroads* (White Plains: International Arts and Sciences Press, 1969), which draws extensively upon the discussion in the *Grundrisse.*

as a class, between the feudal landlords and the serfs, in feudal society.

The second interpretation is that the increasingly predominant role of science and technology in production will create the conditions in which the organization and control of production by society as a whole is the essential next stage of development. For on one side, the application of science to production creates immense wealth, making possible high levels of living and greatly increased leisure time; and on the other side, it brings into existence a more educated population whose members can now formulate more clearly the goals of individual self-expression and self-realization. From this viewpoint the creation of a new society can be seen as a long-term process in which, through the progress of the "general intellect," men gradually extend their control over the social conditions that affect their lives. Or, to use an expression which Marx employed in discussing the growth of joint-stock companies, there may be (there may in fact have occurred in the twentieth century) a progressive "abolition of the capitalist mode of production within capitalist production itself."

Neither in the *Grundrisse* nor elsewhere does Marx examine the political implications of these ideas about the future development of capitalist production. His political theory was never expounded in a systematic form. But by looking at its partial formulations in Marx's account of the class structure and in his commentaries on the development of the working-class movement, we may be able to grasp how it would have been worked out in the context of his later economic analysis.

THE THEORY OF CLASSES

The theory of social classes is at the center of Marx's thought. For as he wrote in his early criticism of the Young Hegelians: "*History* does *nothing;* it 'does *not* possess immense riches,' it 'does not fight battles.' It is *men,* real, living men, who do all this, who possess things and fight battles. . . . History is *nothing* but the activity of men in pursuit of their ends." [45] Whatever the contradictions within a given form of society, and whatever abstract forces (such as the progress of science and technology) may be at work, they can only become effective through the conscious, purposive actions of

[45] *The Holy Family;* in Bottomore and Rubel, eds., *op. cit.,* p. 63.

men. And these actions arise out of, are shaped by, the real life experiences of individuals within the division of labor and the class
structure.

The great importance of the concept of class was referred to
earlier, when I noted that Marx's discovery of the proletariat as
the bearer of a social ideal in the world of reality was a crucial
element in the evolution of his thought. In fact, those parts of
Marx's theory of class which are elaborated at all fully concern
particularly the formation and development of the proletariat in
capitalist society. His general view is well set out in *The Poverty of
Philosophy*: "Economic conditions had in the first place transformed
the mass of the people into workers. The domination of capital
created the common situation and common interests of this class.
Thus this mass is already a class in relation to capital, but not yet a
class for itself. In the struggle, of which we have only indicated a
few phases, this mass unites and forms itself into a class for itself.
The interests which it defends become class interests. But the struggle between classes is a political struggle." [46] A similar conception
is formulated in Marx's discussion of the role of the peasantry in
France, in *The 18th Brumaire of Louis Bonaparte*: "The small-
holding peasants form a vast mass, the members of which live in
similar conditions but without entering into manifold relations with
one another. Their mode of production isolates them from one
another instead of bringing them into mutual intercourse. . . . In
so far as millions of families live under economic conditions of
existence that separate their mode of life, their interests and their
culture from those of the other classes, and put them in hostile
opposition to the latter, they form a class. In so far as there is merely
a local interconnection among these small-holding peasants, and
the identity of their interests begets no community, no national
bond and no political organization among them, they do not form
a class." [47]

The proletariat, unlike the peasantry, is a modern—not a traditional—class, created by the growth of large-scale industry, and able,
because of its concentration in factories and towns, to develop a class
consciousness and independent political organizations. Marx emphasizes strongly the distinctive character of modern classes—the
bourgeoisie and proletariat—in relation to earlier social groups such

---

[46] Bottomore and Rubel, eds., *op. cit.*, p. 187.
[47] *Ibid.*, pp. 188–89.

as feudal estates;[48] and the elaboration of his general theory would have required a systematic analysis of the different forms that social classes (in the broad meaning of "class," which refers to all the historical social groups constituted by the "masters of the system of production" and the "direct producers") had assumed in the various stages of social development. As it is, Marx only indicates very briefly some of the specific features of modern classes by suggesting that the conditions of capitalist society permit the rapid development of classes on a national, rather than a local, scale; and at the same time capitalist society brings out more clearly the economic character and interests of the classes. The bourgeoisie and the proletariat are, in this sense, "pure" classes.

However, the most distinctive feature of modern classes is that they are also the "final" classes; and capitalism is, in Marx's words, "the last antagonistic form of society." Just as the third estate abolished estates when it rose to power, so the working class will abolish classes and inaugurate the classless society. This idea of the social mission of the working class runs through Marx's work from his very early writings (the essay on Hegel's philosophy of right in the *Deutsch–Französische Jahrbücher*, 1844)[49] to one of his last publications (the preface to the *Enquête Ouvrière*, 1880).[50] It may well have had, as Avineri argues,[51] a speculative origin, as a reformulation of Hegel's concept of a "universal class"; and Marx certainly attributed this historical importance to the proletariat before he had undertaken any serious analysis of the economic structure of modern society. But it should not be forgotten that Marx was already very familiar with the more empirical writings of the French socialists, especially the Saint-Simonians, and with Lorenz von Stein's study of the situation of the working class in the modern industrial system. His life's work can be regarded as an attempt to show, by an empirical investigation, how the development of modern capitalism necessarily leads to a social transformation in which the working-class movement will abolish all classes.

At all events, this conception has generally been seen as the predominant and distinctive theme of Marx's social theory, so that, as Ossowski observes,[52] it became in a sense "the symbol of his whole

---

[48] See above, pp. 14–15.
[49] See Bottomore, ed., *op. cit.*, pp. 58–59.
[50] See below, pp. 178–79.
[51] See the selection in this volume, pp. 102–12.
[52] See the selection in this volume, pp. 79–91.

doctrine," expressed by such terms as "class point of view." But as I indicated earlier, the theory of modern classes was not expounded systematically by Marx, and the conception that he outlined in a fragmentary way presents both theoretical and empirical problems that appear even within the context of Marx's own analysis of capitalism. In his earlier writings Marx emphasized very strongly the polarization of classes; for example, in *The Communist Manifesto* he asserts that "the epoch of the bourgeoisie possesses . . . this distinctive feature: it has simplified the class antagonisms. Society as a whole is more and more splitting up into two great hostile camps, into two great classes directly facing each other— bourgeoisie and proletariat." But in the unfinished chapter of *Capital,* Vol. III, written much later when Marx was trying to advance from his fundamental economic analysis to an investigation of the social relations that developed from the economic basis, he observed that even in the most highly developed modern society, England, "the class structure does not appear in a pure form. . . . Intermediate and transitional strata obscure the class boundaries even in this case. . . ."

It may be argued, as Ossowski suggests,[53] that Marx was formulating a model of the class structure, an ideal type to which the real social world would gradually conform more closely in the final stage of development of the capitalist system. Even if this view were accepted, it would involve a much more protracted evolution toward the final breakdown of capitalism than Marx envisaged in his writings on class in the period between the 1840s and the 1860s. There is indeed evidence that as he pursued his economic analysis Marx began to conceive a more prolonged development of capitalism; but at the same time there emerged a discrepancy between his political writings (in which he continued to greet every new economic crisis as the harbinger of revolution) and his theoretical investigations. More important, however, is the fact that in his theoretical studies Marx began to sketch a course of social development that directly contradicts the notion of an increasing polarization of classes. The possibility that the intermediate strata in capitalist society would grow, rather than diminish, as a proportion of the population is suggested in a number of ways, and expressed most clearly in a comment on Ricardo in the manuscript of *Theories of Surplus*

[53] See below, p. 82.

Value: "What he [Ricardo] forgets to mention is the continual increase in numbers of the middle classes, . . . situated midway between the workers on one side and the capitalists on the other, who rest with all their weight upon the working class and at the same time increase the social security and power of the upper ten thousand." [54] Elsewhere in *Theories of Surplus Value,* commenting upon Malthus, Marx observes: "His greatest hope—which he himself considers more or less utopian—is that the middle class will grow in size and that the working class will form a continually diminishing proportion of the total population (even if it grows in absolute numbers). That is, in fact, the trend of bourgeois society." [55]

These ideas are developed more fully in the *Grundrisse.* There, especially in the passage which I quoted earlier,[56] Marx seems to envisage a virtual disappearance of the proletariat as he and other nineteenth-century social theorists had generally understood it—the class of manual workers in modern factory industry—at a more advanced stage of capitalist development. The problem which this presents is not that the contradiction between the social character of the production of use-values and the private appropriation of surplus value through exchange is resolved, but that there no longer seems to be a human agency that will bring about the necessary social transformation; and both the process of social change and the form of a new society become unclear. In fact, there is a strong element of technological determinism in the discussion in the *Grundrisse,* as though Marx was insisting that the application of advanced science to production must of necessity bring into existence a society of free and equal individuals. One is tempted to expand another of Marx's more deterministic statements—"The hand mill gives you a society with the feudal lord, the steam mill a society with the industrial capitalist"—by summarizing the doctrine of the *Grundrisse* in the phrase: "The automated mill gives you a classless society."

If Marx had been able to complete his social theory by expounding his theory of classes and his political theory, he would undoubtedly have done so in the same manner as he presented his economic analysis; that is to say, he would have combined a theo-

---

[54] See Bottomore and Rubel, eds., *op. cit.,* pp. 190–91. I have revised my original translation of this passage, which was rather too free.

[55] Translated from the German text in *Werke,* XXVI, iii, 57.

[56] See above, pp. 17–18.

retical discussion with a comprehensive empirical study of the actual development of social classes.[57] Such an investigation would have to deal with three principal sets of problems: (1) the consequences for the class structure, and especially for the polarization of classes, of the rapid increase in productivity and in the size of the surplus, and the concomitant growth of the middle classes; (2) the various cultural and political influences which either favor or impede the development of working-class consciousness, and in particular a revolutionary class consciousness; (3) the conditions which are necessary, beyond the abolition of private property in the means of production, and the disappearance of classes in this sense, to establish the new society of liberated individuals that Marx called "socialism" or "communism."

As to the first of these problems, we can only speculate, on the basis of Marx's brief reference to the "growth of the middle classes," and his discussion in the *Grundrisse,* about what kind of solution he might have proffered. It is obvious that he would not have taken the naïve view, which has sometimes been put forward under the guise of Marxism, that the working class in advanced capitalist societies is to be defined as all those who work for a living and who are not self-employed. Marx clearly meant by the working class the industrial workers who *produce* surplus value; and he distinguished them from the middle classes who *live from* surplus value, but who assist in the realization and distribution of the surplus (and also from various other categories of workers, e.g., domestic servants, whom he described, following Adam Smith and Ricardo, as "unproductive"). The consequences of the growth of the middle classes and the relative (or even absolute) decline in numbers of the working class would seem to strengthen bourgeois rule, as Marx himself notes; and the transition to a socialist society then becomes more problematic. It could be argued, in terms of Marx's own analysis, either that the transition will never be made at all (and that there will emerge from capitalism; a type of society which none of the socialist thinkers had foreseen; or that it will be made in a different way from that which Marx originally expected, through social conflicts in which the working-class movement will be only one— though an important—element. At the extreme, however, as Marx

---

[57] Not only did Marx not accomplish this, but no later Marxist has even attempted a thorough historical and sociological study of modern social classes. What we have, for the most part, is either abstract philosophical discourse or the tedious repetition of political slogans.

sketched the course of capitalist development in the *Grundrisse,* the role of the working class seems to become quite insignificant. It is difficult to interpret Marx's ideas here because of the tentative and fragmentary character of the text; but it seems reasonable to suppose that he had in mind a technologically advanced economy, something we should refer to as "computerized" or "automated," in which a large proportion of the population would be engaged in scientific, technical, and administrative occupations. The nature of the social conflict that would then bring about the breakdown of capitalism and the creation of a socialist society remains unclear, and is not discussed by Marx; but it seems to me that it might take the form suggested by some recent sociological analyses,[58] in which a direct political struggle would develop between those who control the instruments of economic and political decision-making and those who have been reduced to a condition of "dependence." Whether such groups, engaged in a conflict about the future form of society, should be called "classes," is partly a question of terminology, but mainly one to be settled by theoretical and empirical inquiry. They can fit perfectly well within Marx's general scheme of the opposition between the "masters of the system of production" and the "direct producers"; but just as the social classes of nineteenth-century capitalism had to be distinguished from feudal estates, so these new classes would have to be distinguished from the bourgeoisie and proletariat of nineteenth-century theory, even though there may be elements of continuity.

The second problem—concerning the development of class consciousness—has to be examined in the context of the preceding discussion. For the most part, Marx emphasized, especially in his earlier writings, those influences which were favorable to the development of working-class consciousness, though he also recognized, implicitly or explicitly, that there were strong countervailing forces: the dominant position of ruling-class ideas, the effects of social mobility,[59] the growth of the middle classes. But Marx

[58] See especially Alain Touraine, *The Post-Industrial Society* (New York: Random House, Inc., 1971).

[59] In *Capital,* Vol. III, Marx noted that the situation in which ". . . a man without wealth, but with energy, strength of character, ability, and business sense, is able to become a capitalist . . . brings an unwelcome number of new soldiers of fortune into the field, and into competition with the existing individual capitalists . . . also consolidates the rule of capital itself, enlarges its basis, and enables it to recruit ever new forces for itself out of the lower layers of society." See Bottomore and Rubel, eds., *op. cit.,* p. 190.

neglected other powerful influences which have proved to be of great importance. One is the strength of national or ethnic consciousness, not only in the creation of new nation-states in nineteenth-century Europe and of a new rivalry between them, but also in the nationalism of the twentieth century, whether in the form of national liberation movements, conflicts between nations, or social movements based upon national or ethnic groups within existing nation-states.[60] A second influence, which works in quite a different direction, comes from the increasing social differentiation in modern societies (analyzed most fully by Simmel) that is associated with the more complex division of labor and with a growing cultural diversity and individualism. This social differentiation tends to break down the uniformity of working-class consciousness, to create a greater diversity of status positions (which, as Max Weber argued, constitute another form of stratification inhibiting the development of "pure" class antagonism), and to strengthen the influence of the "intermediate strata," or middle classes. The effect of the forces that impede the growth of working-class consciousness, especially a revolutionary consciousness, is naturally greater if there is a long-term trend for the middle classes to increase and the working class to decline in relative or absolute numbers.

An assessment of the strength of these positive and negative influences would require a profound sociological and historical investigation and would be, in fact, a proper continuation of Marx's own work. It is plain enough, however, that the growth of working-class consciousness in the most advanced capitalist countries during the twentieth century has not followed the course that Marx anticipated, at least in his earlier writings. In most of these countries (but not in the United States, which must be regarded as a highly significant exception) there has been a steady development of working-class consciousness, in the sense that independent workers' parties have been formed and have gained the allegiance of a major part of the working class. But in no country has the working class become predominantly revolutionary in outlook—that is to say, deeply committed to bringing about a rapid and radical transformation of society. The high point of revolutionary conscious-

---

[60] Among later Marxist schools only the Austro-Marxists, as might be expected from their situation in the multinational Hapsburg Empire, paid serious attention to the problem of nationalism; the classic study is Otto Bauer, *Die Nationalitätenfrage und die Sozialdemokratie* (Vienna, 1907). For the most part, however, Marxists have continued to neglect or underestimate such phenomena.

ness among workers (at that time even among American workers) was probably in the period just before the First World War, during the war, and immediately afterwards. Since then, the general evolution of the working-class movement has been toward more reformist policies, and there are few indications in the present course of economic and social development that this trend is likely to change abruptly. At all events it is now scarcely possible to conceive the political system of the advanced capitalist countries as fostering the kind of dramatic confrontation between bourgeoisie and proletariat which Marx, especially in his romantic youth, foresaw.

The last set of problems in Marx's theory of class concerns the transition to a socialist society. Occasionally, as I have already indicated, Marx wrote in the language of technological determinism, as if the advance of science and its application to production must necessarily bring into existence a classless, liberated society. But I do not think such passages represent his most profound thought on the processes of social change. Marx's fundamental conception is rather that the advance of science will create both the material conditions (the abolition of scarcity in the satisfaction of basic human needs) and the intellectual or cultural prerequisites (understanding of the means to control and shape social life in order to achieve the maximum of human enjoyment) for a new society.[61] The complex interplay between the development of production, the emergence of new human needs and aspirations, the development of political consciousness, and the formation of organizations to engage in a political struggle would have been the subject of Marx's political theory. Unfortunately this, like the theory of class, can only be examined in the fragmentary, incomplete form in which Marx left it.

SOCIAL MOVEMENTS AND IDEOLOGIES

When nineteenth-century writers referred to "the social movement," they meant the labor movement in its various manifestations[62]— political clubs, trade unions, cooperatives, utopian communities, or mass movements such as Chartism—just as, in referring to "the social question," they meant the labor question, the condition of the industrial working class. Marx too wrote of the labor movement,

---

[61] This is unmistakably a version of the Enlightenment doctrine of the beneficent progress of human reason.

[62] See Lorenz von Stein, *op. cit.*

or workers' movement, but he also used the term "party" for some of its forms; however, it is clear that he was not referring, in the main, to the modern type of political party,[63] and in fact used the term to describe very different kinds of organization.[64] For example, Marx referred to the Communist League (of which he was a member from 1847 to 1852) as "our party," although this was a party only in the sense of a political club, or *société de pensée*. In a different context, he and Engels regarded the Chartist movement as "the first working-men's party of modern times," and saw the Chartist traditions as a possible basis for the creation of a new working-class party in England.

Marx also spoke of "our party" in a more transcendental sense, as Monty Johnstone has noted: "For Marx the party in this sense was the embodiment of his conception of the 'mission' of the working class, concentrating in itself the 'revolutionary interests of society.' . . ."[65] From this standpoint "party" and "class" are identical; the party is simply the class organized for a political struggle, the final stage in the development of the "class for itself." This conception, however, is quite compatible with the view that Marx seems generally to have expressed: namely, that the political development of the working class (its organization, in a broad sense) would give rise to a variety of particular organizations that would be linked together by the class itself, not by a centralized, disciplined party. Thus the Paris Commune, which was not at all the achievement of a party in the modern sense, was described by Marx as "the political form at last discovered under which to work out the emancipation of labor."[66] The predominant theme of all Marx's writing on the development of working-class politics is that it should result in the creation of autonomous organizations, inde-

---

[63] Only towards the end of Marx's life did the German workers' party begin to develop some of the characteristics of the modern mass party, and it was mainly Engels who observed and commented on this development. See J. P. Nettl, "The German Social-Democratic Party 1890–1914 as a Political Model," *Past and Present*, XXX (1965), 65–95.

[64] There has been surprisingly little discussion of Marx's ideas about the nature of a working-class party, partly no doubt because of the preeminence which the Bolshevik Party acquired as a universal model. One useful review of the subject is Monty Johnstone, "Marx and Engels and the Concept of the Party," *The Socialist Register* (London: Merlin Press, 1967), pp. 121–58.

[65] *Ibid.*, p. 129.

[66] *The Civil War in France* (London: Edward Truelove, 1871). It was first published anonymously.

pendent of the bourgeois parties and movements; it would not necessarily culminate in the establishment of a single supreme organization that would direct the whole working-class struggle.

Marx did not live to see the full development of mass political
parties, and so he did not have to confront, in its most acute form,
the problem of a divergence between the party as an organization,
with its central offices, funds, newspapers and journals, and large
numbers of officials, and the class as a potential community or social
movement. When, later, Michels analyzed the socialist parties, particularly the German Social Democratic party, he concluded that
there is an inescapable concentration of power at the top, or "oligarchy," in all large-scale organizations, and a consequent division
of interest between the leaders and officials and the masses that have
combined to form the party.[67] The interests of the officials, Michels
says, "are always conservative, and in a given political situation
these interests may dictate a defensive and even a reactionary policy
when the interests of the working class demand a bold and aggressive policy." [68] Michels buttressed his argument by analyzing what
he called the "incompetence of the masses," who in his view "are
incapable of taking part in the decision-making process and desire
strong leadership." This is quite similar to the conception that
Lenin formulated, though from a different perspective and in a
different context, which also established a strong distinction between party and class by asserting that the working class by itself
can never attain more than a "trade union consciousness" (i.e., a
preoccupation with immediate economic questions) and that a revolutionary consciousness has to be brought to the working class from
outside, by the Marxist theorists of the party. This notion, which
Lenin expressed in practical political terms, was elaborated in a
philosophical argument by Georg Lukács as one of the central
themes in his distinctive interpretation of Marxism; in the form of
a distinction between a "psychological consciousness" (the empirically given consciousness of workers) and an "imputed rational consciousness," which Lukács also described as "the correct class con-

[67] Robert Michels, *Political Parties* (1911; English translation, New York: The
Free Press, 1966).
[68] In the second edition of his work (1915) Michels observed that the actions
of the German Social Democratic leaders in abruptly reversing their policy and
supporting the war provided an effective confirmation of what he had said about
the future of socialist parties.

sciousness of the proletariat and its organizational form, the communist party." [69]

The arguments of Lenin and Lukács (influenced in one case by
the backwardness of Russian society, and in the other by the failure
of the European revolutions after 1917) seem to me historically false,
since the working-class movement had already arrived at socialist
ideas before Marx himself became a socialist or worked out his social
theory; they are also inconsistent with the fundamental orientation
of Marx's own thought, which places the main emphasis upon a
spontaneous development of working-class consciousness. Nevertheless, these arguments, like those of Michels, raise serious problems
that remain largely unexplored in Marx's work, and which have
received less attention than they merit from later Marxist writers.
There are two principal issues to consider. One concerns the relation of the party as an organization to the class—the problems of
leadership, of the role of a revolutionary elite, of oligarchy and bureaucracy. Michels' view of the dominant position of party leaders
and officials and the "incompetence of the masses" was based partly
upon a consideration of the profound differences of education and
culture that separated the leaders from the rank-and-file members
and from the working class as a whole. Another socialist thinker,
Waclaw Machajski, expounded this line of thought still more force-
fully, again with particular reference to German social democracy,
by arguing that the socialist movement actually expressed the ideology of dissatisfied intellectuals, and that its outcome would be the
creation of a new ruling class of intellectuals—though he continued
to believe that a classless society might still be attained eventually
as a result of a general improvement in the level of education and
culture.[70] It is worth noting that the few Marxists who have responded to Michels' argument have likewise attached great importance to the development of popular education and culture;
Bukharin,[71] for example, argued that the "incompetence of the
masses" was a product of economic and technical conditions

[69] See the selection below, pp. 92–101. I have outlined a criticism of Lukács'
argument in my essay "Class Consciousness and Social Structure," in Istvan
Mészáros, ed., *Aspects of History and Class Consciousness* (London: Routledge &
Kegan Paul Ltd., 1971).

[70] W. Machajski, *The Intellectual Worker* (in Russian, 1905). The argument of
the book is summarized in Max Nomad, *Rebels and Renegades* (New York: The
Macmillan Company, 1932).

[71] Nicolai Bukharin, *Historical Materialism: A System of Sociology* (1921; English translation, New York: International Publishers, 1925).

". . . expressing themselves in the general culture and in educational conditions," and would disappear in a socialist society. It might be claimed—going beyond Bukharin's argument, which deals only with the situation *after* the revolution—that a high level of general education is a *precondition* for the social transformation which will create a socialist society; and this accords quite well with Marx's own ideas about the course of social and intellectual development in an advanced capitalist society as they are sketched in the *Grundrisse*.[72] But such ideas are still not adequate to dispose of the problem raised by Michels; for his main argument was that the very structure of large organizations engenders a bureaucratic style, a dominant elite group, and a sharp division between the leaders, the rank-and-file members, and even more the class as a whole. This is a problem which Marx himself, as I have said, did not have to confront, but it has become ever more acute for later Marxist thinkers, for a variety of reasons. One is that the scale and complexity of organizations in modern societies has greatly increased since Marx's time, so that the question of mass participation and control has itself become more complex and difficult. Another is that the oligarchic tendencies in working-class political parties have appeared in new, and still more blatant forms; these phenomena have now to be studied not only in the social democratic type of party, but also in the Bolshevik type in a single-party political system. And because Marxism itself was dominated for decades by the Bolshevik ideology, there is still no serious Marxist political sociology capable of analyzing systematically, by theoretical and empirical investigations, these aspects of present-day society.

The second important issue raised by the ideas of Lenin and Lukács on the development of working-class consciousness concerns the relation between class, political doctrine, and social theory—and in a general way, the role of intellectuals in the working-class movement. There seems to me little warrant in Marx's own writing for the view that a working-class party has to become a "Marxist" party. Indeed, late in life Marx explicitly dissociated himself from some of the attempts to create such parties, especially in France, by declaring that he himself was not a "Marxist." Marx's theory of society would, of course, influence working-class consciousness and enter in various ways into the political doctrines of the working

[72] See above, p. 17. Among later Marxist writers Antonio Gramsci and the Austro-Marxists, with their particular interest in the development of workers' education, gave most attention to these cultural questions.

class; as a theory, however, its principal object was to reveal the nature of class relations in capitalist society, to analyze the economic and social tendencies in the development of capitalism, and to show the working class as an independent political force engaged in conflict with existing society. The manner in which the working class in each particular society would become organized as a political movement, and the form in which it would express its opposition to capitalism and its aspirations for a new society, would depend upon cultural traditions and historical circumstances; and its doctrine would necessarily go beyond any science, since it would embrace an imaginative vision of the society of the future.

Marx clearly distinguished between scientific theory and social doctrine (or ideology) in his critique of political economy; the bourgeois economic doctrines were certainly ideological, in the sense of presenting a distorted, misleading picture of capitalist society, but at the same time the political economy of Adam Smith and Ricardo was a genuine theoretical science. The distinction is set in a historical context. Marx's view seems to be that a rising class (for example, the bourgeoisie in feudal society) is able to develop, through its representative intellectuals, a realistic science of society, whereas the social thought of a class that is established in power becomes more ideological as the need emerges to conceal the special interests and privileges of the rulers and to prevent social changes which would diminish their power.[73] From this point of view it can be said that Marx's theory stands in the same relation to the proletariat as classical political economy stood to the bourgeoisie. But further: the Bolshevik ideology can then be seen as the doctrine of a new dominant class, resembling the vulgar apologias for capitalism which in Marx's judgment had succeeded the classical works of political economy. Of course, this historical development is not what Marx himself expected. He seems to have conceived the future socialist society as having a thoroughly rational and scientific character so that men's social relationships, and their relation to nature, would be more or less completely transparent and accessible to reason, while the scope of ideological thought, with its distorting influence, would be severely restricted if not eliminated altogether.

It needs to be emphasized that although Marx discussed theory and ideology in their historical context, the distinction that he made

[73] This is not a matter of *conscious* deception. Marx always emphasized that the production of ideology is a social and cultural process that occurs without individual thinkers being aware of it.

between them had an absolute and universal character. Marx undoubtedly believed that genuine theoretical progress was possible in the science of society, and that he himself had contributed to this progress through his discoveries in political economy—a science which, as he observed to Engels, had not advanced since the time of Adam Smith and Ricardo until his own work was undertaken. There is a profound difference, therefore, between Marx's outlook and the later interpretations of Marxism by Lukács or Karl Mannheim. For in Lukács' essays in *History and Class Consciousness* the distinction between theory and ideology becomes blurred, and Marxist theory is presented mainly in its ideological form by being identified with the class consciousness of the proletariat. And in Mannheim's principal contribution to this problem, *Ideology and Utopia,* the distinction is explicitly dissolved in a conception that makes all social thought, including Marxism, inescapably ideological—that is, endowed with a particular, biased orientation because of the thinker's social position.[74]

Marx's thought, which separates yet connects theory and ideology, and relates both to the development of classes, presents a number of difficulties that require critical examination.[75] One such difficulty concerns the role of social classes as the sole or principal source of ideologies. If we characterize an ideology, following Kolakowski's usage[76] (which I think represents quite faithfully the intention of Marx's thought), as the sum of conceptions by means of which a social group systematizes its values, then it is evident that there are many potential sources of ideology—ethnic and linguistic groups, occupational groups, generations, groups resulting from cultural or regional affinities and traditions, as well as social classes —and the question of where ideologies do mainly originate has to be settled by empirical study, not by conceptual discussion or philosophical reflection. I have already drawn attention to the importance of nationalist movements and ideologies; and in the past two decades many other social movements and ideologies have developed from very diverse social groups that are quite distinct

[74] In a confused way, however, Mannheim retained a vestigial hope (which became stronger in his later writings) that ideology could be transcended in a more comprehensive, more objective synthesis that might be achieved by a particular social group in which all the diverse streams of thought came together, the "socially unattached intelligentsia."

[75] Some of the problems are treated in the selections from H. B. Acton and Leszek Kolakowski; see below, pp. 113–18 and pp. 119–22.

[76] See p. 119 below.

from, or only loosely connected with, social classes (e.g., the student movement, women's liberation, the Black Power movement). Moreover, it can well be argued that the production of ideology is unlikely to come to an end even in a classless society as long as any differentiated social groups continue to exist.[77]

Other difficulties arise concerning the role of intellectuals—the "thinking" representatives of classes or other groups who actually construct theories and ideologies. Marx's political theory makes use of an analogy between the rise of the bourgeoisie in feudal society, and the rise of the proletariat in capitalist society, but in several respects the analogy is not exact. So far as the intellectuals are concerned, the main difference is that while the intellectual representatives of the bourgeoisie were themselves, for the most part, bourgeois, and participated directly in the social life that they expressed in thought, those of the proletariat—the socialist intellectuals—are not proletarians; and there emerges a potential divergence between the practical life and aspirations of the working class and the interpretation of that life in socialist doctrines. This situation makes plausible Lenin's idea that a socialist consciousness is brought to the working class from outside, and on the other hand, the view of Machajski and others that socialism is after all only the ideology of the intellectuals in their struggle for political dominance.[78]

GENERAL VIEW OF MARXIST SOCIOLOGY

The preceding discussion will have suggested the complexity of the problems confronting any attempt to analyze the relations, of dependence or mutual influence, between the development of a system of production, the formation of classes, and the crystallization of interests and values (of classes and other social groups) in political movements and doctrines. The immense historical significance of Marx's thought is that it formulated these problems in such a manner as to create a "wholly new attitude to social and historical questions," [79] and to open up entire new fields of social inquiry.

[77] There is an interesting discussion of this question in the book by Radovan Richta, *Civilization at the Crossroads,* which I mentioned earlier (p. 18 above, note 44).

[78] Or as might now be said, of the experts and managers as a "new class" or elite. See especially, on this subject, Milovan Djilas, *The New Class* (New York: Frederick A. Praeger, Inc., 1957).

[79] Isaiah Berlin; see the selection on pp. 56–58 below.

To a large extent these new fields constituted the domain of sociology; and it is not surprising, therefore, that Marxism came to be regarded, at the end of the nineteenth century, as a system of sociology.[80] At all events there can be no doubt about the extent of Marx's influence upon the formation and development of sociology. In some degree almost all the classical thinkers—Tönnies, Max Weber, Simmel, Michels, Pareto, and Mosca[81] were affected by Marxism, either in the elaboration of their whole problematic (as is largely the case with Weber), or in their selection of particular crucial problems (for example, in Pareto's theory of elites). But this is not to say that there was any notable development of an independent Marxist sociology. On the contrary, as the problems which Marx had posed were absorbed into the mainstream of sociology and became objects of study from perspectives quite different from that of Marx himself, Marxist thinkers began to distinguish more sharply between Marxism and any kind of sociological theory; and they were encouraged in this direction by the increasingly political character of Marxism as it became the official doctrine of organized parties.

Only a few Marxist thinkers attempted to present and develop Marx's thought as a sociological theory. Among them the most talented and consistent were the Austro-Marxists, and in particular, so far as purely theoretical questions are concerned, Max Adler.[82] According to Adler, Marx's great discoveries were: first, the concept of man as a social being, or "socialized humanity," which laid the basis for a general social science on the same level as the natural sciences;[83] second, the notion of social evolution as a sociological

[80] It was treated from this point of view by Tönnies and others at the first international congress of sociology (*Annales de l'Institut International de Sociologie,* ed. René Worms, Vol I [Paris, 1895]); and Georges Sorel examined at length the differences between the social theories of Durkheim and Marx in an essay, "Les théories de M. Durkheim," published in *Le Devenir social* (Paris, Nos. 1 and 2 [April and May, 1895]).

[81] Durkheim is the outstanding exception. His sociological theory was developed in quite a different context of ideas, deriving from Comte and positivism, and from the conservative reaction to the French Revolution; and within his own cultural tradition he had little occasion to confront the Marxist theory.

[82] There is still no adequate account of the Austro-Marxists in English, and this whole school of thought has been quite unjustifiably neglected. Some of Adler's major writings on social theory have been republished recently under the title *Soziologie des Marxismus,* 3 vols (Vienna, 1964), but they are not available in English.

[83] In the tenth thesis on Feuerbach, Marx asserts that "the standpoint of the new materialism is human society or socialized humanity."

category, derived by a transformation of the philosophical idea of development; third, the conception of human society as an antagonistic unity, divided by the class struggle, which also constitutes the driving force in social change. Adler's exposition is distinctive because of his emphasis upon Marxism as a social science that conceives human behavior as law-governed and strives to formulate social laws, and at the same time his effort to find a place for purposive behavior. His chief preoccupation is the logic of Marxism, and within this framework he poses and attempts to resolve the problems of causation and teleology, of the differences between the natural and social sciences, with which Max Weber, similarly, was wrestling at this time. The strong emphasis upon Marxism as a social science, which needs to be consolidated and extended, led the Austro-Marxists to undertake investigations that still deserve attention for their combination of theoretical analysis and empirical reference. Among these studies are Otto Bauer's work on nationality,[84] and Karl Renner's examination of law in capitalist society, which remains one of the very few serious contributions to an analysis of the relationship between the economic structure and the sphere of ideology.[85]

The other main attempt to expound Marxism as a sociological theory is Bukharin's popular textbook, *Historical Materialism,*[86] which also discusses, though in a less profound way (and drawing upon Max Adler's work), the problems of causation and teleology. One of the most interesting aspects of Bukharin's book, which has also been undeservedly neglected (mainly for political reasons, after his condemnation and execution by Stalin), is that it deals seriously with other sociological theories and with the criticisms of Marxism that arise from them, and attempts to meet these criticisms in a scientific way.[87]

Bukharin's work, though neglected in substance, is known through two critical essays by Lukács and Gramsci.[88] These essays

[84] See above, p. 26, note 60.
[85] See the selection on pp. 123–27 below.
[86] See above, p. 30.
[87] For example, Michels' analysis of oligarchy (see above, p. 31), and Max Weber's account of the Protestant ethic and the origins of capitalism.
[88] Lukács' review, published in 1925, appears in an English translation under the title "Technology and Social Relations" in *New Left Review*, XXXIX (1966). Gramsci's discussion of the book, written in prison, has been published in English in Quintin Hoare and Geoffrey Nowell Smith, eds., *Selections from the Prison Notebooks of Antonio Gramsci* (London: Lawrence and Wishart, 1971), pp. 419–72.

provide a convenient starting point for considering the opposite view, in which Marxism is treated as a philosophy ("historical materialism") characterized by a distinctive method (the "dialectic"), and is contrasted with sociology as a "positive science" employing a natural science method. Thus Lukács writes of Bukharin that as a "necessary consequence of his natural-scientific approach, sociology . . . develops into an independent science with its own substantive goals. The dialectic can do without such independent substantive achievements; its realm is that of the historical process as a whole, whose individual, concrete, unrepeatable moments reveal its dialectical essence precisely in the qualitative differences between them and in the continuous transformation of their objective structure. The *totality* is the territory of the dialectic. A 'scientific' general sociology, on the other hand, . . . must have its own independent substantive achievements allowing only one kind of law." The criticism is clear (and Gramsci's argument follows a similar course); it is directed against a positivistic sociology which would express regularities of social behavior in causal laws. However, sociology has rarely been developed in an extreme positivist manner; and many sociological thinkers have been concerned above all with the fundamental problem of the possibility, or scope, of causal explanation as against the interpretation of purposive action in the social sciences. As I have shown, Max Adler was preoccupied with this question, and it is raised more briefly in Bukharin's book.

Lukács and Gramsci, however, go to the other extreme and present the dialectic in a stark contrast with a presumed positivistic sociology; and they do this in a highly abstract way so that the actual method which they call dialectic—the selection of problems, the rules of evidence, the procedures for testing empirical propositions, and so on—remains obscure.[89] Marx himself never expounded his methodological views in the manner of Durkheim or Weber, and we cannot be sure how he would have dealt with the problems of method that have become the subject of later discussion. Nevertheless, I think it can be claimed—partly on the basis of Marx's references to the empirical nature of his studies, and to the similarities between the natural sciences and his own social science—that he regarded his work as the construction of an empirical science, not as a new form of "critical philosophy." And there is one fairly long

[89] István Mészáros' study, *Lukács' Concept of Dialectic* (London: Merlin Press, 1972), throws light on one aspect of the method, the conceptualization of problems, but not on the nature of its proofs.

passage on method which seems to confirm this claim directly. In his preface to the second German edition of *Capital* in 1873, Marx responded to some of the criticisms of his work, especially those which alleged that it had a metaphysical character, by quoting and commenting upon the observations made by a Russian reviewer[90] of the first edition: "After quoting from . . . the preface to my *Zur Kritik der politischen Oekonomie,* Berlin, 1859, in which I set forth the materialist foundation of my method, the writer continues as follows: 'For Marx, only one thing is important: to discover the laws of the phenomena he is investigating. . . . Consequently, Marx is concerned with only one thing: to show by exact scientific investigation the necessity of a definite and orderly succession in social conditions, and to establish, as accurately as possible, the facts that serve him as the starting point and grounds for his views. For this purpose it is quite enough if he proves, at one and the same time, the necessity of the present order and the necessity of another order into which the first must inevitably pass, regardless of whether men believe it or do not believe it, are conscious or unconscious of it. Marx regards the social movement as a natural sequence of historical phenomena, governed by laws which are not only independent of the will, the consciousness, and the purposes of men, but on the contrary, determine their volition, consciousness, and purposes.' . . . When the writer describes so aptly . . . the method I have actually used, what else is he describing but the dialectical method?" If this *is* the dialectical method, then it is scarcely distinguishable from the method of all empirical science. Of course, it raises all the problems with which studies in the logic of the social sciences have been concerned for the past century (and which Max Adler analyzed within Marxist thought), and it is open to anyone to argue that such a scientific method is inappropriate for the study of human behavior; but he should not then pass off his views as being those of Marx himself.

What distinguishes Marx's social theory is not a unique method; nor is it the preeminence of a concept such as "totality," upon which Lukács lays so much stress, for this idea has had an important place in almost all sociological thought. The distinctive feature is a particular conception of the scope and main problems of a general social science. Unlike other sociological systems that treat society as

---

[90] The review, published in a St. Petersburg journal, *Vestnik Evropy,* No. 4 (1872), was written by I. I. Kaufmann, a professor at the University of St. Petersburg, whom Marx later described in a letter as "my very intelligent critic."

an autonomous subject and take its existence in the natural world as something given, Marx's theory is based firmly upon the idea of a relationship between society and nature. Its fundamental concept is "human labor," viewed in a historical perspective; it is the developing interchange between man and nature, which at the same time creates, and progressively transforms, social relationships among men. From this notion of labor, worked out for the first time in the *Economic and Philosophical Manuscripts*,[91] all the principal categories of Marx's social thought can be derived: the system of production, the division of labor, the alienation of labor, the formation of classes, the development of political movements and ideologies. Equally, Marx's conception of the future socialist society is expressed in terms of the same fundamental idea, for in the passage on freedom and necessity in the third volume of *Capital* he writes that: "Freedom in this field [of material production] cannot consist of anything else but the fact that socialized mankind, the associated producers, regulate their interchange with nature rationally, bring it under their common control, instead of being ruled by it as by some blind power . . .";[92] and the discussion of science and technology in the *Grundrisse* is only an elaboration of this theme.

In Marx's conception there is not a one-sided determinism of society by nature, or of nature by society, but an interchange and a mutual influence. Moreover, as social relations develop and cultural forms are elaborated in more complex ways, the various elements of social life assume the appearance, and to some extent the reality, of independent existence; and the general notion of human labor and production can provide only a guide for an analysis in detail of the interrelationships.[93] Thus, in assessing Marx's social

[91] See especially the section, "Private Property and Communism," where Marx writes, ". . . for socialist man, the *whole of what is called world history* is nothing but the creation of man by human labor, and the emergence of nature for man . . ." (Bottomore, ed., *op. cit.*, p. 166). There is an excellent discussion of the crucial importance of this notion of human labor in Alfred Schmidt, *The Concept of Nature in Marx* (1962; English translation, London: New Left Books, 1971), especially Chapter 2.

[92] Bottomore and Rubel, eds., *op. cit.*, pp. 254-55.

[93] As Marx observed in the course of discussing the fundamental relationship between the "masters of production" and the "direct producers": "This does not prevent an economic basis which in its principal characteristics is the same, from manifesting infinite variations and gradations, owing to the effect of innumerable external circumstances, climatic and geographical influences, historical influences from the outside, etc. These variations can only be discovered by analyzing these empirically given circumstances" (*Capital*, Vol. III; see Bottomore and Rubel, eds., *op. cit.*, pp. 99-100).

theory we have to distinguish between questions concerning the value of his general approach and fundamental concepts, and questions concerning the truth or falsity of his empirical propositions (and those of later Marxists) about particular forms of society at definite stages in their development. As to the first, it is difficult to dissent from Max Weber's judgment on the "materialist conception of history": "The analysis of social and cultural phenomena from the particular aspect of their economic conditioning and significance was a creative and fecund scientific principle . . . and will remain so for a long time to come." [94] This is not to say that the principle or approach itself is incapable of any further development and modification, or that it can be accepted dogmatically without any confrontation with alternative principles and approaches, especially as these have been formulated in sociology since Marx's time.

In the last resort the value of the principle is shown by the research it stimulates, and the problems it solves. Here we must ask how well established are Marx's empirical propositions—mainly about the development of capitalist society; whether some of them have to be substantially revised; and if so, how this might affect the basic principles of the Marxist approach. Finally, we must ask whether there has been any significant extension of Marx's "new science" to those aspects of social life which he himself was unable to study with any thoroughness, or to the massive historical changes, including the emergence of "postcapitalist" or "socialist" societies, which have occurred since the end of the nineteenth century. In this field, as I showed earlier, major criticisms can be formulated which, if they do not refute, at least cast doubt upon some of Marx's statements and raise a host of new problems. But perhaps the most serious criticism of all is that, in the course of the twentieth century, the scientific development of Marx's theory seems to have come to a stop. Where is an analysis of modern capitalism to be found that can be set beside Marx's *Capital*? Where is the Marxist theory of classes developed on the basis of profound historical and sociological research? Where is any Marxist theory at all of modern political parties? The questions could be multiplied. In the past few decades Marxist theory has assumed, in some circles, an increasingly metaphysical and dogmatic character as a result of a one-sided emphasis upon the philosophical context of Marx's thought;

[94] Max Weber, "Objectivity in Social Science and Social Policy" (1904), English translation in Max Weber, *The Methodology of the Social Sciences*, edited by Edward A. Shils and Henry A. Finch (New York: The Free Press, 1949).

while elsewhere it has become immured within the sphere of methodological disputation. Only as the inspiration of a "critical outlook," not as a science of society, does it seem to bear upon the real features of social development in the present age. If the intention of Marx's thought can properly be interpreted (and this is my own view) as the foundation of a general social science—a sociology, then it must be said that this Marxist sociology has still to be constructed. The task may prove impossible and may lead in the end to a scheme of thought quite different from Marxism; and if the construction is to be attempted at all, a profound reorientation of Marxist thought as it now exists will be needed.

A NOTE ON THE SELECTIONS

The vast literature on Marx and the very diverse interpretations of his thought render exceptionally difficult a choice of writings that will adequately represent the range of his theory, the distinctive ideas that it has contributed to social science, and the problems that it poses to its critics and defenders. Any selection can hardly escape being itself another interpretation. However, I have included texts written from very different standpoints, by Marxists and non-Marxists; and I have chosen them for the contribution they make to understanding the fundamental conceptions of Marx's theory.

The first three selections discuss the general conceptual framework of "historical materialism" in its relation to the philosophy of history and to sociology. They draw attention to the difficulty of interpreting Marx's theory, especially because, as Croce notes, the doctrine was not embodied in a classical and definitive book; and they show how different emphases (arising very largely out of the intellectual formation and interests of the interpreter himself) can result in the theory being portrayed as more philosophical or more sociological in its orientation.

The following three selections deal with the central concept of class, and consider, from different points of view, how Marx's notion of class was developed, what theoretical difficulties it presents, and in what ways it needs to be extended, systematized, or revised. These texts, and especially Lukács' discussion of class consciousness, lead on to the question of ideology, which is discussed in general terms in the selections by Acton and Kolakowski, and then illustrated by an excerpt from Renner's pioneering study of the economic and social foundations of law.

The last three selections concern some particular aspects of Marx's theory that have been unduly neglected. The study by Miliband presents in a coherent form Marx's scattered reflections on the state, and elicits from them a view of his political doctrine. Lichtheim analyzes Marx's conception of the "Asiatic mode of production," which has been a source of problems and controversies in the interpretation of Marx's theory of social development; and in the course of this analysis he makes some illuminating comments on the general Marxist conception of stages in the development of society. Finally, Hilde Weiss's introduction to Marx's *Enquête Ouvrière* supplies a much-needed emphasis upon the persistent strand of empiricism in Marx's work, and at the same time poses the problem, over which controversy has raged again in the past decade, of the relation between science and criticism in social research. It provokes further reflection on a question that has been too often ignored—namely, what would be the distinctive character of Marxist sociological research?

ONE

MARX THE SOCIOLOGIST.

J. A. SCHUMPETER

. . . German-trained and speculative-minded as [Marx] was, he had a thorough grounding and a passionate interest in philosophy. Pure philosophy of the German kind was his starting point and the love of his youth. For a time he thought of it as his true vocation. He was a Neo-Hegelian, which roughly means that while accepting the master's fundamental attitudes and methods he and his group eliminated, and replaced by pretty much their opposites, the conservative interpretations put upon Hegel's philosophy by many of its other adherents. This background shows in all his writings wherever the opportunity offers itself. It is no wonder that his German and Russian readers, by bent of mind and training similarly disposed, should seize primarily upon this element and make it the master key to the system.

I believe this to be a mistake and an injustice to Marx's scientific powers. He retained his early love during the whole of his lifetime. He enjoyed certain formal analogies which may be found between his and Hegel's argument. He liked to testify to his Hegelianism and to use Hegelian phraseology. But this is all. Nowhere did he betray positive science to metaphysics. He says himself as much in the preface to the second edition of the first volume of *Das Kapital,* and that what he says there is true and no self-delusion can be proved by analyzing his argument, which everywhere rests upon social fact, and the true sources of his propositions none of which lies in the domain of philosophy. Of course, those commentators or critics who themselves started from the philosophic side were unable to do this because they did not know enough about the social sciences involved. The propensity of the philosophic system-builder, moreover, made them averse to any other interpretation but the one which proceeds from some philosophic principle. So they saw philosophy in the most matter-of-fact statements about economic experience, thereby shunting discussion on to the wrong track, misleading friends and foes alike.

Marx the sociologist brought to bear on his task an equipment which consisted primarily of an extensive command over historical and contemporaneous fact. His knowledge of the latter was always somewhat antiquated, for he was the most bookish of men and therefore fundamental materials, as distinguished from the material of the newspapers, always reached him with a lag. But hardly any historical work of his time that was of any general importance or scope escaped him, although much of the monographic literature did. While we cannot extol the completeness of his information in this field as much as we shall his erudition in the field of economic theory, he was yet able to illustrate his social visions not only by large historical frescoes but also by many details most of which were as regards reliability rather above than below the standards of other sociologists of his time. These facts he embraced with a glance that pierced through the random irregularities of the surface down to the grandiose logic of things historical. In this there was not merely passion. There was not merely analytic impulse. There were both. And the outcome of his attempt to formulate that logic, the so-called Economic Interpretation of History,[1] is doubtless one of the greatest individual achievements of sociology to this day. Before it, the question sinks into insignificance whether or not this achievement was entirely original and how far credit has in part to be given to predecessors, German and French.

The economic interpretation of history does *not* mean that men are, consciously or unconsciously, wholly or primarily, actuated by economic motives. On the contrary, the explanation of the role and mechanism of non-economic motives and the analysis of the way in which social reality mirrors itself in the individual psyches is an essential element of the theory and one of its most significant contributions. Marx did not hold that religions, metaphysics, schools of art, ethical ideas and political volitions were either reducible to economic *motives* or of no importance. He only tried to unveil the economic *conditions* which shape them and which account for their rise and fall. The whole of Max Weber's[2] facts and arguments fits

---

[1] First published in that scathing attack on Proudhon's *Philosophie de la Misère*, entitled *Das Elend der Philosophie*, 1847. Another version was included in the *Communist Manifesto*, 1848.

[2] The above refers to Weber's investigations into the sociology of religions and particularly to his famous study, *Die protestantische Ethik und der Geist des Kapitalismus*, republished in his collected works.

perfectly into Marx's system. Social groups and classes and the ways in which these groups or classes explain to themselves their own existence, location and behavior were of course what interested him most. He poured the vials of his most bilious wrath on the historians who took those attitudes and their verbalizations (the ideologies or, as Pareto would have said, *derivations*) at their face value and who tried to interpret social reality by means of them. But if ideas or values were not for him the prime movers of the social process, neither were they mere smoke. If I may use the analogy, they had in the social engine the role of transmission belts. We cannot touch upon that most interesting post-war development of these principles which would afford the best instance by which to explain this, the Sociology of Knowledge.[3] But it was necessary to say this much because Marx has been persistently misunderstood in this respect. Even his friend Engels, at the open grave of Marx, defined the theory in question as meaning precisely that individuals and groups are swayed primarily by economic motives, which in some important respects is wrong and for the rest piteously trivial.

While we are about it, we may as well defend Marx against another misunderstanding: the *economic* interpretation of history has often been called the *materialistic* intepretation. It has been called so by Marx himself. This phrase greatly increased its popularity with some, and its unpopularity with other people. But it is entirely meaningless. Marx's philosophy is no more materialistic than is Hegel's, and his theory of history is not more materialistic than is any other attempt to account for the historic process by the means at the command of empirical science. It should be clear that this is logically compatible with any metaphysical or religious belief—exactly as any physical picture of the world is. Medieval theology itself supplies methods by which it is possible to establish this compatibility.[4]

What the theory really says may be put into two propositions: (1) The forms or conditions of production are the fundamental determinant of social structures which in turn breed attitudes, actions and civilizations. Marx illustrates his meaning by the famous state-

[3] The German word is *Wissenssoziologie*, and the best names to mention are those of Max Scheler and Karl Mannheim. The latter's article on the subject in the German Dictionary of Sociology (*Handwörterbuch der Soziologie*) can serve as an introduction.

[4] I have met several Catholic radicals, a priest among them, all devout Catholics, who took this view and in fact declared themselves Marxists in everything except in matters relating to their faith.

ment that the "hand-mill" creates feudal, and the "steam-mill,"
capitalist societies. This stresses the technological element to a dangerous extent, but may be accepted on the understanding that mere
technology is not all of it. Popularizing a little and recognizing
that by doing so we lose much of the meaning, we may say that it
is our daily work which forms our minds, and that it is our location within the productive process which determines our outlook
on things—or the sides of things we see—and the social elbowroom
at the command of each of us. (2) The forms of production themselves have a logic of their own; that is to say, they change according to necessities inherent in them so as to produce their successors
merely by their own working. To illustrate by the same Marxian
example: the system characterized by the "hand-mill" creates an
economic and social situation in which the adoption of the mechan-
ical method of milling becomes a practical necessity that individuals
or groups are powerless to alter. The rise and working of the
"steam-mill" in turn creates new social functions and locations,
new groups and views, which develop and interact in such a way
as to outgrow their own frame. Here, then, we have the propeller
which is responsible first of all for economic and, in consequence
of this, for any other social change, a propeller the action of which
does not itself require any impetus external to it.

Both propositions undoubtedly contain a large amount of truth
and are, as we shall find at several turns of our way, invaluable
working hypotheses. Most of the current objections completely fail,
all those for instance which in refutation point to the influence of
ethical or religious factors, or the one already raised by Eduard
Bernstein, which with delightful simplicity asserts that "men have
heads" and can hence act as they choose. After what has been said
above, it is hardly necessary to dwell on the weakness of such arguments: of course men "choose" their course of action which is
not directly enforced by the objective data of the environment; but
they choose from standpoints, views and propensities that do not
form another set of independent data but are themselves molded
by the objective set.

Nevertheless, the question arises whether the economic interpretation of history is more than a convenient approximation which
must be expected to work less satisfactorily in some cases than it
does in others. An obvious qualification occurs at the outset. Social
structures, types and attitudes are coins that do not readily melt.
Once they are formed they persist, possibly for centuries, and since

different structures and types display different degrees of this ability to survive, we almost always find that actual group and national
behavior more or less departs from what we should expect it to be
if we tried to infer it from the dominant forms of the productive
process. Though this applies quite generally, it is most clearly seen
when a highly durable structure transfers itself bodily from one
country to another. The social situation created in Sicily by the
Norman conquest will illustrate my meaning. Such facts Marx did
not overlook but he hardly realized all their implications.

A related case is of more ominous significance. Consider the emergence of the feudal type of landlordism in the kingdom of the
Franks during the sixth and seventh centuries. This was certainly
a most important event that shaped the structure of society for
many ages and *also influenced conditions of production, wants and
technology included.* But its simplest explanation is to be found in
the function of military leadership previously filled by the families
and individuals who (retaining that function however) became feudal landlords after the definitive conquest of the new territory. This
does not fit the Marxian schema at all well and could easily be so
construed as to point in a different direction. Facts of this nature
can no doubt also be brought into the fold by means of auxiliary
hypotheses but the necessity of inserting such hypotheses is usually
the beginning of the end of a theory.

Many other difficulties that arise in the course of attempts at
historical interpretation by means of the Marxian schema could be
met by admitting some measure of interaction between the sphere
of production and other spheres of social life.[5] But the glamour of
fundamental truth that surrounds it depends precisely on the strict-
ness and simplicity of the one-way relation which it asserts. If this
be called in question, the economic interpretation of history will
have to take its place among other propositions of a similar kind—
as one of many partial truths—or else to give way to another that
does tell more fundamental truth. However, neither its rank as an
achievement nor its handiness as a working hypothesis is impaired
thereby.

To the faithful, of course, it is simply the master key to all the
secrets of human history. And if we sometimes feel inclined to smile
at rather naïve applications of it, we should remember what sort of

[5] In his later life, Engels admitted that freely. Plekhanov went still further in
this direction.

arguments it replaced. Even the crippled sister of the economic interpretation of history, the Marxian Theory of Social Classes, moves into a more favorable light as soon as we bear this in mind.

Again, it is in the first place an important contribution that we have to record. Economists have been strangely slow in recognizing the phenomenon of social classes. Of course they always classified the agents whose interplay produced the processes they dealt with. But these classes were simply sets of individuals that displayed some common character: thus, some people were classed as landlords or workmen because they owned land or sold the services of their labor. Social classes, however, are not the creatures of the classifying observer but live entities that exist as such. And their existence entails consequences that are entirely missed by a schema which looks upon society as if it were an amorphous assemblage of individuals or families. It is fairly open to question precisely how important the phenomenon of social classes is for research in the field of purely economic theory. That it is very important for many practical applications and for all the broader aspects of the social process in general is beyond doubt.

Roughly speaking, we may say that the social classes made their entrance in the famous statement contained in the *Communist Manifesto* that the history of society is the history of class struggles. Of course, this is to put the claim at its highest. But even if we tone it down to the proposition that historical events may often be interpreted in terms of class interests and class attitudes and that existing class structures are always an important factor in historical interpretation, enough remains to entitle us to speak of a conception nearly as valuable as was the economic interpretation of history itself.

Clearly, success on the line of advance opened up by the principle of class struggle depends upon the validity of the particular theory of classes we make our own. Our picture of history and all our interpretations of cultural patterns and the mechanism of social change will differ according to whether we choose, for instance, the racial theory of classes and like Gobineau reduce human history to the history of the struggle of races or, say, the division of labor theory of classes in the fashion of Schmoller or of Durkheim and resolve class antagonisms into antagonisms between the interests of vocational groups. Nor is the range of possible differences in analysis confined to the problem of the nature of classes. Whatever view we may hold about it, the different interpretations will result from different definitions of class interest[6] and from different opinions about how class action manifests itself. The subject is a hotbed of prejudice to this day, and as yet hardly in its scientific stage.

Curiously enough, Marx has never, as far as we know, worked out systematically what it is plain was one of the pivots of his thought. It is possible that he deferred the task until it was too late, precisely because his thinking ran so much in terms of class concepts that he did not feel it necessary to bother about definitive statement at all. It is equally possible that some points about it remained unsettled in his own mind, and that his way toward a full-fledged theory of classes was barred by certain difficulties he had created for himself by insisting on a purely economic and over-simplified conception of the phenomenon. He himself and his disciples both offered applications of this under-developed theory to particular patterns of which his own *History of the Class Struggles in France* is the outstanding example.[7] Beyond that no real progress has been achieved. The theory of his chief associate, Engels, was of the division of labor type and essentially un-Marxian in its implications. Barring this we have only the sidelights and *aperçus*—some of them of striking force and brilliance—that are strewn all over the writings of the master, particularly in *Das Kapital* and the *Communist Manifesto.*

The task of piecing together such fragments is delicate and cannot be attempted here. The basic idea is clear enough, however. The stratifying principle consists in the ownership, or the exclusion from ownership, of means of production such as factory buildings, machinery, raw materials and the consumers' goods that enter into the workman's budget. We have thus, fundamentally, two and only two classes, those owners, the capitalists, and those have-nots who are compelled to sell their labor, the laboring class or proletariat. The

---

[6] The reader will perceive that one's views about what classes are and about what calls them into existence do not uniquely determine what the *interests* of those classes are and how each class will act on what "it"—its leaders for instance or the rank and file—considers or feels, in the long run or in the short, erroneously or correctly, to be its interest or interests. The problem of group interest is full of thorns and pitfalls of its own, quite irrespective of the nature of the groups under study.

[7] Another example is the socialist theory of imperialism. . . . O. Bauer's interesting attempt to interpret the antagonisms between the various races that inhabited the Austro-Hungarian Empire in terms of the class struggle between capitalists and workers (*Die Nationalitätenfrage*, 1905) also deserves to be mentioned, although the skill of the analyst only serves to show up the inadequacy of the tool.

existence of intermediate groups, such as are formed by farmers or artisans who employ labor but also do manual work, by clerks and by the professions is of course not denied; but they are treated as anomalies which tend to disappear in the course of the capitalist process. The two fundamental classes are, by virtue of the logic of their position and quite independently of any individual volition, essentially antagonistic to each other. Rifts within each class and collisions between subgroups occur and may even have historically decisive importance. But in the last analysis, such rifts or collisions are incidental. The one antagonism that is not incidental but inherent in the basic design of capitalist society is founded upon the private control over the means to produce: the very nature of the relation between the capitalist class and the proletariat is strife—class war.

. . . Marx tries to show how in that class war capitalists destroy each other and eventually will destroy the capitalist system too. He also tries to show how the ownership of capital leads to further accumulation. But this way of arguing as well as the very definition that makes the ownership of something the constituent characteristic of a social class only serves to increase the importance of the question of "primitive accumulation," that is to say, of the question how capitalists came to be capitalists in the first instance or how they acquired that stock of goods which according to the Marxian doctrine was necessary in order to enable them to start exploiting. On this question Marx is much less explicit.[8] He contemptuously rejects the bourgeois nursery tale (*Kinderfibel*) that some people rather than others became, and are still becoming every day, capitalists, by superior intelligence and energy in working and saving. Now he was well advised to sneer at that story about the good boys. For to call for a guffaw is no doubt an excellent method of disposing of an uncomfortable truth, as every politician knows to his profit. Nobody who looks at historical and contemporaneous fact with anything like an unbiased mind can fail to observe that this children's tale, while far from telling the whole truth, yet tells a good deal of it. Supernormal intelligence and energy account for industrial success and in particular for the *founding* of industrial positions in nine cases out of ten. And precisely in the initial stages of capitalism and of every individual industrial career, saving was and is an important element in the process though not quite as ex-

---

[8] See *Das Kapital*, vol. i, ch. xxvi: "The Secret of Primitive Accumulation."

plained in classic economics. It is true that one does not ordinarily attain the status of capitalist (industrial employer) by saving from a wage or salary in order to equip one's factory by means of the fund thus assembled. The bulk of accumulation comes from profits and hence presupposes profits—this is in fact the *sound* reason for distinguishing saving from accumulating. The means required in order to start enterprise are typically provided by borrowing other people's savings, the presence of which in many small puddles is easy to explain or the deposits which banks create for the use of the would-be entrepreneur. Nevertheless, the latter does save as a rule: the function of his saving is to raise him above the necessity of submitting to daily drudgery for the sake of his daily bread and to give him breathing space in order to look around, to develop his plans and to secure cooperation. As a matter of economic theory, therefore, Marx had a real case—though he overstated it— when he denied to saving the role that the classical authors attributed to it. Only his inference does not follow. And the guffaw is hardly more justified than it would be if the classical theory were correct.[9]

The guffaw did its work, however, and helped to clear the road for Marx's alternative theory of primitive accumulation. But this alternative theory is not as definite as we might wish. Force—robbery—subjugation of the masses facilitating their spoliation and the results of the pillage in turn facilitating subjugation—this was all right of course and admirably tallied with ideas common among intellectuals of all types, in our day still more than in the day of Marx. But evidently it does not solve the problem, which is to explain how some people acquired the power to subjugate and to rob. Popular literature does not worry about it. I should not think of addressing the question to the writings of John Reed. But we are dealing with Marx.

Now at least the semblance of a solution is afforded by the historical quality of all the major theories of Marx. For him, it is essential for the *logic* of capitalism, and not only a matter of *fact*, that

[9] I will not stay to stress, though I must mention, that even the classical theory is not as wrong as Marx pretended it was. "Saving up" in the most literal sense has been, especially in earlier stages of capitalism, a not unimportant method of "original accumulation." Moreover, there was another method that was akin to it though not identical with it. Many a factory in the seventeenth and eighteenth centuries was just a shed that a man was able to put up by the work of his hands, and required only the simplest equipment to work it. In such cases the manual work of the prospective capitalist plus a quite small fund of savings was all that was needed—and brains, of course.

it grew out of a feudal state of society. Of course the same question about the causes and the mechanism of social stratification arises also in this case, but Marx substantially accepted the bourgeois view that feudalism was a reign of force[10] in which subjugation and exploitation of the masses were already accomplished facts. The class theory devised primarily for the conditions of capitalist society was extended to its feudal predecessor—as was much of the conceptual apparatus of the economic theory of capitalism[11]—and some of the most thorny problems were stowed away in the feudal compound to reappear in a settled state, in the form of data, in the analysis of the capitalist pattern. The feudal exploiter was simply replaced by the capitalist exploiter. In those cases in which feudal lords actually turned into industrialists, this alone would solve what is thus left of the problem. Historical evidence lends a certain amount of support to this view: many feudal lords, particularly in Germany, in fact did erect and run factories, often providing the financial means from their feudal rents and the labor from the agricultural population (not necessarily but sometimes their serfs).[12] In all other cases the material available to stop the gap is distinctly inferior. The only frank way of expressing the situation is that from a Marxian standpoint there is no satisfactory explanation, that is to say, no explanation without resorting to non-Marxian elements suggestive of non-Marxian conclusions.[13]

[10] Many socialist writers besides Marx have displayed that uncritical confidence in the explanatory value of the element of force and of the control over the physical means with which to exert force. Ferdinand Lassalle, for instance, has little beyond cannons and bayonets to offer by way of explanation of governmental authority. It is a source of wonder to me that so many people should be blind to the weakness of such a sociology and to the fact that it would obviously be much truer to say that power leads to control over cannons (and men willing to use them) than that control over cannons generates power.

[11] This constitutes one of the affinities of the teaching of Marx to that of K. Rodbertus.

[12] W. Sombart, in the first edition of his *Theorie des modernen Kapitalismus*, tried to make the most of those cases. But the attempt to base primitive accumulation entirely on the accumulation of ground rent showed its hopelessness as Sombart himself eventually recognized.

[13] This holds true even if we admit robbery to the utmost extent to which it is possible to do so without trespassing upon the sphere of the intellectual's folklore. Robbery actually entered into the building up of commercial capital at many times and places. Phoenician as well as English wealth offers familiar examples. But even then the Marxian explanation is inadequate because in the last resort successful robbery must rest on the personal superiority of the robbers. And as soon as this is admitted, a very different theory of social stratification suggests itself.

This, however, vitiates the theory at both its historical and its logical source. Since most of the methods of primitive accumulation also account for later accumulation—primitive accumulation, as it were, continues throughout the capitalist era—it is not possible to say that Marx's theory of social classes is all right *except* for the difficulties about processes in a distant past. But it is perhaps superfluous to insist on the shortcomings of a theory which not even in the most favorable instances goes anywhere near the heart of the phenomenon it undertakes to explain, and which never should have been taken seriously. These instances are to be found mainly in that epoch of capitalist evolution which derived its character from the prevalence of the medium-sized owner-managed firm. Beyond the range of that type, class positions, though in most cases reflected in more or less corresponding economic positions, are more often the cause than the consequence of the latter: business achievement is obviously not everywhere the only avenue to social eminence and only where it is can ownership of means of production causally determine a group's position in the social structure. Even then, however, it is as reasonable to make that ownership the defining element as it would be to define a soldier as a man who happens to have a gun. The water-tight division between people who (together with their descendants) are supposed to be capitalists once for all and others who (together with their descendants) are supposed to be proletarians once for all is not only, as has often been pointed out, utterly unrealistic but it misses the salient point about social classes—the incessant rise and fall of individual families into and out of the upper strata. The facts I am alluding to are all obvious and indisputable. If they do not show on the Marxian canvas, the reason can only be in their un-Marxian implications.

It is not superfluous, however, to consider the role which that theory plays within Marx's structure and to ask ourselves what analytic intention—as distinguished from its use as a piece of equipment for the agitator—he meant it to serve.

On the one hand, we must bear in mind that for Marx the theory of Social Classes and Economic Interpretation of History were not what they are for us, viz., two independent doctrines. With Marx, the former implements the latter in a particular way and thus restricts—makes more definite—the *modus operandi* of the conditions or forms of production. These determine the social structure and, through the social structure, all manifestations of civilization and the whole march of cultural and political history. But the social

structure is, for all non-socialist epochs, defined in terms of classes
—those two classes—which are the true dramatis personae and at
the same time the only *immediate* creatures of the logic of the capitalist system of production which affects everything else through
them. This explains why Marx was forced to make his classes purely
economic phenomena, and even phenomena that were economic in
a very narrow sense: he thereby cut himself off from a deeper view
of them, but in the precise spot of his analytic schema in which he
placed them he had no choice but to do so.

On the other hand, Marx wished to define capitalism by the same
trait that also defines his class division. A little reflection will convince the reader that this is not a necessary or natural thing to do.
In fact it was a bold stroke of analytic strategy which linked the fate
of the class phenomenon with the fate of capitalism in such a way
that socialism, which in reality has nothing to do with the presence
or absence of social classes, became, by definition, the only possible
kind of classless society, excepting primitive groups. This ingenious
tautology could not equally well have been secured by any definitions of classes *and* of capitalism other than those chosen by Marx
—the definition by private ownership of means of production.
Hence there had to be just two classes, owners and non-owners, and
hence all other principles of division, much more plausible ones
among them, had to be severely neglected or discounted or else
reduced to that one.

The exaggeration of the definiteness and importance of the dividing line between the capitalist class in that sense and the proletariat
was surpassed only by the exaggeration of the antagonism between
them. To any mind not warped by the habit of fingering the Marxian rosary it should be obvious that their relation is, in normal times,
primarily one of cooperation and that any theory to the contrary
must draw largely on pathological cases for verification. In social
life, antagonism and synagogism are of course both ubiquitous and
in fact inseparable except in the rarest of cases. But I am almost
tempted to say that there was, if anything, less of absolute nonsense
in the old harmonistic view—full of nonsense though that was too—
than in the Marxian construction of the impassable gulf between
tool owners and tool users. Again, however, he had no choice, not
because he wanted to arrive at revolutionary results—these he could
have derived just as well from dozens of other possible schemata—
but because of the requirements of his own analysis. *If* class struggle
was the subject matter of history and also the means of bringing

about the socialist dawn, and *if* there had to be just those two classes, then their relation had to be antagonistic on principle or else the force in his system of social dynamics would have been lost.

Now, though Marx *defines* capitalism sociologically, i.e., by the institution of private control over means of production, the *mechanics* of capitalist society are provided by his economic theory. This economic theory is to show how the sociological data embodied in such conceptions as class, class interest, class behavior, exchange between classes, work out through the medium of economic values, profits, wages, investment, etc., and how they generate precisely the economic process that will eventually break its own institutional framework and at the same time create the conditions for the emergence of another social world. This particular theory of social classes is the analytic tool which, by linking the economic interpretation of history with the concepts of the profit economy, marshals all social facts, makes all phenomena confocal. It is therefore not simply a theory of an individual phenomenon which is to explain that phenomenon and nothing else. It has an organic function which is really much more important to the Marxian system than the measure of success with which it solves its immediate problem. This function must be seen if we are to understand how an analyst of the power of Marx could ever have borne with its shortcomings. . . .

TWO

HISTORICAL MATERIALISM
ISAIAH BERLIN

No formal exposition of historical materialism was ever published by Marx himself. It occurs in a fragmentary form in all his early work written during the years 1843–48, and is taken for granted in his later thought. He did not regard it as a new philosophical system so much as a practical method of social and historical analysis, and a basis for political strategy. Later in life he often complained of the use made of it by his followers, some of whom appeared to think that it would save them the labour of historical study by providing a kind of algebraic "table," from which, given enough factual data, automatic answers to all historical questions could be mechanically "read off." In a letter which, towards the end of his life, he wrote to a Russian correspondent, he gave as an example of dissimilar development, despite analogous social conditions, the history of the Roman plebs and of the European industrial proletariat. "When one studies these forms of evolution separately," he wrote, "and then compares them, one can easily find the clue to this phenomenon; but one will never get there by the universal *passe partout* of particular historico-philosophical theory which explains everything because it explains nothing, the supreme virtue of which consists in being super-historical."

The theory matured gradually in his mind. It is possible to trace its growth in the essays on the *Hegelian Philosophy of Right* and on the *Jewish Question*; in these the proletariat is for the first time identified as the agent destined to change society in the direction adumbrated by philosophy, which because it is as yet philosophy divorced from action, is itself a symptom and an expression of impotence. It is further developed in *The Holy Family*—an amalgam of polemical outbursts against the "critical critics," i.e. the young Hegelians—principally the brothers Bauer and Stirner—interspersed with fragments on the philosophy of history, social criticism of literature, and other oddities; it is most fully stated in a volume, over six hundred pages in length, which he composed with Engels in

From Isaiah Berlin, *Karl Marx: His Life and Environment,* 3rd ed. (London: Oxford University Press, 1963), pp. 122–25, 136–43, 151–58. Copyright © 1963 by Oxford University Press, Amen House. Reprinted by permission.

1846, entitled *The German Ideology,* but never published. This, for the most part, confused, verbose and ponderous work, which deals with authors and views long dead and justly forgotten, contains in its lengthy introduction the most sustained, imaginative and impressive exposition of Marx's theory of history. Like the terse and brilliant *Theses on Feuerbach* which belong to the same period, and the *Philosophico-economic Manuscripts* of 1844 with their new application of Hegel's concept of alienation, the greater part of *The German Ideology* did not see the light until the present century. It is philosophically far more interesting than any other work by Marx, and represents a submerged, but a most crucial and original stage of his thought, the total ignorance or neglect of which by his immediate followers (including the makers of the Russian Revolution) led to an exclusive emphasis on the historical and economic aspects, and defective understanding of the sociological and philosophical content, of his ideas. This fact is responsible for the clear, half positivist, half Darwinian interpretation of Marx's thought, which we owe mainly to Kautsky, Plekhanov, and above all to Engels—a tradition that has decisively influenced both the theory and the practice of the movement which goes by Marx's name.

The framework of the new theory is undeviatingly Hegelian. It recognizes that the history of humanity is a single, non-repetitive process, which obeys discoverable laws. These laws are different from the laws of physics or of chemistry, which being unhistorical, record unvarying conjunctions and successions of interconnected phenomena, whenever or wherever these may repeat themselves; they are similar rather to those of geology or botany, which embody the principles in accordance with which a process of continuous change takes place. Each moment of this process is new in the sense that it possesses new characteristics, or new combinations of known characteristics; but unique and unrepeatable though it is, it nevertheless follows from the immediately preceding state in obedience to the same laws, as this last state from its own predecessor. But whereas according to Hegel the single substance in the succession of whose states history consists, is the eternal universal Spirit, the internal conflict of whose elements is made concrete, e.g. in religious conflicts or the wars of national states, each being the embodiment of the self-realizing Idea which it requires a supersensible intuition to perceive, Marx, following Feuerbach, denounces this as a piece of mystification on which no knowledge could be founded. For if the world were a metaphysical substance of this type; its behaviour could not be tested by the only reliable method in our power, namely, empirical observation; and an account of it could not, therefore, be verified by the methods of any science. The Hegelian can, of course, without fear of refutation, attribute anything he wishes to the unobservable activity of an impalpable world-substance, much as the believing Christian or theist attributes it to the activity of God, but only at the cost of explaining nothing, of declaring the answer to be an empirically impenetrable mystery. It is such translation of ordinary questions into less intelligible language that makes the resultant obscurity look like a genuine answer. To explain the knowable in terms of the unknowable is to take away with one hand what one affects to give with the other. Whatever value such procedure may have, it cannot be regarded as equivalent to a scientific explanation, that is, to the ordering by means of a comparatively small number of interrelated laws of the great variety of distinct, *prima facie* unconnected, phenomena. So much for orthodox Hegelianism.

*   *   *

Like Hegel, Marx treats history as a phenomenology. In Hegel the Phenomenology of the human Spirit is an attempt to show, often with great insight and ingenuity, an objective order in the development of human consciousness and in the succession of civilizations that are its concrete embodiment. Influenced by a notion prominent in the Renaissance, but reaching back into earlier mystical cosmogony, Hegel looked upon the development of mankind as being similar to that of an individual human being. Just as in the case of a man a particular capacity, or outlook, or way of dealing with reality cannot come into being until and unless other capacities have first become developed—that is, indeed the essence of the notion of growth or education in the case of individuals—so races, nations, churches, cultures, succeed each other in a fixed order, determined by the growth of the collective faculties of mankind expressed in arts, sciences, civilization as a whole. Pascal had perhaps meant something of this kind when he spoke of humanity as a single, centuries old, being, growing from generation to generation. For Hegel all change is due to the movement of the dialectic, that works by a constant logical criticism, that is, struggle against, and final self-destruction of, ways of thought and constructions of reason and feeling, which, in their day, had embodied the highest point reached by the ceaseless growth (which for Hegel is the logical self-realization) of the human spirit; but which, embodied in rules or institutions, and erroneously taken as final and absolute by a given society or outlook, thereby become obstacles to progress, dying survivals of a logically "transcended" stage, which by their very one-sidedness breed logical antinomies and contradictions by which they are exposed and destroyed. Marx accepted this vision of history as a battlefield of incarnate ideas, but translated it into social terms, of the struggle between classes. For him alienation (for that is what Hegel, following Rousseau and Luther and an earlier Christian tradition, called the perpetual self-divorce of men from unity with nature, with each other, with God, which the struggle of thesis against antithesis entailed) is intrinsic to the social process, indeed it is the heart of history itself. Alienation occurs when the results of men's acts contradict their true purposes, when their official values, or the parts they play, misrepresent their real motives and needs and goals. This is the case, for example, when something that men have made to respond to human needs—say, a system of laws, or the rules of musical composition—acquires an independent status of its own, and is seen by men, not as something created by them to satisfy a common social want (which may have disappeared long ago), but as an objective law or institution, possessing eternal, impersonal authority in its own right, like the unalterable laws of Nature as conceived by scientists and ordinary men, like God for a believer. For Marx the capitalist system is precisely this kind of entity, a vast instrument brought into being by intelligible material demands—a progressive improvement and broadening of life in its own day, that generates its own intellectual, moral, religious beliefs, values and forms of life. Whether those who hold them know it or not, such values are simply props to the power of the class whose interests the capitalist system embodies; nevertheless, they come to be viewed by all sections of society as being objectively valid for all mankind. Thus, for example, industry and the capitalist mode of exchange are not timelessly valid institutions, but were generated by the mounting resistance by peasants and artisans to dependence on the blind forces of nature.

Production is a social activity. Any form of co-operative work or division of labour, whatever its origin, creates common purposes and common interests, not analysable as the mere sum of the individual aims or interests of the human beings involved. If, as in capitalist society, the product of the total social labour of a society is appropriated by one section of that society for its own exclusive benefit, as a result of an inexorable historical development, which Engels, more explicitly (and much more mechanistically) than Marx, attempts to describe, this goes against the "natural" needs of human society—against what men, whose essence, as human beings, is to be social, require, in order to develop freely and fully. According to Marx, those who accumulate in their hands the means of production, and thereby also its fruits in the form of capital, forcibly deprive the majority of the producers—the workers—of what they create, and so split society into exploiter and exploited; the interests of these classes are opposed; the survival of each class depends on its ability to defeat its adversary in a continuous war, a war that determines all the institutions of that society. In the course of the struggle technological skills develop, the culture of the class-divided society becomes more complex, its products grow richer, and the needs which its material progress breeds, more varied and more artificial—that is, more "unnatural." Unnatural, because both the warring classes became "alienated," by the conflict which has replaced co-operation for common ends, from the integrated common life and creation, that, according to this theory, is demanded by the social nature of man. The monopoly of the means of production held by a particular group of men, enables it to bind its will on the others and to force them to perform tasks alien to their own needs. Thereby the unity of society is destroyed, and the lives of both classes become distorted. The majority—that is the propertyless proletarians—now work for the benefit, and according to the ideas, of others: the fruit of their labour as well as its instruments are taken from them; their mode of existence, their ideas and ideals correspond not to their own real predicament—that of human beings artificially prevented from living as their natures demand (namely as members of a unified society, capable of understanding the reasons for doing what they do, and of enjoying the fruits of their own united, free and rational activity)—but to the aims of their oppressors. Hence their lives rest on a lie. Their masters, in their turn, whether consciously or not, cannot help seeking to justify their own parasitic existence as being both natural and desirable. In the course of this, they generate ideas, values, laws, habits of life, institutions (a complex which Marx sometimes calls "ideology"), the whole purpose of which is to prop up, explain away, defend, their own privileged, unnatural, and therefore unjustified, status and power. Such ideologies—national, religious, economic and so on, are forms of collective self-deception; the victims of the ruling class—the proletarians and peasants—imbibe it as part of their normal education, of the general outlook of the unnatural society, and so come to look upon it, and accept it, as objective, just, necessary, a part of the natural order which pseudo-sciences are then created to explain. This, as Rousseau had taught, serves to deepen still further human error, conflict and frustration.

The symptom of alienation is the attribution of ultimate authority, either to some impersonal power—say the laws of supply and demand—from which the rationality of capitalism is represented as being logically deducible, or to imaginary persons or forces—divinities, churches, the mystical person of the king or priest, or interims of other oppressive myths, whereby men, torn from a "natural" mode of life (which alone makes it possible for entire societies to perceive the truth and live harmoniously), seek to explain their unnatural condition to themselves. If men are ever to liberate themselves, they must be taught to see through these myths. The most oppressive of all, in Marx's demonology, is bourgeois economic science, which represents the movement of commodities or of money —indeed the process of production, consumption and distribution— as an impersonal process, similar to those of nature, an unalterable pattern of objective forces before which men can only bow, and which it would be insane to resist.[1] Deterministic as he was, Marx nevertheless resolved to show that the conception of any given economic or social structure as a part of an unchangeable world order was an illusion brought about by man's alienation from the form of life natural to him—a typical "mystification," the effects of purely human activities masquerading as a law of nature; it would be removed only by other, equally human activities—the application of "demystifying" reason and science; ultimately by the weapon of revolution. These liberating activities may themselves be determined by objective laws, but what these laws determine is the activity of human thought and will (particularly of men taken in the mass), and not merely the movement of material bodies, obeying their own inexorable patterns that are independent of human decisions and actions. If, as Marx believed, human choices can affect the course of events, then, even if these choices are themselves ultimately determined and scientifically predictable, such a situation is one in which

[1] For Marx classical economics or sociology are so many attempts to disguise transient and largely irrational arrangements, as the operations of universally valid laws: a quasi-religion of which bourgeois economists, sociologists, philosophers and so forth, are the priests.

Hegelians and Marxists think it legitimate to call men free, since such choices are not, like the rest of nature, mechanically determined. Indeed this kind of determination, according to thinkers of this school, is all that can be meant by the notion of freedom.

Because the historical function of capitalism, and its relation to the interests of a specific class, are not understood, it comes not to enrich but to crush and distort the lives of millions of workers, and indeed of their oppressors too, like everything that is not rationally grasped and therefore blindly worshipped as a fetish. Money for instance, which played a progressive role in the days of liberation from barter, has now become an absolute object of pursuit and reverence for its own sake, brutalizing and destroying man whom it was invented to liberate. Men are divorced from the products of their own toil and from the instruments with which they produce: these acquire a life and status of their own, and in the name of their survival or improvement, living human beings are oppressed and treated like cattle or saleable commodities. This is true of all institutions, churches, economic systems, forms of government, moral codes, which, through being misunderstood, become more powerful than their inventors, monsters worshipped by their makers—the blind, unhappy Frankensteins whose lives they frustrate and twist. At the same time, merely to see through or criticize this predicament, which the young Hegelians thought sufficient, will not destroy it. To be effective, the weapons with which one fights, among them ideas, must be those called for by the historical situation—neither those that served a previous period, nor those for which the historical process has not yet called. Men must ask themselves, first and foremost, what stage the class war—which is the dialectic at work—has reached, and then act accordingly. This is to be "concrete" and not timeless, or idealistic or "abstract." Alienation—the substitution of imaginary relations between, or worship of, inanimate objects or ideas for real relations between, or respect for, persons—will come to an end only when the final class—the proletariat—defeats the bourgeoisie. Then the ideas which this victory will generate, will automatically be those expressive of, and beneficial to, a classless society, that is, all mankind. Neither institutions nor ideas which rest on falsifying the character of any section of the human race, and so leading to (or expressive of) their oppression, will survive. Capitalism, under which the labour of human beings is bought and sold, and the workers are treated merely as sources of labour power, is plainly a system which distorts the truth about what men are and can be, and seeks to subordinate history to a class interest (which is injustice), and is therefore due to be superseded by the gathering power of its indignant victims which its own victories call into existence. All frustration, for Marx, is the product of alienation—the barriers and distortions that are created by the inevitable war of classes, and shut out this or that body of men from the harmonious co-operation with one another for which their nature craves.

*   *   *

For Marx, no less than for earlier rationalists, man is potentially wise, creative and free. If his character has deteriorated beyond recognition, that is due to the long and brutalizing war in which he and his ancestors have lived ever since society ceased to be that primitive communism out of which, according to the current anthropology, it has developed. Until this state is reached again, embodying, however, all the conquests, technological and spiritual, which mankind has won in the course of its long wandering in the desert, neither peace nor freedom can be obtained. The French Revolution was an attempt to bring this about by altering political forms only—which was no more than the bourgeoisie required, since it already possessed the economic reality: and, therefore, all it succeeded in doing (as indeed was its appointed historical task at the stage of development at which it occurred) was to establish the bourgeoisie in a dominant position by finally destroying the corrupt remnant of an obsolete feudal régime. This task could not but be continued by Napoleon whom no one could suspect of wishing consciously to liberate humanity; whatever his personal motive for acting as he did, the demands of his historical environment inevitably made him an instrument of social change; by his agency, as Hegel had indeed perceived, Europe advanced yet another step towards the realization of its destiny.

The gradual freeing of mankind has pursued a definite, irreversible direction: every new epoch is inaugurated by the liberation of a hitherto oppressed class; nor can a class, once it has been destroyed, ever return. History does not move backwards, or in cyclical movements: all its conquests are final and irrevocable. Most previous ideal constitutions were worthless because they ignored actual laws of historical development, and substituted in their place the subjective caprice or imagination of the thinker. A knowledge of these laws is essential to effective political action. The ancient world gave way to the medieval, slavery to feudalism, and feudalism to the industrial bourgeoisie. These transitions were not peaceful, but sprang from wars and revolutions, for no established order gives way to its successor without a struggle.

And now only one stratum remains submerged below the level of the rest, one class alone remains enslaved, the landless, propertyless proletariat, created by the advance of technology, perpetually assisting classes above itself to shake off the yoke of the common oppressor, always, after the common cause has been won, condemned to be oppressed by its own former allies, the new victorious class, by masters who were themselves but lately slaves. The proletariat is on the lowest possible rung of the social scale: there is no class below it; by securing its own emancipation the proletariat will therefore emancipate mankind. It has, unlike other classes, no specific claim, no interests of its own which it does not share with all men as such: for it has been stripped of everything but its bare humanity: its very destitution causes it to represent human beings as such—what it is entitled to, is the minimum to which all men are entitled. Its fight is thus not a fight for the natural rights of a particular section of society: for natural rights are but the ideal aspect of the bourgeois attitude to the sanctity of private property; the only real rights are those conferred by history, the right to act the part which is historically imposed upon one's class. The bourgeoisie, in this sense, has a full right to fight its final battle against the masses, but its task is hopeless: it will necessarily be defeated, as the feudal nobility was defeated in its day. As for the masses, they fight for freedom not because they choose, but because they must, or rather they choose because they must: to fight is the condition of their survival; the future belongs to them, and in fighting for it, they, like every rising class, are fighting against a foe doomed to decay, and thereby fighting for the whole of humanity. But whereas all other victories placed in power a class itself doomed to ultimate disappearance, this conflict will be followed by no other, being destined to end the condition of all such struggles, by abolishing classes as such; by dissolving the state itself, hitherto the instrument of a single class, into a free, because classless, society. The proletariat must be made to understand that no real compromise with the enemy is possible: that, while it may conclude temporary alliances with him in order to defeat some common adversary, it must ultimately turn against him. In backward countries, where the bourgeoisie itself is still fighting for power, the proletariat must throw in its lot with it, asking itself not what the ideals of the bourgeoisie may be, but what it is *compelled* to do in the particular situation: and must adapt its tactics to this. And while history is determined—and the victory will, therefore, be won by the rising class whether any given individual wills it or not—how rapidly this will occur, how efficiently, how far in accordance with the conscious popular will, depends on human initiative, on the degree of understanding of their task by the masses and the courage and efficiency of their leaders.

To make this clear, and to educate the masses for their destiny is, therefore, according to Marx, the whole duty of a contemporary philosopher. But, it has often been asked, how can a moral precept, a command to do this or that, be deduced from the truth of a theory of history? Historical materialism may account for what does in fact occur, but cannot, precisely because it is concerned solely with what is, provide the answer to moral questions, that is, tell us what ought to be. Marx, like Hegel, flatly rejected this distinction. Judgments of fact cannot be sharply distinguished from those of value: all one's judgments are conditioned by practical activity in a given social milieu which, in its turn, are functions of the stage reached by one's class in its historical evolution: one's views as to what one believes to exist and what one wishes to do with it, modify each other. If ethical judgments claim objective validity—and unless they do, they cannot, according to Marx, be either true or false—they must be definable in terms of empirical activities and be verifiable by reference to them. He rejected any notion of a non-empirical, purely contemplative or specifically moral intuition or moral reason. The only sense in which it is possible to show that something is good or bad, right or wrong, is by demonstrating that it accords or discords with the historical process, i.e. the collective activity of men, that it assists it or thwarts it, will survive or will inevitably perish. All causes permanently lost or doomed to fail, are, by that very fact, made bad and wrong, and indeed this is what constitutes the meaning of these terms. But this is a dangerous empirical criterion, since causes which may appear lost may, in fact, have suffered only a temporary setback, and will in the end prevail.

His view of truth in general derives directly from this position. He is sometimes accused of maintaining that, since a man is wholly determined to think as he does by his social environment, even if some of his statements are objectively true, he cannot know it, being conditioned to think them true by material causes, not by their truth. Marx's statements on this subject are vague to a degree; but in general it may be said that he would have accepted the normal interpretation of what is meant by saying that a theory or a proposition of natural science or of ordinary sense experience is true or false. But he was scarcely interested in this, the most common, type of truth discussed by philosophers. He was concerned with the reasons for which social, moral, historical verdicts are thought true or false, where arguments between opponents can so easily not be settled by direct appeal to empirical facts accessible to both. He might have agreed that the bare proposition that Napoleon died in exile, would have been accepted as equally true by a bourgeois and a socialist historian. But he would have gone on to say that no true historian confines himself to a list of events and dates: that the plausibility of his account of the past, its claim to be more than a bare chronicle, depends, at the very least, upon his choice of fundamental concepts, his power of emphasis and arrangement, that the very process of selection of material betrays an inclination to stress this or that event or act as important or trivial, adverse or favourable to human progress, good or bad. And in this tendency the social origin and environment and class affiliation and interests of the historian tell only too clearly.

This attitude underlies his purely Hegelian view of rationality as identical with the knowledge of the laws of necessity. If you know in what direction the world process is working, you can either identify yourself with it or not; if you do not, if you fight it, you thereby compass your own certain destruction, being necessarily defeated by the forward advance of history. To choose to do so deliberately is to behave irrationally. Only a wholly rational being is wholly free to choose between alternatives: where one of these irresistibly leads to his own destruction, he cannot choose it freely, because to say that an act is free, as Marx employs the term, is to deny that it is contrary to reason. The bourgeoisie as a class is indeed fated to disappear, but individual members of it may follow reason and save themselves (as Marx might have claimed to have done himself) by leaving it before it finally founders. True freedom is unattainable until society has been made rational, that is, has overcome the contradictions which breed illusions and distort the understanding of both masters and slaves. But men can work for the free world by discovering the true state of the balance of forces, and acting accordingly; the path to freedom thus entails knowledge of historical necessity. Marx's use of words like "right," or "free," or "rational," whenever he does not slip insensibly into ordinary usage, owes its eccentric air to the fact that it derives from his metaphysical views;

and therefore diverges widely from that of common speech, which is largely intended to record and communicate something scarcely of interest to him—the subjective experience of class-perverted individuals, their states of mind or of body as revealed by the senses or in self-consciousness.

Such in outline is the theory of history and society which constitutes the metaphysical basis of communism. It is a wide and comprehensive doctrine which derives its structure and basic concepts from Hegel and the Young Hegelians, and its dynamic principles from Saint-Simon, its belief in the primacy of matter from Feuerbach, and its view of the proletariat from the French communist tradition. Nevertheless it is wholly original; the combination of elements does not in this case lead to syncretism, but forms a bold, clear, coherent system, with the wide range and the massive architectonic quality that is at once the greatest pride and the fatal defect of all forms of Hegelian thought. But it is not guilty of Hegel's reckless and contemptuous attitude towards the results of the scientific research of his time; on the contrary, it attempts to follow the direction indicated by the empirical sciences, and to incorporate their general results. Marx's practice did not always conform to this theoretical ideal, and that of his followers sometimes did so even less: while not actually distorted, the facts are sometimes made to undergo peculiar transformations in the process of being fitted into the intricate dialectical pattern. It is by no means a wholly empirical theory, since it does not confine itself to the description of the phenomena and the formulation of hypotheses concerning their structure and behaviour; the Marxist doctrine of movement in dialectical collisions is not a hypothesis liable to be made less or more probable by the evidence of facts, but a pattern, uncovered by a non-empirical, historical method, the validity of which is not questioned. To deny this would be tantamount, according to Marx, to a return to "vulgar" materialism, which, ignoring the crucial discoveries of Hegel and indeed Kant, recognizes only those connexions as real, for which there is the corrigible evidence of the physical senses.

In the sharpness and the clarity with which this theory formulates its questions, in the rigour of the method by which it proposes to search for the answers, in the combination of attention to detail and power of wide comprehensive generalization, it is without parallel. Even if all its specific conclusions were proved false, its importance in creating a wholly new attitude to social and historical questions, and so opening new avenues of human knowledge, would be unimpaired. The scientific study of historically evolving economic relations, and of their bearing on other aspects of the lives of communities and individuals, began with the application of Marxist canons of interpretation. Previous thinkers—for example, Vico, Hegel, Saint-Simon—drew up general schemata, but their direct results, as embodied, for instance, in the gigantic systems of Comte or Spencer, are at once too abstract and too vague, and as little remembered in our day as they deserve to be. The true father of modern economic history, and, indeed, of modern sociology, in so far as any one man may claim that title, is Karl Marx. If to have turned into truisms what had previously been paradoxes is a mark of genius, Marx was richly endowed with it. His achievements in this sphere are necessarily ignored in proportion as their effects have become part of the permanent background of civilized thought.

THREE

CONCERNING THE LIMITATION
OF THE MATERIALISIC
THEORY OF HISTORY

BENEDETTO CROCE

Historical materialism, if it is to express something critically acceptable, can . . . be neither a new *a priori* notion of the philosophy of history, nor a new method of historical thought; it must be simply a *canon* of historical interpretation. This canon recommends that attention be directed to the so-called economic basis of society, in order that the forms and mutations of the latter may be better understood.

The concept canon ought not to raise difficulty, especially when it is remembered that *it imples no anticipation of results,* but only an aid in seeking for them; and is entirely of empirical origin. When the critic of the text of Dante's *Comedia* uses Witte's well-known canon, which runs: *"the difficult reading is to be preferred to the easy one,"* he is quite aware that he possesses a mere instrument, which may be useful to him in many cases, useless in others, and whose correct and advantageous employment depends entirely on his caution. In like manner and with like meaning it must be said that historical materialism is a mere *canon;* although it be in truth a canon *most rich in suggestion.*

But was it in this way that Marx and Engels understood it? and is it in this way that Marx's followers usually understand it?

Let us begin with the first question. Truly a difficult one, and offering a multiplicity of difficulties. The first of these arises so to speak, from the *nature of the sources.* The doctrine of historical materialism is not embodied in a classical and definite book by those authors, with whom it is as it were identified; so that, to discuss that book and to discuss the doctrine might seem all one thing. On the contrary it is scattered through a series of writings, composed in the course of half a century, at long intervals, where only the most casual mention is made of it, and where it is sometimes merely un-

From Benedetto Croce, *Historical Materialism and the Economics of Karl Marx,* translated by C. M. Meredith, with an Introduction by A. D. Lindsay (London: Howard Latimer Ltd., 1913), pp. 77–93.

derstood or implied. Anyone who desired to reconcile all the forms
with which Marx and Engels have endowed it, would stumble
upon contradictory expressions, which would make it impossible
for the careful and methodical interpreter to decide what, on the
whole, historical materialism meant for them.

Another difficulty arises in regard to the weight to be attached
to their expressions. I do not think that there has yet been a study
of what might be called Marx's *forma mentis;* with which Engels
had something in common, partly owing to congeniality, partly
owing to imitation or influence. Marx, as has been already remarked,
had a kind of abhorrence for researches of purely scholastic interest.
Eager for knowledge of *things* (I say, of concrete and individual
things) he attached little weight to discussions of *concepts* and the
forms of concepts; this sometimes degenerated into an exaggeration
in his own concepts. Thus we find in him a curious opposition between statements which, interpreted strictly, are erroneous; and yet
appear to us, and indeed are, loaded and pregnant with truth. Marx
was addicted, in short, to a kind of *concrete logic*.[1] Is it best then
to interpret his expressions literally, running the risk of giving them
a meaning different from what they actually bore in the writer's
inmost thoughts? Or is it best to interpret them broadly, running
the opposite risk of giving them a meaning, theoretically perhaps
more acceptable, but historically less true?

The same difficulty certainly occurs in regard to the writings of
numerous thinkers; but it is especially great in regard to those of
Marx. And the interpreter must proceed with caution: he must do
his work bit by bit, book by book, statement by statement, connect-
ing indeed these various indications one with another, but taking
account of differences of time, of actual circumstances, of fleeting
impressions, of mental and literary habits; and he must submit to
acknowledge ambiguities and incompleteness where either exists,
resisting the temptation to confirm and complete by his own judgment. It may be allowed for instance, as it appears to me for various
reasons, that the way in which historical materialism is stated above
is the same as that in which Marx and Engels understood it in their
inmost thoughts; or at least that which they would have agreed to
as correct if they had had more time available for such labours of

---

[1] The over-abused Dühring was not mistaken when he remarked that in Marx's
works expressions occur frequently "which appear to be universal without being
actually so" (Allgemein aussehen ohne es zu sein). *Kritische Geschichte der
Nationalökonomie und des Socialismus,* Berlin, 1871, p. 527.

scientific elaboration, and if criticism had reached them less tardily. And all this is of importance up to a certain point, for the interpreter and historian of ideas; since for the history of science, Marx and Engels are neither more nor less than they appear in their books and works; real, and not hypothetical or possible persons.[2]

But even for science itself, apart from the history of it, the hypothetical or possible Marx and Engels have their value. What concerns us theoretically is to understand the various possible ways of interpreting the problems proposed and the solutions thought out by Marx and Engels, and to select from the latter by criticism those which appear theoretically true and welcome. What was Marx's intellectual standpoint with reference to the Hegelian philosophy of history? In what consisted the criticism which he gave of it? Is the purport of this criticism always the same for instance in the article published in the *Deutsch-französische Jahrbücher*, for 1844, in the *Heilige Familie* of 1845, in the *Misère de la philosophie* of 1847, in the appendix to *Das Kommunistische Manifest* of 1848, in the preface to the *Zur Kritik* of 1859, and in the preface to the 2nd edition of *Das Kapital* of 1873? Is it so again in Engels' works in the *Antidühring*, in the article on *Feuerbach*, etc.? Did Marx ever really think of substituting, as some have believed, *Matter* or material fact for the Hegelian *Idea*? And what connection was there in his mind between the concepts *material* and *economic*? Again, can

---

[2] Gentile, *Una critica del materialismo storico* in the *Studî storici* of Crivellucci, vol. VI, 1897, pp. 379–423, throws doubt on the interpretation offered by me of the opinions of Marx and Engels, and on the method of interpretation itself. I gladly acknowledge that in my two earlier essays I do not clearly point out where precisely the textual interpretation ends and the really theoretical part begins; which theoretical exposition, only by conjecture and in the manner described above, can be said to agree with the inmost thoughts of Marx and Engels. In his recent book, *La filosofia di Marx*, Pisa, Spoerri, 1899 (in which the essay referred to is reprinted), Gentile remarks (p. 104), that, although it is a very convenient practice, and in some cases legitimate and necessary "to interpret doctrines, by calling a part of their statement worthless or accidental in form and external and weak, and a part the real substance and essential and vital, it is yet necessary to justify it in some way." He means certainly, "justify it as historical interpretation," since its justification as correction of theory cannot be doubtful. It seems to me that even historically the interpretation can be justified without difficulty when it is remembered that Marx *did not insist*, (as Gentile himself says) on his metaphysical notions; and did certainly insist on his historical opinions and on the political policy which he defended. Marx's personality as a sociological observer and the teacher of a social movement, certainly outweighs Marx as a metaphysician which he was almost solely as a young man. That it is worth the trouble to study Marx from all sides is not denied, and Gentile has now admirably expounded and criticised his youthful metaphysical ideas.

the explanation given by him, of his position with regard to Hegel: "the ideas determined by facts and not the facts by the ideas," be called an inversion of Hegel's view, or is it not rather the inversion of that of the ideologists and doctrinaires? [3] These are some of the questions pertaining to the *history of ideas,* which will be answered some time or other: perhaps at present the time has not yet arrived to write the history of ideas which are still in the process of development. [4]

But, putting aside this historical curiosity, it concerns us now to work at these ideas in order to advance in theoretical knowledge. How can historical materialism justify itself scientifically? This is the question I have proposed to myself, and to which the answer is given by the critical researches referred to at the beginning of this paragraph. Without returning to them I will give other examples, taken from the same source, that of the Marxian literature. How ought we to understand scientifically Marx's *neodialectic?* The final opinion expressed by Engels on the subject seems to be this: the dialect is the rhythm of the development of things, *i.e.* the inner law of things in their development. This rhythm is not determined *a priori,* and by metaphysical deduction, but is rather observed and gathered *a posteriori,* and only through the repeated observations and verifications that are made of it in various fields of reality, can it be presupposed that all facts develop through negations, and negations of negations. [5] Thus the dialect would be the discovery of a

---

[3] I confess that I have never been able to *understand*—however much I have considered the matter—the meaning of this passage (which ought however to be very evident, since it is quoted so often without any comment), in the preface to the second edition of *Das Kapital*: "Meine dialektische Methode ist der Grundlage nach von der Hegel'schen nicht nur verschieden, sondern ihr direktes Gegentheil. Für Hegel is *der Denkprocess,* den er sogar unter dem Namen *Idee* in ein selbständiger subjeckt verwandelt, der Demjurg des Wirklichen, das nur seine aüssere Erscheinung bildet. Bei mir ist umgekehrt *das Ideelle* nichts Andres als das im Menschenkopf umgesetzte und ubersetzte Materielle." (*Das Kapital* I, p. xvii.) Now it seems to me that the *Ideelle* of the last phrase has *no relation* to the *Denkprocess* and to the Hegelian *Idea* of the preceding phrase. . . . Some have thought that by the objections [I] stated, I intended to deny Marx's Hegelian *inspiration*. It is well to repeat that I merely deny the *logical relation* affirmed between the two philosophical theories. To deny Marx's Hegelian inspiration would be to contradict the evidence.

[4] Answers to several of the questions suggested above are now supplied in the book already referred to, by Gentile: *La Filosofia di Marx*.

[5] *Antidühring*, pt. I. ch. xlii., especially pp. 138–145, which passage is translated into Italian in the appendix to the book by Labriola referred to above: *Discorrendo di socialismo e di filosophia, cf. Das Kapital,* I. p. xvii, "Gelingt dies und spiegelt sich nun das Leben des stoffs ideell wieder, *so mag es aussehen,* als habe man es mit einer Konstruction a priori zu thun."

great natural law, less empty and formal than the so-called *law of evolution* and it would have nothing in common with the old Hegelian dialect except the name, which would preserve for us an historical record of the way in which Marx arrived at it. But does this natural rhythm of development exist? This could only be stated from observation, to which indeed, Engels appealed in order to assert its existence. And what kind of a law is one which is revealed to us by observation? Can it ever be a law which governs things absolutely, or is it not one of those which are now called tendencies, or rather is it not merely a simple and limited generalisation? And this recognition of rhythm through negations of negations, it is not some rag of the old metaphysics, from which it may be well to free ourselves.[6] This is the investigation needed for the progress of science. In like manner should other statements of Marx and Engels be criticised. What for example shall we think of Engels' controversy with Dühring concerning the basis of history: whether this is *political force* or *economic fact?* Will it not seem to us that this controversy can perhaps retain any value in face of Dühring's assertion that political fact is that *which is essential historically,* but in itself has not that general importance which it is proposed to ascribe to it? We may reflect for a moment that Engels' thesis: "force protects (*schutzt*) but does not cause (*verursacht*) usurpation," might be directly inverted into another that: "force *causes* usurpation, but economic interest *protects* it," and this by the well-known principle of the interdependence and competition of the social factors.

And the class war? In what sense is the general statement true that *history is a class war?* I should be inclined to say that history is a class war (1) when there are classes, (2) when they have antagonistic interests, (3) when they are aware of this antagonism, which would give us, in the main, the humourous equivalence that history is a class war only when it is a class war. In fact sometimes classes have not had antagonistic interests, and very often they are not conscious of them; of which the socialists are well aware when they endeavour, by efforts not always crowned with success (with the peasantry, for example, they have not yet succeeded), to arouse this consciousness in the modern proletariat. As to the possibility of the non-existence

---

[6] Lange, indeed, in reference to Marx's *Das Kapital,* remarked that the Hegelian dialectic, "the development by antithesis and synthesis, might almost be called an *anthropological discovery.* Only in history, as in the life of the individual, development by antithesis *certainly does not accomplish itself so easily and radically, nor with so much precision and symmetry as in speculative thought.*" (*Die Arbeiterfrage,* pp. 248–49.)

of classes, the socialists who prophesy this non-existence for the society of the future, must at least admit that it is not a matter intrinsically necessary to historical development, since in the future,
and without classes, history, it may well be hoped will continue. In
short even the particular statement that "history is a class war," has
that limited value of a canon and of a point of view, which we have
allowed in general to the materialist conception.[7]

The second of the two questions proposed at the beginning is:
How do the Marxians understand historical materialism? To me it
seems undeniable that in the Marxian literature, *i.e.* the writings
of the followers and interpreters of Marx, there exists in truth a
metaphysical danger of which it is necessary to beware. Even in the
writings of Professor Labriola some statements are met with which
have recently led a careful and accurate critic to conclude that Labriola understands historical materialism in the genuine and original sense of a metaphysic, and that of the worst kind, a metaphysic
of the contingent.[8] But although I have myself, on another occasion,
pointed out those statements and formulae which seem to me doubtful in Labriola's writings, I still think, as I thought then, that they
are superficial outgrowths on a system of thought essentially sound;
or to speak in a manner agreeing with the considerations developed
above, that Labriola, having educated himself in Marxism, may
have borrowed from it also some of its over-absolute style, and at
times a certain carelessness about the working out of concepts, which
are somewhat surprising in an old Herbartian like himself,[9] but
which he then corrects by observations and limitations always useful, even if slightly contradictory, because they bring us back to the
ground of reality.

Labriola, moreover, has a special merit, which marks him off from
the ordinary exponents and adapters of historical materialism. Although his theoretical formulae may here and there expose him
to criticism, when he turns to history, *i.e.* to concrete facts, he

---

[7] With regard to the *abstract* classes of Marxian economics and the *real* or
historical classes, see some remarks by Sorel in the article referred to in the
Journal des Economistes, p. 229. [Croce refers to Sorel's article "Sur la théorie
marxiste de la valeur," *Journal des Economistes*, March 1897.—Ed.]

[8] G. Gentile, *o.c.* in *Studî storici*, p. 421. *cf.* 400-401.

[9] Labriola has indeed an exaggerated dislike for what he calls the *scholastic*:
but even this exaggeration will not appear wholly unsuitable as a reaction against
the method of study which usually prevails among the mere men of letters, the
niggardly scholars, the empty talkers and jugglers with abstract thought, and all
those who lose their sense of close connection between science and life.

changes his attitude, throws off as it were, the burden of theory and becomes cautious and circumspect: *he possesses, in a high degree, respect for history*. He shows unceasingly his dislike for formulae of every kind, when concerned to establish and scrutinise definite processes, nor does he forget to give the warning that there exists "no theory, however good and excellent in itself, which will help us to a summary knowledge of every historical detail." [10]

In his last book we may note especially a full inquiry into what could possibly be the nature of a *history of Christianity*. Labriola criticises those who set up as an historical subject the *essence* of Christianity, of which it is unknown where or when it has existed; since the history of the last centuries of the Roman Empire shows us merely the origin and growth of what constituted the Christian society, or the church, a varying group of facts amidst varied historical conditions. This critical opinion held by Labriola seems to me perfectly correct; since it is not meant to deny (what I myself, do not deny) the justification of that method of historical exposition, which for lack of another phrase, I once called *histories by concepts*,[11] thus distinguishing it from the historical exposition of the life of a given social group in a given place and during a given period of time. He who writes the *history of Christianity,* claims in truth, to accomplish a task somewhat similar to the tasks of the historians of *literature,* of *philosophy,* of *art: i.e.* to isolate a body of facts which enter into a fixed concept, and to arrange them in a chronological series, without however denying or ignoring the source which these facts have in the other facts of life, but keeping them apart for the convenience of more detailed consideration. The worst of it is that whereas literature, philosophy, art and so on are determined or determinable concepts, Christianity is almost solely a bond, which unites beliefs often intrinsically very diverse; and, in writing the history of Christianity, there is often a danger of writing in reality the history of a *name, void without substance*.[12]

But what would Labriola say if his cautious criticism were turned against that *history of the origin of the family, of private property*

---

[10] *Discorrendo di socialismo e di filosophia,* l. ix.

[11] *Intorno alla storia della cultura* (Kulturgeschichtein *Atti* dell Accad. Pont.; vol. xxv. 1895, p. 8.)

[12] "If by Christianity is meant merely the sum of the beliefs and expectations concerning human destiny, these beliefs"—writes Labriola—"vary as much, in truth, as in the difference, to mention only one instance, between the free will of the Catholics after the Council of Trent, and the absolute determination of Calvin!" (*L.c.* ix.)

and of class distinctions, which is one of the most extensive historical applications made by the followers of Marx: desired by Marx,
sketched out by Engels on the lines of Morgan's investigations, carried on by others. Alas, in this matter, the aim was not merely to
write, as could, perhaps, have been done, a useful manual of the
historical facts which enter into these three concepts, but actually
an *additional history* was produced: A history, to use Labriola's own
phrase, of the *essence* family, of the *essence* class and of the *essence*
private property, with a predetermined cadence. A "history of the
family," to confine ourselves to one of the three groups of facts,—
can only be an enumeration and description of the particular forms
taken by the *family* amongst different races and in the course of
time: a series of particular histories, which unite themselves into a
general concept. It is this which is offered by Morgan's theories,
expounded by Engels, which theories modern criticism have cut
away on all sides.[13] Have they not allowed themselves to presup-
pose, as an historical stage, through which all races are fated to
pass, that chimerical matriarchate, in which the mere reckoning of
descent through the mother is confused with the predominance of
woman in the family and that of woman in society? Have we not
seen the reproofs and even the jeers directed by some Marxians
against those cautious historians who deny that it is possible to assert, in the present condition of the criticism of sources, the existence of a primitive communism, or a matriarchate, amongst the
Hellenic races? Indeed, I do not think that throughout this investigation proof has been given of much critical foresight.

I should also like to call Labriola's attention to another confusion, very common in Marxian writings, between *economic forms
of organisation* and *economic epoch.* Under the influence of evolu-
tionist positivism, those divisions which Marx expressed in general:
the *Asiatic,* the *antique,* the *feudal* and the *bourgeois* economic organisation, have become four historical *epochs: communism, slave
organisation, serf organisation,* and *wage-earning organisation.* But
the modern historian, who is indeed not such a superficial person
as the ordinary Marxians are accustomed to say, thus sparing themselves the trouble of taking a share in his laborious procedure, is
well aware that there are four *forms* of economic organisation,
which succeed and intersect one another in actual history, often

---

[13] Without referring to the somewhat unmethodical work of Westermarck,
History of Human Marriage, see especially Ernst Grosse's book, *Die Formen der
Familie und die Formen des Wirthschaft,* Freiburg in B., 1896.

forming the oddest mixtures and sequences. He recognizes an Egyptian mediævalism or feudalism, as he recognises an Hellenic mediævalism or feudalism; he knows too of a German *neo-mediævalism* which followed the flourishing bourgeois organisation of the German cities before the Reformation and the discovery of the New World; and he willingly compares the general economic conditions of the Greco-Roman world at its zenith with those of Europe in the sixteenth and seventeenth centuries.

Connected with this arbitrary conception of historical epochs, is the other of the inquiry into *the cause* (note carefully; into the cause) of the transition from one form to another. Inquiry is made, for instance, into the *cause* of the abolition of slavery, which must be the *same*, whether we are considering the decline of the Greco-Roman world or modern America; and so for serfdom, and for primitive communism and the capitalist system: amongst ourselves the famous Loria has occupied himself with these absurd investigations, the perpetual revelation of a single cause, of which he himself does not know exactly whether it be the earth, or population or something else—yet it should not take much to convince us (it would suffice for the purpose to read, with a little care, some books of narrative history), that the transition from one form of economic, or more generally, social, organisation, to another, is not the result of a *single cause,* nor even of *a group of causes which are always the same;* but is due to causes and circumstances which need examination for each case since they usually vary for each case. Death is death; but people die of many diseases.

But enough of this; and I may be allowed to conclude this paragraph by reference to a question which Labriola also brings forward in his recent work, and which he connects with the criticism of historical materialism.

Labriola distinguishes between historical materialism as an interpretation of history, and as a general conception of life and of the universe (*Lebens-und-Weltanschauung*), and he inquires what is the nature of the *philosophy immanent* in historical materialism; and after some remarks, he concludes that this philosophy is the *tendency to monism,* and is a *formal* tendency.

Here I take leave to point out that if into the terms *historical materialism two different things* are intruded, *i.e.:* (1) a method of interpretation; (2) a definite conception of life and of the universe; it is natural to find a philosopy in it, and moreover with a tendency to monism, because it was included therein at the outset. What close connection is there between these two orders of thought? Perhaps a logical connection of *mental coherence?* For my part, I confess that I am unable to see it. I believe, on the contrary, that Labriola, this time, is simply stating *à propos* of historical materialism what he thinks to be the necessary attitude of modern thought with regard to the problems of ontology; or what, according to him, should be the standpoint of the socialist opinion in regard to the conceptions of optimism and pessimism; and so on. I believe, in short, that he is not making an *investigation* which will reveal the philosophical conceptions underlying historical materialism; but merely a *digression,* even if a digression of interest and importance. And how many other most noteworthy opinions and impressions and sentiments are welcomed by socialist opinion! But why christen this assemblage of new facts by the name of historical materialism, which has hitherto expressed the well-defined meaning of a way of interpreting history? Is it not the task of the scientist to distinguish and analyse what in empirical reality and to ordinary knowledge appears mingled into one?

THE MARXIAN SYNTHESIS

STANISLAW OSSOWSKI

THE CONCEPT OF SOCIAL CLASS
IN MARXIAN DOCTRINE

The concept of social class is something more than one of the fundamental concepts of Marxian doctrine. It has in a certain sense become the symbol of his whole doctrine and of the political programme that is derived from it. This concept is expressed in the terms "class standpoint" and "class point of view," which in Marxist circles used until recently to be synonymous with "Marxist standpoint" or "Marxist point of view." In this sense "class standpoint" simply meant the opposite of "bourgeois standpoint."

According to Engels,[1] Marx effected a revolutionary change in the whole conception of world history. For Marx, so Engels maintained, had proved that "the whole of previous history is a history of class struggles, that in all the simple and complicated political struggles the only thing at issue has been the social and political rule of social classes."

The concept of social class is also linked with what Engels in the same article calls the second great discovery of Marx, to which he attaches so much importance in the history of science—the clarification of the relationship that prevails between capital and labour. Finally, it may be said that the concept of social class is bound up with the entire Marxian conception of culture as the superstructure of class interests.

The role of the class concept in Marxian doctrine is so immense that it is astonishing not to find a definition of this concept, which they use so constantly, anywhere in the works of either Marx or Engels. One might regard it as an undefined concept of which the meaning is explained contextually. But in fact one has only to com-

From Stanislaw Ossowski, *Class Structure in the Social Consciousness* (New York: The Free Press, 1963; London: Routledge & Kegan Paul Ltd., 1963), pp. 71–84. Copyright © 1963 by Stanislaw Ossowski. Reprinted with the permission of Macmillan Publishing Co., Inc. and Routledge & Kegan Paul Ltd.

[1] ME, Vol. II, p. 149; the quotation comes from F. Engels, *Karl Marx*. [ME refers to Karl Marx and Frederick Engels, *Selected Works in Two Volumes* (Moscow: Foreign Languages Publishing House, 1951).—Ed.]

pare the various passages in which the concept of social class is used by either writer to realize that the term "class" has for them a variable denotation: that is, that it refers to groups differentiated in various ways within a more inclusive category, such as the category of social groups with common economic interests, or the category of groups whose members share economic conditions that are identical in a certain respect. The sharing of permanent economic interests is a particularly important characteristic of social classes in Marxian doctrine, and for this reason it has been easy to overlook the fact that although it is, in the Marxian view, a *necessary condition* it does not constitute a *sufficient condition* for a valid definition of social class.

Marx left the problem of producing a definition of the concept of social class until much later. The manuscript of the third volume of his *magnum opus, Das Kapital,* breaks off dramatically at the moment when Marx was about to answer the question: "What constitutes a class?" We do not know what answer he would have given if death had not interrupted his work. Nor do we know whether he would have attempted to explain the discrepancies in his earlier statements.

After the death of Marx, Engels did not take up the question which the manuscript of *Das Kapital* left unanswered. Lenin's later definition, which has been popularized by Marxist text-books and encyclopaedias, links two different formulations but fails to explain how we are to regard them. Does the author see them as two equivalent definitions and does he link them in order to give a fuller characteristic of the designate of the concept of class? Or is the conjunction of the two formulations essential because the characteristics given in one of them are not necessarily conjoint to the characteristic given in the second? Independently of this, such metaphorical expressions as the "place in the historically determined system of social production" may be variously interpreted and Lenin's definition is sufficiently loose to be applicable to all the shades of meaning found in the term "class" as used by Marx and Engels.[2] Bucharin's

---

[2] Classes are large groups of people which differ from each other by the place they occupy in a historically determined system of social production, by their relation (in most cases fixed and formulated in law) to the means of production, by their role in the social organization of labour and, consequently, by the dimensions and method of acquiring the share of social wealth of which they dispose. Classes are groups of people one of which can appropriate the labour of another owing to the different places they occupy in a definite system of social economy." (V. I. Lenin, *A Great Beginning,* in *The Essentials of Lenin* in Two Volumes, London, Lawrence & Wishart, 1947, p. 492.)

definition,[3] which is also intended to reflect the Marxian conception of social class, affords room for even wider possibilities of interpretation, and it is only Bucharin's classification of social classes that enables one to grasp the denotation assigned by the author to the concept of social class.[4]

In using the concept of class based on economic criteria, Marx sometimes restricts the scope of this concept by introducing psychological criteria. An aggregate of people which satisfies the economic criteria of a social class becomes a class in the full meaning of this term only when its members are linked by the tie of class consciousness, by the consciousness of common interests, and by the psychological bond that arises out of common class antagonisms.[5] Marx is aware of the ambiguity and makes a terminological distinction between *Klasse an sich* and *Klasse für sich,* but he does not in general make much further use of these more narrowly defined concepts.

Marx sometimes uses a different term to denote a class which is not a class in the fullest sense because it lacks psychological bonds. For instance, he sometimes uses the term "stratum"; on other occasions he avoids using a more general term and confines himself to the name of a specified group such as the "small peasantry." At times he may even call certain classes which are conscious of their class interests "fractions" of a more inclusive class. In the case of capitalists and landowners, for instance, Marx sometimes sees them as two separate classes, at others as two fractions of a single class, the bourgeoisie.

All these discrepant uses of the term "class" were probably the

[3] N. Bucharin, *Historical Materialism, A System of Sociology,* London, 1926, p. 267 (English translation).
[4] *Ibid.* pp. 282–84.
[5] Cf. the following passages:
"The separate individuals form a class in so far as they have to carry on a common battle against another class." (K. Marx and F. Engels, *The German Ideology* (The Marxist-Leninist Library, Volume XVII, London, Lawrence & Wishart, 1940, pp. 48–49). "The organization of the proletarians into a class, and consequently into a political party." ("Manifesto of the Communist Party," ME, Vol. I, p. 41.) "In so far as millions of families live under economic conditions of existence that separate their mode of life, their interests and their culture from those of the other classes, and put them in hostile opposition to the latter, they form a class. In so far as there is merely a local interconnection among these small-holding peasants, and the identity of their interests begets no community, no national bond and no political organization among them, they do not form a class. They are consequently incapable of enforcing their class interest." (ME, Vol. I, p. 303; quotation from K. Marx.) "Bonaparte represented the most numerous class of the French society at that time, the small-holding (*Parzellen*) peasants" (ME, Vol. I, p. 302; quotation from "The Eighteenth Brumaire of Louis Bonaparte").

less important for Marx because, according to his theory, further
social development would render them obsolete. This was to result
from the growth of the social consciousness and from the predicted
disappearance of the difference between the *Klasse an sich* and the
Klasse für sich as well as from the progressive process of class polarization in the social structure.

The matter can however be put in a different way. We may take
it that Marx, instead of providing a definition of social class which
would make it possible to fix the scope of this concept, is giving
the model of a social class, the ideal type which is to be fully realized in the future, in the last stage of the development of the capitalist system. In the period in which Marx wrote, the industrial
proletariat of Western Europe was approximating to the ideal type
of a social class. Other social groups separated on the basis of economic criteria could be called classes only to a greater or lesser extent, and could approximate to the ideal type only in some respects.
Hence endeavours to apprehend them by means of conceptual categories with sharply-drawn boundaries of application must lead to
confusion.

However that may be, one should, when considering the Marxian
conception of class structure, remember that the component elements of this structure are confined to those groups which Marx
calls "classes" when contrasting them with "strata," in which "the
identity of their interests (those of the members of a 'stratum') begets no unity, no national union and no political organization."

As we shall see below, the Marxian concept of social class involves
certain conceptual complications which are more than a matter of
terminology.

*   *   *

THE BASIC DICHOTOMY

Marx and Engels are above all the inheritors of the dichotomic perceptions found in folklore and of the militant ideology of popular
revolutions. Reading their works, one never loses sight of the age-
old conflict between the oppressing classes and the oppressed classes.
I have already mentioned the dichotomic perceptions of the drama
of history that appear in the Communist Manifesto and in Engels'
work written three years earlier. The reader will recall the two-fold
way of conceiving human relations within the social structure in
terms of a dichotomic division: the manifold polar division of the

various oppressor and oppressed classes in earlier societies gives way to a single all-inclusive dichotomy. According to the forecast of the Communist Manifesto, the capitalist society was to achieve this dichotomy in full in the penultimate act of the drama, in the period that precedes the catastrophe. In approximating to such a dichotomy, the social structure of the capitalist world would then be nearing its end.

According to the founders of Marxian doctrine, the society in which they lived was characterized by a tendency to develop in the direction indicated above. In this society Marx discerned "the inevitable destruction of the middle bourgeois classes and of the so-called peasant estate." [6] In Engels' version, the era marked the accomplishment of "the division of society into a small, excessively rich class and a large, propertyless class of wage-workers." [7] The workers' rising in Paris on 22 June, 1848, was regarded by Marx as "the first great battle . . . between the two classes that split modern society . . . the war of labour and capital." [8]

TWO CONCEPTIONS OF THE INTERMEDIATE CLASSES

Marx the revolutionary and Marx the dramatist of history developed a dichotomic conception of a class society. Marx the sociologist was compelled in his analysis of contemporary societies to infringe the sharpness of the dichotomic division by introducing intermediate classes. He could not overlook the "mass of the nation . . . standing between the proletariat and the bourgeoisie." [9] These intermediate classes were a very important element in the pictures of his own era given us by Marx in his historical studies. Sometimes he speaks of "intermediate strata" when giving a narrower definition of a social class. Elsewhere the term "middle estate" appears, although in this context it does not denote an institutionalized group such as the French tiers état.

There is such a variety of social statuses and economic positions in these intermediate classes that it is difficult to confine them within a uniform scheme. The term "intermediate classes" suggests a scheme of gradation. And in fact one sometimes finds in Marx's

[6] ME, Vol. I, p. 75; quotation from K. Marx, Wage, Labour and Capital.

[7] ME, Vol. 1, p. 73; quotation from F. Engels' Introduction to Marx's Wage, Labour and Capital.

[8] ME, Vol. I, pp. 147, 148; quotations from K. Marx, The Class Struggles in France, 1848–1850.

[9] ME, Vol. I, p. 137.

writings the conception of the intermediate classes as groupings of individuals occupying an intermediate position in the economic gradation in respect of their relation to the means of production, or to the variety of their social roles and sources of income. For instance, in the *Address of the Central Committee to the Communist League*, written by Marx and Engels in 1850, the petit bourgeoisie includes the small capitalists, whose interests conflict with those of the industrialists. And again, in his *The Civil War in France*, Marx refers to the "liberal German middle class, with its professors, its capitalists, its aldermen and its penmen." [10] Here he conceives of the middle class in the sense in which the term is used in England or the United States. A capitalist—that is to say an owner of the means of production—may belong to one class or another depending on the amount of capital he owns. One should however bear in mind that Marx is not thinking here of "high society" nor of rows and columns in statistical tables. For him the amount of capital owned by an individual is associated with separate class interests.

It was not, however, this conception of an intermediate class that was incorporated in the set of basic concepts in the Marxian analysis of the capitalist society. In constructing his theoretical system, Marx set up the foundation for another conception of the class which occupies the intermediate position between the class of capitalists and the proletariat. This conception was not in fact formulated in its final form by either Marx or his pupils. It is nevertheless related to the scheme of class structure of the capitalist society that is characteristic for Marx and Marxism, a scheme in which three social classes correspond to three kinds of relations to the means of production.

In this scheme the intermediate class, which Marx usually calls the "petit bourgeoisie" regardless of whether reference is being made to urban or rural dwellers, is determined by the simultaneous application of two criteria. Each of these criteria taken separately forms the basis for a dichotomic division of social classes, although in a different way. One criterion is the ownership of the means of production. This is a criterion which, in a dichotomic scheme, divides society into propertied and propertyless classes. The second criterion is work, which, however, in contradistinction to Saint-Simon's conception, does not include the higher managerial func-

---

[10] ME, Vol. I, p. 447: quotation from the *Second Address of the General Council of the International Working Men's Association on the Franco-Prussian War.*

tions in capitalist enterprises. We have come across this second criterion in the dichotomic scheme as well. It divides society into working classes and idle classes. In this conception, the intermediate class consists of those who belong to both the overlapping categories; those who possess their own means of production and themselves make use of them.

Marxism applies still another version of this trichotomous division, a version which is usually not differentiated from the former one. In the first criterion of division (the ownership of the means of production) remains the same. On the other hand, the second criterion is not work but the fact of not employing hired labour. In this version, the intermediate class is more narrowly defined than in the earlier one. It does not include all those working people who possess their own means of production but only those who work on their own account without employing hired labour. According to this version, a wealthy farmer who employs two or three regular hired labourers, or who has small-holders working for him in exchange for an advance in cash or kind, is included in the class of rural capitalists. In the first version the petit bourgeoisie includes two strata; those who work in their own work-shops and employ hired labour, and those who do not employ such labour. Sociologically speaking, the first version is more suited to describe some conditions, the second more suited to others; thus it depends on various circumstances which need not be discussed here. The combination of the two versions gives two functionally differentiated intermediate classes, as the diagram . . . shows.

From the viewpoint of the Marxian assumptions concerned with the tendencies of development in capitalism, the position of the petit bourgeoisie, which is intermediate between the two basic classes, is sometimes interpreted in yet another way. The petit bour-

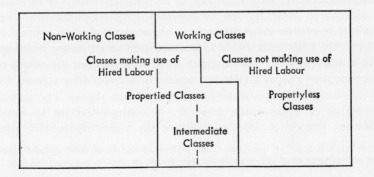

geoisie is said to belong to the propertied class so far as present conditions are concerned, to the proletariat with regard to its future prospects. Thus not only the craftsman but also the small-holder are potential proletarians.[11]

There is also an economic gradation that corresponds to this trichotomous scheme. The capitalist class is that class which owns large-scale means of production or at least sufficient to make possible the employment of hired labour; the petit bourgeoisie consists of those who dispose of the means of production on a modest scale; while the proletariat is in principle the class that owns no means of production whatsoever. In this functional scheme, however, it is not the degree of wealth that determines the boundaries between classes but the social roles, namely their relation to the means of production, work and their relation to the hiring of labour. In the scheme of gradation referred to earlier, on the other hand, the middle class could also include *rentiers,* the owners of small industrial establishments and other capitalists with property not exceeding the limits of "moderate wealth."

A strict observance of functional economic criteria in distinguishing the three classes—capitalists, petit bourgeoisie, and proletariat—leads, however, to conflicts with sociological criteria. For instance, an engineer would in his capacity as hired labour in a capitalistic establishment have to be included amongst the proletariat, as would a doctor employed in a private sanatorium. As we know, Marx associated the concept of the proletariat with the conception of a fundamental dichotomy. The proletarian is a man who is unprotected from the extremes of exploitation by any special qualifications which would prevent him from being replaced by another worker with equal physical strength. According to Marx's intentions, this criterion would exclude the engineer or doctor from the class of the proletariat.

Moreover, according to the Marxian assumption that a class is united by the common interests of its members in great social conflicts, yet another factor may help to correct a scheme based on "relations to the means of production." For instance, the salary of the engineer employed by the capitalist includes a portion of the

[11] Cf. Engels: *The Peasant Question in France and Germany,* ME, Vol. I, pp. 384, 395. Bucharin, in developing Marx's theory of social classes, differentiates the category of classes intermediate between the two basic classes in a different way than is done in our scheme; he distinguishes intermediate classes, transition classes and classes of mixed types (*op. cit.,* pp. 283-84).

"surplus value" produced by the workers and appropriated by the capitalist.

In summing up our discussion of this classical Marxian scheme of social roles in relation to the various ways of conceiving the social structure which were discussed earlier, we may consider it as an overlapping of a dichotomic view and a scheme of gradation. In this conception the intermediate class is determined by the boundaries of the two basic and antagonistic classes. It is separated from the others by virtue of the fact that these two basic classes are divided against each other, not by one single criterion, but by two or three criteria to which correspond class-groupings of varying extensions. The intermediate class is made up of people who are connected with each of the two basic classes but in differing respects. This connexion exists both in the logical sense (characteristics which enter into the definition of two basic classes) and in the sociological sense. At the same time, as I have already pointed out, the petit bourgeoisie, as determined by its peculiar "relations to the means of production," occupies a central position in the trichotomous economic gradation (the extent of ownership of the means of production).

A TRICHOTOMOUS FUNCTIONAL SCHEME
WITHOUT AN INTERMEDIATE CLASS

With Marx the revolutionary, the dichotomic conception of social structure is dominant. With Marx the theorist, we sometimes have to deal not only with the trichotomous scheme with a middle class between the two opposing classes but also with a scheme which is inherited from bourgeois economics. This is the trichotomous functional scheme of Adam Smith. This scheme appears rarely in the works of Marx and Engels,[12] but its importance is increased by the fact that it is the starting-point of the last chapter of the third volume of *Das Kapital,* the chapter which is devoted exclusively to an analysis of classes in modern society. This uncompleted chapter, entitled "Classes," opens with the words:

> The owners merely of labour-power, owners of capital, and land-owners, whose respective sources of income are wages, profit and

[12] Cf. *Ludwig Feuerbach and the End of Classical German Philosophy* (ME, Vol. II, p. 356); Marx's letter to Engels of April 30, 1868 (K. Marx and F. Engels, *Selected Correspondence,* Moscow, Foreign Languages Publishing House, n.d., pp. 245-50).

ground-rent, in other words, wage-labourers, capitalists and landowners, constitute then three big classes of modern society based upon
the capitalist mode of production.[13]

And a little further on, when he is dealing with the question
"What constitutes a class?" Marx again takes precisely this conception of the social structure as his starting-point.

In the dichotomic conception and in the trichotomous Marxian
conception which I have discussed earlier the emphasis is placed
on human relationships. In Smith's conception, on the other hand,
the viewpoint of an economist rather than of a sociologist is dominant. The main stress falls on the relations of people to things.
Clear economic categories, that is criteria concerned with relationships to things, leave no place in the social structure for the intermediate classes which a sociologist cannot overlook. In Adam
Smith's scheme those who own their own means of production and
yet work themselves do not form a separate class but belong to two
or three classes simultaneously.

> It sometimes happens, indeed, that a single independent workman
> has stock sufficient both to purchase the materials of his work and to
> maintain himself till it be completed. He is both master and workman,
> and enjoys the whole produce of his own labour, or the whole value
> which it adds to the materials upon which it is bestowed. It includes
> what are usually two distinct revenues, belonging to two distinct per-
> sons, the profits of stock, and the wages of labour.[14]

Marx considers this point in the third volume of *Das Kapital*, and
even accords it conditional approval.[15]

Thus we find two different trichotomous schemes of social structure in Marx, to both of which may be applied the definition of
class as a group determined by the relation to the means of production. In the first case (capitalists, petit bourgeoisie, proletariat), the

[13] K. Marx, *Capital*, Vol. III, Moscow, Foreign Languages Publishing House,
1959, p. 862.

[14] *Op. cit.*, Vol. I, Everyman's Library, p. 58.

[15] "When an independent labourer—let us take a small farmer, since all three
forms of revenue may here be applied—works for himself and sells his own
product, he is first considered as his own employer (capitalist), who makes use
of himself as a labourer, and second as his own landlord, who makes use of himself as his own tenant. To himself as wage-worker he pays wages, to himself as
capitalist he gives the profit, and to himself as landlord he pays rent. Assuming
the capitalist mode of production and the relations corresponding to it to be the
general basis of society, this subsumption is correct, in so far as it is not thanks
to his labour, but to his ownership of the means of production . . . that he is
in a position to appropriate his own surplus labour." *Capital*, Vol. III, Lawrence
& Wishart, London, 1960, p. 853.

various classes have correspondingly *various relationships to the means of production.* In the second case (land-owners, owners of capital and those who own nothing but their own labour), the classes are determined by the *relation to the various means of production,* the capacity to work being regarded here as a category of the means of production.

A MULTI-DIVISIONAL STRUCTURE

A functional scheme can contain more than three classes, as we saw with Madison [James Madison, *The Federalist,* No. 10 (1787)]. In Marx's writings a direct formulation which would conceive of social structure in terms of such a multi-divisional scheme is nowhere to be found. But if we bring together statements made in various works we find that even an image of this kind can be derived from his works. In his *German Ideology* we find the bourgeoisie and the class of the large industrialists set against each other as classes of different and in a certain respect even opposite social functions; for the interests of the bourgeoisie are contained within national boundaries, while the large industrialists form a cosmopolitan class on an international scale.[16] In his *Class Struggles in France* Marx shows us how the class interests of the French financial aristocracy clash with those of the industrial bourgeoisie.[17] Marx attributes to the financial aristocracy the "desire to enrich themselves not by production but by cleverly appropriating to themselves riches that already exist," and calls them ironically "the *lumpenproletariat* on the heights of bourgeois society." [18] Apart from these two rival classes, Marx mentions the petit bourgeoisie which is removed from political power. A year or so later, in his description of the same society in *The Eighteenth Brumaire,* Marx once again shifts the line dividing the bourgeoisie into two antagonistic factions. This antagonism, for which the ideological superstructure was the conflict between Orleanists and Legitimists, is seen as the outcome of the competition between capital and ownership of land.[19] These factions,

---

[16] K. Marx and F. Engels, *The German Ideology,* Lawrence & Wishart, 1939, pp. 24–26.

[17] "The mania to get rich not by production, but by pocketing the already available wealth of others." *The Class Struggles in France 1848–1850,* ME, Vol. I, pp. 128–29.

[18] *The Class Struggles in France 1848–1850,* ME, Vol. I, p. 131.

[19] K. Marx, *The Eighteenth Brumaire of Louis Bonaparte,* ME, Vol. I, pp. 247–53.

based on the ownership of different types of wealth, are the two basic classes from Adam Smith's scheme.

If we now take the class differentiation of the rural population, as it is presented for instance by Engels in the introduction to his work *The Peasant Wars in Germany*,[20] and if we do not overlook the *lumpenproletariat*—which is not a "class" according to the Marxian definition but a "stratum"—"a mass sharply differentiated from the industrial proletariat" [21]—a stratum which can play a specific role in social movements—we obtain an image in which the capitalist society is functionally differentiated into seven, eight or even nine classes or strata.

THE OVERLAPPING OF VIEWPOINTS

In his character of revolutionary, economist and sociologist, Marx inherited all three basic types of conceiving the class structure which are encountered in the history of European thought. These are the dichotomic scheme, the scheme of gradation and the functional scheme. At the same time he introduced a characteristic way of conceiving this structure, by intersecting two or three dichotomic divisions. It is this latter way that has come to be regarded as the classic Marxian scheme, although Marx does not employ it when he is discussing the concept of class in the last pages of his greatest work.

We have noted in Marx's writings two versions of this classic Marxian scheme, and also an explicit formulation of Adam Smith's trichotomous functional scheme; there is also an implied multi-class version of a functional scheme which recalls that of Madison. Thus it may be maintained that the works of Marx and Engels contain at least six different ways of conceiving the structure of contemporary capitalist societies. The definition of a social class which refers to the relations to the means of production is just as applicable to the classic Marxian scheme as it is to the schemes of Adam Smith and of Madison.

The schemes may differ, but this does not involve contradictory assumptions. The dichotomic aspect of the Marxian theory of classes indicates the direction in which capitalist societies will develop; seen in this perspective the multi-divisional schemes are intended to refer to transitory phenomena. But even without a ref-

[20] F. Engels, Prefatory Note to *The Peasant War in Germany*, ME, Vol. I, pp. 584–86.

[21] *The Class Struggles in France 1848–1850*, ME, Vol. I, p. 142.

erence to trends of development the Smithian scheme cited in the third volume of *Das Kapital* and elsewhere need not run counter to the basic dichotomy. It is sufficient to group land-owners and owners of capital in a single more inclusive "superior" category of "propertied classes" and to set them against "those who own nothing but their own labour" as the "propertyless class." The trichotomous scheme of gradation may be reconciled with the dichotomic conception by treating the middle class as a grouping resulting from overlapping class extensions or as one determined by the boundaries of the two opposite classes.

We may still seek other explanations. In the Marxian image of capitalist society the dichotomy refers to the classes that participate in capitalist production, which, it should be noted, is not the only form of production in existing capitalist societies. The dichotomy is a basic scheme for the Marxian model of a capitalist society, with its two large classes which appear *"à l'interieur de l'atelier capitaliste,"* as Labriola puts it. But this dichotomous class-division of capitalist society is not inconsistent with the existence of other social groups, so long as one accepts the view that other forms of relations of production and their corresponding classes have survived from the past within this society. The dichotomic scheme is intended to characterise capitalist society with regard to its dominant and peculiar form of relations of production, while the multidivisional scheme reflects the actual social structure. . . .[22]

[22] "Dire que le capitalisme est caractérisé par l'organisation autoritaire de la fabrique et la division en classes—capitalistes et salariés—qui en découle, ce n'est pas nier qu'avec le capitalisme survivent d'autres régimes économiques. . . . Si Marx s'occupait des deux grandes classes qui existent à l'intérieur de l'atelier capitaliste, il ne pouvait pour cela supprimer d'un trait de sa plume autoritaire petite bourgeoisie, groupes professionnels et autres métiers inclassables." (Arturo Labriola, *Karl Marx—L'économiste—Le socialiste*, Paris, 1909, pp. 185–86). Sorel points out that Marx frequently confuses logical constructions with his descriptions of actual phenomena, and conjectures that Marx did not always realize the abstract character of his theory of classes.

CLASS CONSCIOUSNESS
GEORG LUKÁCS

Marx's chief work breaks off just as he is about to embark on the definition of class. This omission was to have serious consequences both for the theory and the practice of the proletariat. For on this vital point the later movement was forced to base itself on interpretations, on the collation of occasional utterances by Marx and Engels and on the independent extrapolation and application of their method. In Marxism the division of society into classes is determined by position within the process of production. But what, then, is the meaning of class consciousness? The question at once branches out into a series of closely interrelated problems. First of all, how are we to understand class consciousness (in theory)? Second, what is the (practical) function of class consciousness, so understood, in the context of the class struggle? This leads to the further question: is the problem of class consciousness a "general" sociological problem or does it mean one thing for the proletariat and another for every other class to have emerged hitherto? And lastly, is class consciousness homogeneous in nature and function or can we discern different gradations and levels in it? And if so, what are their practical implications for the class struggle of the proletariat?

I

In his celebrated account of historical materialism[1] Engels proceeds from the assumption that although the essence of history consists in the fact that "nothing happens without a conscious purpose or an intended aim," to understand history it is necessary to go further than this. For on the one hand, "the many individual wills active in history for the most part produce results quite other than those intended—often quite the opposite; *their motives, therefore,*

From George Lukács, *History and Class Consciousness* (London: The Merlin Press Ltd., 1971), pp. 46–55. Copyright 1968 by Hermann Luchterand Verlag. Translation copyright 1971 by The Merlin Press Ltd. Reprinted with the permission of The Merlin Press Ltd.

[1] *Feuerbach and the End of Classical German Philosophy*, S.W. [Marx/Engels, *Selected Works* (2 vols.) (London: Lawrence and Wishart, 1950)] II, pp. 354 ff.

in relation to the total result are likewise of only secondary importance. On the other hand, the further question arises: *what driving forces in turn stand behind these motives?* What are the historical causes which transform themselves into these motives in the brain of the actors?" He goes on to argue that these driving forces ought themselves to be determined, in particular those which "set in motion great masses, whole peoples and again whole classes of the people; and which create *a lasting action resulting in a great transformation.*" The essence of scientific Marxism consists, then, in the realisation that the real motor forces of history are independent of man's (psychological) consciousness of them.

At a more primitive stage of knowledge this independence takes the form of the belief that these forces belong, as it were, to nature and that in them and in their causal interactions it is possible to discern the "eternal" laws of nature. As Marx says of bourgeois thought: "Man's reflections on the forms of social life and consequently also his scientific analysis of those forms, take a course directly opposite to that of their actual historical development. He begins post festum, with the results of the process of development ready to hand before him. The characters . . . have already acquired the stability of natural self-understood forms of social life, before man seeks to decipher not their historical character (for in his eyes they are immutable) but their meaning." [2]

This is a dogma whose most important spokesmen can be found in the political theory of classical German philosophy and in the economic theory of Adam Smith and Ricardo. Marx opposes to them a critical philosophy, a theory of theory and a consciousness of consciousness. This critical philosophy implies above all historical criticism. It dissolves the rigid, unhistorical, natural appearance of social institutions; it reveals their historical origins and shows therefore that they are subject to history in every respect including historical decline. Consequently history does not merely unfold *within* the terrain mapped out by these institutions. It does not resolve itself into the evolution of *contents,* of men and situations, etc., while the *principles* of society remain eternally valid. Nor are these institutions the *goal* to which all history aspires, such that when they are realised history will have fulfilled her mission and will then be at an end. On the contrary, history is precisely *the history of these institutions,* of the changes they undergo *as* institutions which

[2] *Capital,* I, p. 75.

bring men together in societies. Such institutions start by controlling economic relations between men and go on to permeate all human relations (and hence also man's relations with himself and with nature, etc.).

At this point bourgeois thought must come up against an insuperable obstacle, for its starting-point and its goal are always, if not always consciously, an apologia for the existing order of things or at least the proof of their immutability.[3] "Thus there has been history, but there is no longer any," [4] Marx observes with reference to bourgeois economics, a dictum which applies with equal force to all attempts by bourgeois thinkers to understand the process of history. (It has often been pointed out that this is also one of the defects of Hegel's philosophy of history.) As a result, while bourgeois thought is indeed able to conceive of history as a problem, it remains an *intractable* problem. Either it is forced to abolish the process of history and regard the institutions of the present as eternal laws of nature which for "mysterious" reasons and in a manner wholly at odds with the principles of a rational science were held to have failed to establish themselves firmly, or indeed at all, in the past. (This is characteristic of bourgeois sociology.) Or else, everything meaningful or purposive is banished from history. It then becomes impossible to advance beyond the mere "individuality" of the various epochs and their social and human representatives. History must then insist with Ranke that every age is "equally close to God," i.e. has attained an equal degree of perfection and that—for quite different reasons—there is no such thing as historical development.

In the first case it ceases to be possible to understand the *origin* of social institutions.[5] The objects of history appear as the objects of immutable, eternal laws of nature. History becomes fossilised in a *formalism* incapable of comprehending that the real nature of socio-historical institutions is that they consist of *relations between men*. On the contrary, men become estranged from this, the true source of historical understanding and cut off from it by an unbridgeable gulf. As Marx points out,[6] people fail to realise "that

---

[3] And also of the "pessimism" which *perpetuates* the present state of affairs and represents it as the uttermost limit of human development just as much as does "optimism." In this respect (and in this respect alone) Hegel and Schopenhauer are on a par with each other.

[4] *The Poverty of Philosophy*, p. 135.

[5] *Ibid.*, p. 117.

[6] *Ibid.*, p. 122.

these definite social relations are just as much the products of men as linen, flax, etc."

In the second case, history is transformed into the irrational rule of blind forces which is embodied at best in the "spirit of the people" or in "great men." It can therefore only be described pragmatically but it cannot be rationally understood. Its only possible organisation would be aesthetic, as if it were a work of art. Or else, as in the philosophy of history of the Kantians, it must be seen as the instrument, senseless in itself, by means of which timeless, suprahistorical, ethical principles are realised.

Marx resolves this dilemma by exposing it as an illusion. The dilemma means only that the contradictions of the capitalist system of production are reflected in these mutually incompatible accounts of the same object. For in this historiography with its search for "sociological" laws or its formalistic rationale, we find the reflection of man's plight in bourgeois society and of his helpless enslavement by the forces of production. "To them, *their own social action,*" Marx remarks,[7] "takes the form of the action of objects which rule the producers instead of being ruled by them." This law was expressed most clearly and coherently in the purely natural and rational laws of classical economics. Marx retorted with the demand for a historical critique of economics which resolves the totality of the reified objectivities of social and economic life into *relations between men*. Capital and with it every form in which the national economy objectifies itself is, according to Marx, "not a thing but a social relation between persons mediated through things." [8]

However, by reducing the objectivity of the social institutions so hostile to man to relations between men, Marx also does away with the false implications of the irrationalist and individualist principle, i.e. the other side of the dilemma. For to eliminate the objectivity attributed both to social institutions inimical to man and to their historical evolution means the restoration of this objectivity to their underlying basis, to the relations between men; it does not involve the elimination of laws and objectivity independent of the will of man and in particular the wills and thoughts of individual men. It simply means that this objectivity is the self-objectification of human society at a particular stage in its development; its laws

---

[7] *Capital,* I, p. 75 (my italics). Cf. also Engels, *The Origin of the Family, Private Property and the State,* S.W. II, pp. 292–93.

[8] *Capital,* I, p. 766. Cf. also *Wage Labour and Capital,* S.W. II, p. 83; on machines see *The Poverty of Philosophy,* p. 149; on money, *ibid.,* p. 89, etc.

hold good only within the framework of the historical context which produced them and which is in turn determined by them.

It might look as though by dissolving the dilemma in this manner we were denying consciousness any decisive role in the process of history. It is true that the conscious reflexes of the different stages of economic growth remain historical facts of great importance; it is true that while dialectical materialism is itself the product of this process, it does not deny that men perform their historical deeds themselves and that they do so consciously. But as Engels emphasises in a letter to Mehring,[9] this consciousness is false. However, the dialectical method does not permit us simply to proclaim the "falseness" of this consciousness and to persist in an inflexible confrontation of true and false. On the contrary, it requires us to investigate this "false consciousness" concretely as an aspect of the historical totality and as a stage in the historical process.

Of course bourgeois historians also attempt such concrete analyses; indeed they reproach historical materialists with violating the concrete uniqueness of historical events. Where they go wrong is in their belief that the concrete can be located in the empirical individual of history ("individual" here can refer to an individual man, class or people) and in his empirically given (and hence psychological or mass-psychological) consciousness. And just when they imagine that they have discovered the most concrete thing of all: *society as a concrete totality,* the system of production at a given point in history and the resulting division of society into classes— they are in fact at the furthest remove from it. In missing the mark they mistake something wholly abstract for the concrete. "These relations," Marx states, "are not those between one individual and another, but between worker and capitalist, tenant and landlord, etc. Eliminate these relations and you abolish the whole of society; your Prometheus will then be nothing more than a spectre without arms or legs. . . ."[10]

Concrete analysis means then: the relation to society *as a whole.* For only when this relation is established does the consciousness of their existence that men have at any given time emerge in all its essential characteristics. It appears, on the one hand, as something which is *subjectively* justified in the social and historical situation, as something which can and should be understood, i.e.

[9] *Dokumente des Sozialismus,* II, p. 76.
[10] *The Poverty of Philosophy,* p. 112.

as "right." At the same time, *objectively*, it by-passes the essence of the evolution of society and fails to pinpoint it and express it adequately. That is to say, objectively, it appears as a "false consciousness." On the other hand, we may see the same consciousness as something which fails *subjectively* to reach its self-appointed goals, while furthering and realising the *objective* aims of society of which it is ignorant and which it did not choose.

This twofold dialectical determination of "false consciousness" constitutes an analysis far removed from the naïve description of what men *in fact* thought, felt and wanted at any moment in history and from any given point in the class structure. I do not wish to deny the great importance of this, but it remains after all merely the *material* of genuine historical analysis. The relation with concrete totality and the dialectical determinants arising from it transcend pure description and yield the category of objective possibility. By relating consciousness to the whole of society it becomes possible to infer the thoughts and feelings which men would have in a particular situation if they were *able* to assess both it and the interests arising from it in their impact on immediate action and on the whole structure of society. That is to say, it would be possible to infer the thoughts and feelings appropriate to their objective situation. The number of such situations is not unlimited in any society. However much detailed researches are able to refine social typologies there will always be a number of clearly distinguished basic types whose characteristics are determined by the types of position available in the process of production. Now class consciousness consists in fact of the appropriate and rational reactions "imputed" [*zugerechnet*] to a particular typical position in the process of production.[11] This consciousness is, therefore, neither the sum nor the average of what is thought or felt by the single individuals who make up the class. And yet the historically significant actions of the class as a whole are determined in the last resort by this consciousness and not by the thought of the individual —and these actions can be understood only by reference to this consciousness.

This analysis establishes right from the start the distance that

---

[11] In this context it is unfortunately not possible to discuss in greater detail some of the ramifications of these ideas in Marxism, e.g. the very important category of the "economic persona." Even less can we pause to glance at the relation of historical materialism to comparable trends in bourgeois thought (such as Max Weber's ideal types).

separates class consciousness from the empirically given, and from the psychologically describable and explicable ideas which men form about their situation in life. But it is not enough just to state that this distance exists or even to define its implications in a formal and general way. We must discover, firstly, whether it is a phenomenon that differs according to the manner in which the various classes are related to society as a whole and whether the differences are so great as to produce *qualitative distinctions.* And we must discover, secondly, the *practical* significance of these different possible relations between the objective economic totality, the imputed class consciousness and the real, psychological thoughts of men about their lives. We must discover, in short, the *practical, historical function* of class consciousness.

Only after such preparatory formulations can we begin to exploit the category of objective possibility systematically. The first question we must ask is how far is it *in fact* possible to discern the whole economy of a society from inside it? It is essential to transcend the limitations of particular individuals caught up in their own narrow prejudices. But it is no less vital not to overstep the frontier fixed for them by the economic structure of society and establishing their position in it.[12] Regarded abstractly and formally, then, class consciousness implies a class-conditioned *unconsciousness* of one's own socio-historical and economic condition.[13] This condition is given as a definite structural relation, a definite formal nexus which appears to govern the whole of life. The "falseness," the illusion implicit in this situation is in no sense arbitrary; it is simply the intellectual reflex of the objective economic structure. Thus, for example, "the value or price of labour-power takes on the appearance of the price or value of labour itself . . ." and "the illusion is created that the totality is paid labour. . . . In contrast to that, under slavery even that portion of labour which is paid for appears unpaid for." [14] Now it requires the most painstaking historical analysis to use the category of objective possibility so as to isolate the conditions in which this illusion can be exposed and a real connection with the totality established. For if from the vantage point of a particular

[12] This is the point from which to gain an historical understanding of the great utopians such as Plato or Sir Thomas More. Cf. also Marx on Aristotle, *Capital,* I, pp. 59–60.

[13] "But although ignorant of this, yet he says it," Marx says of Franklin, *Capital,* I, p. 51. And similarly: "They know not what they do, but they do it." *Ibid.,* p. 74.

[14] *Wages, Price and Profit,* S.W., I, pp. 388–89.

class the totality of existing society is not visible; if a class thinks the thoughts imputable to it and which bear upon its interests right through to their logical conclusion and yet fails to strike at the heart of that totality, then such a class is doomed to play only a subordinate role. It can never influence the course of history in either a conservative or progressive direction. Such classes are normally condemned to passivity, to an unstable oscillation between the ruling and the revolutionary classes, and if perchance they do erupt then such explosions are purely elemental and aimless. They may win a few battles but they are doomed to ultimate defeat.

For a class to be ripe for hegemony means that its interests and consciousness enable it to organise the whole of society in accordance with those interests. The crucial question in every class struggle is this: which class possesses this capacity and this consciousness at the decisive moment? This does not preclude the use of force. It does not mean that the class-interests destined to prevail and thus to uphold the interests of society as a whole can be guaranteed an automatic victory. On the contrary, such a transfer of power can often only be brought about by the most ruthless use of force (as e.g. the primitive accumulation of capital). But it often turns out that questions of class consciousness prove to be decisive in just those situations where force is unavoidable and where classes are locked in a life-and-death-struggle. Thus the noted Hungarian Marxist Erwin Szabó is mistaken in criticizing Engels for maintaining that the Great Peasant War (of 1525) was essentially a reactionary movement. Szabó argues that the peasants' revolt was suppressed *only* by the ruthless use of force and that its defeat was not grounded in socio-economic factors and in the class consciousness of the peasants. He overlooks the fact that the deepest reason for the weakness of the peasantry and the superior strength of the princes is to be sought in class consciousness. Even the most cursory student of the military aspects of the Peasants' War can easily convince himself of this.

It must not be thought, however, that all classes ripe for hegemony have a class consciousness with the same inner structure. Everything hinges on the extent to which they can become conscious of the actions they need to perform in order to obtain and organise power. The question then becomes: how far does the class concerned perform the actions history has imposed on it "consciously" or "unconsciously"? And is that consciousness "true" or "false." These distinctions are by no means academic. Quite apart from problems of culture where such fissures and dissonances are crucial, in all practical matters too the fate of a class depends on its ability to elucidate and solve the problems with which history confronts it. And here it becomes transparently obvious that class consciousness is concerned neither with the thoughts of individuals, however advanced, nor with the state of scientific knowledge. For example, it is quite clear that ancient society was broken economically by the limitations of a system built on slavery. But it is equally clear that neither the ruling classes nor the classes that rebelled against them in the name of revolution or reform could perceive this. In consequence the practical emergence of these problems meant that the society was necessarily and irremediably doomed.

The situation is even clearer in the case of the modern bourgeoisie, which, armed with its knowledge of the workings of economics, clashed with feudal and absolutist society. For the bourgeoisie was quite unable to perfect its fundamental science, its own science of classes: the reef on which it foundered was its failure to discover even a theoretical solution to the problem of crises. The fact that a scientifically acceptable solution does exist is of no avail. For to accept that solution, even in theory, would be tantamount to observing society *from a class standpoint other than that of the bourgeoisie*. And no class can do that—unless it is willing to abdicate its power freely. Thus the barrier which converts the class consciousness of the bourgeoisie into "false" consciousness is objective; it is the class situation itself. It is the objective result of the economic set-up, and is neither arbitrary, subjective nor psychological. The class consciousness of the bourgeoisie may well be able to reflect all the problems of organisation entailed by its hegemony and by the capitalist transformation and penetration of total production. But it becomes obscured as soon as it is called upon to face problems that remain within its jurisdiction but which point beyond the limits of capitalism. The discovery of the "natural laws" of economics is pure light in comparison with mediaeval feudalism or even the mercantilism of the transitional period, but by an internal dialectical twist they became "natural laws based on the unconsciousness of those who are involved in them." [15]

It would be beyond the scope of these pages to advance further and attempt to construct a historical and systematic typology of the

---

[15] Engels, *Umriss zu einer Kritik der Nationalökonomie*, Nachlass [*Aus dem literarischen Nachlass von Karl Marx, Friedrich Engels und Ferdinand Lassalle* (4 vols.) edited by Franz Mehring (Stuttgart: 1902)] I, p. 449.

possible degrees of class consciousness. That would require—in the first instance—an exact study of the point in the total process of production at which the interests of the various classes are most immediately and vitally involved. Secondly, we would have to show how far it would be in the interest of any given class to go beyond this immediacy, to annul and transcend its immediate interest by seeing it as a factor within a totality. And lastly, what is the nature of the totality that is then achieved? How far does it really embrace the true totality of production? It is quite evident that the quality and structure of class consciousness must be very different if, e.g. it remains stationary at the separation of consumption from production (as with the Roman *Lumpenproletariat*) or if it represents the formation of the interests of circulation (as with merchant capital). Although we cannot embark on a systematic typology of the various points of view it can be seen from the foregoing that these specimens of "false" consciousness differ from each other both qualitatively, structurally and in a manner that is crucial for the activity of the classes in society.

SIX

THE PROLETARIAT

SHLOMO AVINERI

Only at this late stage does the proletariat appear in Marx's thinking and social criticism. Its appearance at this point has systematic significance, because it explains Marx's interest in the proletariat within the theoretical framework of this thought. As we shall see later in this chapter, the proletariat, for Marx, is not just an historical phenomenon: its suffering and dehumanization are, according to Marx, a paradigm for the human condition at large. It is not the proletarians' concrete conditions of life but their relation to an anthropological determination of man which primarily interest Marx. Consequently, though Marx is certainly not the first to discuss the proletariat and its position in industrial society, he is the first to relate it to general terms of reference which, for their part, draw very heavily on the Hegelian heritage and tradition.

Marx is fully cognizant of his debt to his predecessors, though there is a significant difference between his readily admitted indebtedness to French Restoration historians and his more ambivalent acknowledgment to Lorenz von Stein. Most of Marx's reading notes for the crucial summer of 1843, when his views on state and society took shape, deal with historical accounts of the role of social classes in the French Revolution, and most of his sources are naturally French; Marx even arranged an index to his various notebooks, according to the social background of the different constitutional instruments of the Revolution.[1] In 1852 Marx tells Weydemeyer that the "bourgeois historians" discovered the role of the classes in determining developments in modern society.[2] Two years later, in a letter to Engels, he specifically refers to Thierry's contribution, but points out that like other Restoration historians Thierry overlooked the fact that social struggles did not end with the emergence and hegemony of the bourgeoisie. The real and final struggle, according to Marx, occurs at the moment of the bourgeoi-

From Shlomo Avineri, *The Social and Political Thought of Karl Marx* (Cambridge: Cambridge University Press, 1968), pp. 52–63. Reprinted with the permission of Cambridge University Press.

[1] *MEGA*, I, 1/2, pp. 118–36; the index pp. 122–23.

[2] Marx to Weydemeyer, 5 March 1852 (*Selected Correspondence*, p. 86).

sie's victory, when it becomes a ruling class and ceases to be a *tiers état* alongside the clergy and the nobility.[3]

Marx's relation to Lorenz von Stein is more complex and remains controversial. Robert Tucker recently pointed out how much Marx's description of the proletariat draws on Stein's *Der Sozialismus und Kommunismus des heutigen Frankreichs*. In this Tucker follows several earlier writers who maintained that Marx had become acquainted with French socialist thinking through Stein's book, and that only later did he read the French authors themselves.[4] Others, however, maintain that, because of the writers' different levels of discussion and conceptualization, Stein's influence on Marx should be rather held at a minimum. It would indeed be difficult to suppose that Marx could be too impressed by Stein's somewhat simplistic arguments.[5]

It is difficult to take issue with these arguments if the problem is posed as if Stein were Marx's only conceivable source. Stein's book does not appear in Marx's reading lists of 1842—but Marx's notes for that year include only books on art and mythology, and he certainly read books on history as well, so the notes as they survive cannot be considered comprehensive. Marx's remarks about Stein are none too clear. In *The Holy Family* Marx reproaches Bruno Bauer for concentrating in his discussion on French socialism and not paying any attention to the English working-class movement on the sole ground that Stein has nothing on it. Marx feels this is a serious weakness of Stein's book. In *The German Ideology,* however, Marx compares Stein's study quite favourably with Karl Grün's book on French and Belgian socialism, and points out that Grün's book is a muddled rehash of Stein's work.[6]

[3] Marx to Engels, 27 July 1854 (*ibid.,* p. 105).

[4] R. C. Tucker, *Philosophy and Myth in Karl Marx* (Cambridge, 1961), pp. 114–16; cf. G. Adler "Die Anfänge der Marxschen Sozialtheorie und ihre Beeinflussung durch Hegel, Feuerbach, Stein und Proudhon," *Festgabe für Adolf Wagner* (Leipzig, 1905), pp. 16 ff.; P. Vogel, *Hegels Gesellschaftsbegriff und seine geschichtliche Fortbildung durch Lorenz Stein, Marx, Engels und Lassalle* (Berlin, 1925); B. Földes, *Das Problem Karl Marx—Lorenz Stein* (Jena, 1927).

[5] F. Mehring, *Nachlass*, I, 186; S. Hook, *From Hegel to Marx,* new edition (Ann Arbor, 1962), p. 199. Hook, however, is mistaken in dating Stein's book at 1845, instead of 1842. For some recent valuable studies of Stein, see K. Mengelberg, "Lorenz v. Stein and his Contribution to Historical Sociology," *Journal of the History of Ideas,* XXII, no. 2 (1961); J. Weiss, "Dialectical Idealism and the Work of Lorenz v. Stein," *International Review of Social History,* VII, no. 1 (1963).

[6] *The Holy Family,* p. 180; *The German Ideology,* pp. 534 f. Engels refers to Stein's book in 1843 as "dull drudgery" (*Werke,* I, 477).

In contrast, Marx refers for the first time to "a propertyless class whose problems "cry out to heaven in Manchester, Paris and Lyons" in an article in the *Rheinische Zeitung* in autumn 1842, a short time after the publication of Stein's book. Though this article ostensibly deals with one of Wilhelm Weitling's books, Marx mentions here writings by Leroux, Considérant, Proudhon and Fourier. They are not mentioned by Weitling at all and Marx could not have read them in the original at that time. He probably got the information about them from Stein's book. But the problem, after all, is not biographical but methodological. Concentrating on the possible—and even quite probable—influence of Stein on Marx begs the question, assuming that Stein's book could have been Marx's only link with French socialist and communist ideas or with a sociological description of the proletariat in industrial society. This is clearly not the case, though some of the evidence has not always been considered. Stein's book caused a minor sensation in Germany, mainly because of the peculiar circumstances of its composition; but Stein was evidently not the first German author to raise the question of the proletariat. Volume XIII of Rotteck's and Welcker's *Lexikon der Staatswissenschaften*, published in 1842, includes the following statement in its entry on "Revolution":

> But this is the content of history: no major historical antagonism disappears or dies out unless there emerges a new antagonism. Thus the general antagonism between the rich and the poor has been recently polarised into the tension between the capitalists and the hirers of labour on the one hand and the industrial workers of all kinds on the other; out of this tension there emerges an opposition whose dimensions become more and more menacing with the proportional growth of the industrial population.

Moreover, discussion of working-class conditions began in Germany many years before the problem existed in Germany itself and this discussion was started not by radicals or socialists, but by conservative romantics, who used it as an argument against *laissez faire* liberalism. Two of the most reactionary German romantics, Adam Müller and Franz von Baader, took up the issue years before the radicals of Rotteck's or Welcker's stamp even considered it. In an essay published shortly after 1815, Adam Müller discussed the conditions of the working class in England in a language which seems to prefigure Marx's analysis in the *Economic-Philosophical Manuscripts* of 1844. Analysing Adam Smith, Müller arrives at the conclusion that political economy breaks the productive process, which should be unitary, into capital and labour.[7] In a work of 1816 Müller maintains that the division of labour emasculates the worker's personality:

> Man needs a many-sided, even an all-rounded, sphere for his activity, limited and restricted as this activity itself may be. . . . But if the division of labour, as it is now being practised in the big cities and the manufacturing and mining areas, cuts-up free man into wheels, cogs, cylinders and shuttles, imposes on him one sphere of activity in the course of his many-sided search for one object—how can one expect this segmented segment to be adequate to the full and fulfilled life or right and law? How can partial forms, which are cut out from the full circle of activity and are being divorced from one another, how can they fit into the full circle of political life and its laws? This is the miserable outcome of the division of labour in all the branches of private industry.[8]

Franz von Baader approaches the same issue in an essay written in 1835, which includes the term *proletair* in its title. Baader says that the moneyed classes impose the burden of taxation almost exclusively on the proletariat and make it simultaneously impossible for the proletarians to participate in political life and become full-fledged *citoyens*. According to Baader, the proletarians pay for the upkeep of the state but do not belong to it. He concludes that, according to the premises of political economy, capitalist competition is doomed to end in a monopoly that would leave the worker in a position far worse than that of the medieval serf:

> One can actually say that serfdom . . . is less terrible and more humane . . . than this reckless, defenceless and welfare-less freedom to which so many parts of the public are exposed in our so-called civilised and enlightened nations. Anyone who looks at this will have to admit that in what is called Christian and enlightened Europe, the civilisation of the few is generally made possible by the lack of civilisation and even barbarism of the many. We approach the state of ancient slavery and helotism far more than the Middle Ages.[9]

That both Müller and Baader sought to avoid this conclusion by a return to neo-feudal, corporative and romantic arrangements does not detract from the demonstration that Lorenz von Stein cannot be regarded as Marx's only source for his characterization of the

[7] A. Müller, *Gesammelte Schriften* (München, 1839), I, 275.

[8] A. Müller, "Die heutige Wissenschaft der Nationalökonomie kurz und fasslich dargestellt," *Ausgewählte Abhandlungen*, ed. J. Baxa (Jena, 1921), p. 46.

[9] F. v. Baader, "Über das dermalige Misverhältnis der Vermögenlosen, oder Proletairs, zu den Vermögen besitzenden Klassen der Sozietät." *Schriften zur Gesellschaftsphilosophie*, ed. J. Sauter (Jena, 1925), p. 325.

industrial proletariat, much as Marx might have drawn from Stein's book some information about individual French writers. Marx draws on a mood and a general malaise prevalent at that time in intellectual circles in Germany among radicals and conservative romantics alike. It would be difficult—and utterly wrong—to choose one writer and make him responsible for moulding Marx's thought. Marx was responding to a *Zeitgeist,* and it was from a common stock far more than from any individual writer, that he drew his ideas and inspiration.

This common background also emphasizes Marx's specific contribution to this discussion of the working class, his suggestion that the condition of the proletariat should not be considered within the narrow historical circumstances of its emergence. Marx's intellectual *tour de force* must be approached by confronting his description of the proletariat with the universal postulates of Hegel's political philosophy.

We have already seen that in the *Critique* Marx is aware that the class of "immediate labour," though vital to the function of civil society, is not cared for by, nor integrated in, the general structure of society. Empirically Marx studied this phenomenon several months earlier when he discussed in some newspaper articles the situation of the village poor in the Rhineland. He comments that it seems inconsistent with Hegelian political philosophy for the village poor to be treated far better by the irrational countryside customs and traditions than by the rational arrangement of the institutional modern state: something must be wrong with the state if it fails to take account of this sector of the population.[10]

In the *Rheinische Zeitung* and in the *Critique* Marx is still obviously thinking in traditional terms of "the poor." This undifferentiated terminology shows that the issue has not yet been approached by philosophical speculation and insight. This happened only after Marx had finished his account of the Hegelian notion of the bureaucracy.

All of Marx's discussions about the bureaucracy conclude that the Hegelian postulate of a "universal class" is an illusion of Hegel's inverted political world. The bureaucracy does not embody universality, but merely usurps it, using the pretexts of the commonwealth for its particular interests, which are no different from other class interests. But if Marx does not accept the Hegelian identifica-

[10] *Rheinische Zeitung,* 27 October 1842 (*Werke,* I, 119).

tion of bureaucracy with universality, he still retains the dialectical concept of a "universal class," i.e. a partial social stratum which is, however, an ideal subject of the universal concept of the *Gemeinwesen*.

If Hegel's "universal class' hypostatizes a given historical phenomenon into a self-fulfilling trans-historical norm, Marx uses it differently. For Marx the term will always be open to the dialectical dynamics of the historical process. He does not invest any one class with the attributes of universality: for him every generation, every historical situation, gives rise to a class which aspires to be the subject of society's general consciousness. Historical developments actually allow this class for a time to represent the *res publica*, society at large, but after a while, with changes in the distribution of social forces and in general conditions, this claim for universality no longer accords with the interests of society as a whole. The class which had hitherto represented society must vacate its place to a new class, which will henceforward claim that *it* represents society. "Rising" classes are those whose claims for universality represent, at a given moment, the general will of society and realize the potential of its development. "Declining" classes are those whose claim for universality is no longer valid and real. They cling to past glories and to present privileges derived from them. In these terms Marx sees the rise and decline of the feudal aristocracy, and applies the same analysis to the bourgeoisie. The Hegelian idea of a "universal class," stripped of its hypostasis, becomes, for Marx, a vehicle for historical explanation.

In the *Introduction to the Critique of Hegel's Philosophy of Right* Marx formulates this for the first time:

> No class in civil society can play this part unless it can arouse, in itself and in the masses, a moment of enthusiasm in which it associates and mingles with society at large, identifies itself with it, and is felt and recognised as the *general representative* of this society. Its aims and interests must genuinely be the aims and interests of society itself, of which it becomes in reality the social head and heart. It is only in the name of the general interest that a particular class can claim general supremacy . . . that genius which pushes material force to political power, that revolutionary daring which throws at its adversary the defiant phrase: *I am nothing and I should be everything.*[11]

And in *The German Ideology*:

---

[11] *Early Writings*, pp. 55–56.

> For each new class which puts itself in the place of one ruling before
> it, is compelled, merely in order to carry through its aims, to represent
> its interest as the common interest of all the members of society, that
> is, expressed in ideal form: it has to give its ideas the form of uni-
> versality. . . . The class making a revolution appears from the very
> start . . . not as a class but as the representative of the whole of
> society.[12]

This tension between particularism and universality—between a
class's appearance as a protagonist of the general will and its search
for its own interests—comes to a head, according to Marx, with the
emergence of the modern proletariat. It can be overcome only by
the simultaneous abolition of the proletariat as a separate class and
the disappearance of class differences in general. Marx does not
postulate the abolition of class antagonisms because any economic
mechanism points in that direction. No economic analysis precedes
his dictum about the abolition of classes; they will be abolished
(*aufgehoben*) because historical development has brought the tension between the general and the particular to a point of no return.
The tension, according to Marx, is now radically general. It per-
meates every nook of society and cannot be transformed into just
another change of the ruling class. Only a dialectical *Aufhebung*
will give rise to a humanity with no dichotomy between the general and the particular.

Only because he sees in the proletariat the contemporary, and
final, realization of universality, does Marx endow the proletariat
with a historical significance and mission. He mentions the proletariat for the first time in the last section of the *Introduction to
the Critique of Hegel's Philosophy of Right,* immediately after the
passage cited above about the role of "universal classes" in history.
The reference to the proletariat is heavily loaded with allusions to
its function as the ultimate "universal class":

> A class must be formed which has *radical chains,* a class in civil society
> which is not a class of civil society, a class which is the dissolution of
> all classes, a sphere of society which has a universal character because
> its sufferings are universal, and which does not claim a *particular
> redress* because the wrong which is done to it is not a *particular
> wrong* but *wrong in general.* There must be formed a sphere of so-
> ciety which claims no *traditional* status but only a human status, a
> sphere which is not opposed to particular consequences but is totally
> opposed to the assumptions of the German political system; a sphere,
> finally, which cannot emancipate itself without emancipating itself

[12] *The German Ideology,* pp. 61–62.

from all the other spheres of society, without, therefore, emancipating all the other spheres, which is, in short, a *total loss* of humanity and which can only redeem itself by a *total redemption of humanity*. This dissolution of society, as a particular class, is the *proletariat*. . . .

When the proletariat announces the *dissolution of the existing social order*, it only declares the *secret of its* own existence, for it *is* the *effective* dissolution of this order. When the proletariat demands the *negation of private property* it only lays down as a *principle for society* what society has already made a principle *for the proletariat*, and what the *latter* already involuntarily embodies as the negative result of society.[13]

The abolition (*Aufhebung*) of private property merely universalizes the situation the proletariat already experiences in society. Communism is not the starting-point of the discussion but its outcome as it emerges from philosophical principles. A political revolution, changing the balance of power within the social framework, will not do, because the proletariat remains in total alienation.[14] Hence the emancipation of the proletariat must be predicated on the emancipation of humanity, as the enslavement of the proletariat is paradigmatic to all forms of human unfreedom:

From the relation of alienated labour to private property it also follows that the emancipation of society from private property, from servitude, takes the political form of the *emancipation of the workers;* not in the sense that only the latters' emancipation is involved, but because this emancipation includes the emancipation of humanity as a whole. For all human servitude is involved in the relation of the worker to production, and all the types of servitude are only modifications or consequences of this relation.[15]

The victory of the proletariat would mean its disappearance as a separate class. In this the proletariat, according to Marx, would differ from other classes, which, on attaining victory, still depended on the continuing existence of their opposite and complementary classes. The feudal baron needed a villein in order to be a baron; a bourgeois needs a proletarian in order to be a bourgeois—only the proletariat as a true, "universal class" does not need its opposite to ensure its own existence. Hence the proletariat can abolish all classes by abolishing itself as a separate class and becoming co-eval with the generality of society. Even the programmatic and necessary

---

[13] *Early Writings*, pp. 58–59; cf. *The German Ideology*, pp. 86–87.

[14] This is the crux of Marx's argument against the narrow view of a political revolution; see his article in *Vorwärts*, 8 August 1844 (*Werke*, I, 408).

[15] *Early Writings*, pp. 132–33.

connection between the proletariat and philosophy becomes possible, because both are universal, and because the proletariat carries out the universal postulates of philosophy: "Just as philosophy finds its material weapons in the proletariat, so the proletariat finds its intellectual weapons in philosophy. . . . Philosophy is the head of this emancipation and the proletariat is its heart. Philosophy can only be realised by the abolition of the proletariat, and the proletariat can only be abolished by the realisation of philosophy." [16]

The universalistic nature of the proletariat does not disappear in Marx's later writings, when his discussion concentrates mainly on the historical causes of the emergence of the proletariat. What was at the outset a philosophical hypothesis is verified by historical experience and observation: the universalistic nature of the proletariat is a corollary of the conditions of production in a capitalist society, which must strive for universality on the geographical level as well.[17]

A careful reading of *The Communist Manifesto* brings the argument from universality to the surface. The proletariat as a "universal," "general," "national" class can only be emancipated universally; its existence defies the norms of bourgeois society:

> In the conditions of the proletariat, those of old society at large are already virtually swamped. The proletarian is without property; his relation to his wife and children has no longer anything in common with the bourgeois family-relations; modern industrial labour, modern subjugation to capital, the same in England as in France, in America as in Germany, has stripped him of every trace of national character. . . .
>
> All previous historical movements were movements of minorities or in the interests of minorities. . . . The proletariat, the lowest stratum of our present society, cannot stir, cannot raise itself up, without the whole superincumbent strata of official society being sprung into the air. . . .
>
> The Communists are distinguished from other working-class parties by this only: 1. In the national struggles of the proletarians of the different countries, they put out and bring to the front the common interests of the entire proletariat, independently of all nationality. 2. In the various stages of development which the struggle of the working class against the bourgeoisie has to pass through, they always and everywhere represent the interests of the movement as a whole. . . .
>
> The working men have no country. We cannot take from them

[16] *Ibid.*, p. 59.
[17] *The German Ideology*, pp. 75–76.

what they have not got. Since the proletariat must first of all acquire political supremacy, must rise to be the leading class of the nation, must constitute itself *the* nation, it is, so far, national, though not in the bourgeois sense of the word.

National differences and antagonisms between peoples are daily more and more vanishing, owing to the development of the bourgeoisie, to freedom of commerce, to the world market, to uniformity in the mode of production and in the conditions of life corresponding thereto.

The supremacy of the proletariat will cause them to vanish still faster. . . .[18]

This strong emphasis on the universal aspects of the proletariat recurs also in the Preamble to the General Rules of the International, drafted by Marx in 1864.[19] It is also behind Marx's opposition to Proudhonist mutualism, which he saw as an avoidance of this universalism. Appropriately enough, when Marx summarizes the deficiencies of the British labour class in 1870, he sees its inability to universalize its experience as its major weakness.[20]

This universalistic element in the proletariat can also explain the systematic nature of Marx's quarrel in the 'forties with Bruno Bauer and the "True Socialists" about the role of the "masses" in the struggle for emancipation. The disdain of Bauer and his disciples for the masses and their tendency to avoid complicity with the proletariat were motivated by a fear lest the general vision of liberty be replaced by advocacy of a particular class and espousal of its cause. For Marx, however, the proletariat was never a particular class, but the repository of the Hegelian "universal class." The debate about the place and significance of the proletariat was again conducted within the conceptual tradition of the Hegelian legacy.[21]

Nevertheless, because Marx's relation to the proletariat is not immediate but is reached through speculative considerations, he does not reveal much empathy or spiritual attachment to the members of the working class. Marx's sceptical view of the proletariat's ability to conceive its own goals and realize them without outside intellectual help has often been documented. It suits his remark that revolutions never start with the "masses" but originate in elite

[18] *Selected Writings,* I, 44, 46, 51.
[19] *Ibid.,* p. 386.
[20] *Werke,* XVI, 415.
[21] Cf. D. Hertz-Eichenrode, "Massenpsychologie bei den Junghegelianer," *International Review of Social History,* VII, no. 2 (1962), 231–59. This excellent study does not, however, bring out the connection between Marx's view of the proletariat and his Hegelian background.

groups.[22] Much as Marx always opposed those socialists who tried explicitly to dissociate themselves from the proletariat, a chief reason for the split in the League of Communists in 1850 was Marx's uncertainty about what would happen to the League if it were to be exclusively proletarian in membership. Marx's opponents within the League even went so far as to accuse him of trying to impose intellectual discipline on the proletarian movement; and Weitling was sometimes snubbed by Marx as the Tailors' King.[23]

This enquiry leads Marx to the conclusion that the conditions of the emergence of the proletariat guarantee their own overcoming. He couples this conclusion with the insight that the same forces produce poverty and wealth within society:

> Private property, as private property, as wealth, is compelled to main-
> tain itself, and thereby its opposite, the proletariat, in existence. That
> is the positive side of the contradiction, self-satisfied private prop-
> erty. . . .
> The proletariat, on the other hand, is compelled as proletariat to
> abolish itself and thereby its opposite, the condition for its existence,
> what makes it the proletariat, i.e. private property. That is the nega-
> tive side of the contradiction, its restlessness within its very self, dis-
> solved and self-dissolving private property.[24]

[22] See Marx's article "The Indian Revolt" (*New York Daily Tribune*, 16 September 1857): "The first blow dealt to the French Monarchy proceeded from the nobility, not from the peasants. The Indian Revolt does not commence with the *ryots*, tortured, dishonoured and stripped naked by the British, but with the sepoys, clad, fed, petted and pampered by them."

[23] Cf. *Werke*, VIII, 598–600. In a letter to Engels (20 July 1852) Marx has this to say about a group of German working-class men: "Asses more stupid than these German workers do not exist" (*Werke*, XXVIII, 93).

[24] *The Holy Family*, p. 51.

SEVEN

IDEOLOGY

H. B. ACTON

We have not so far made use of the word "ideology"—for the use
of the word itself, as well as for discussion of the thing, we have to
turn to *The German Ideology*, which Marx and Engels wrote in
1845–1846, but which remained unpublished until 1932. What we
have so far seen is that according to both Feuerbach and Marx religious and metaphysical ideas convey false views of the world, but
that these false views arise from the aims and desires of men and from
the social arrangements which prevent these aims and desires from
being realized. Feuerbach thought that, once this was clearly recognized, men would free themselves from their obsession with another
world, and would endeavour all the more strongly to realize love,
justice, goodness and wisdom in the human world. Marx, in 1844,
held further that the instrument by which freedom from religious
illusion and the resulting improvement in human living would be
achieved was the proletariat, a class which, if its material strength
were fortified with a correct philosophy, would change the conditions in which they and most men were forced to live lives that were
"debased, enslaved, abandoned, contemptible." At this time both
Feuerbach and Marx held that religion resulted from human failure both in the intellectual and moral spheres, but that it was no
delusion that men with physical bodies live on this earth trying to
achieve ideals of human perfection. In *The German Ideology* Marx
and Engels not only used the word "ideology," but also passed a
long way beyond Feuerbach's conception of the thing it stood for.
This was because they had by this time definitely established their
materialist conception of history. In this book they criticize Feuerbach, and by implication themselves too, for having falsely supposed that there is such a thing as "man" in the abstract rather than
the different sorts of men who exist at different times and places.
Men, they argue, are social beings whose nature changes with the
sort of life they lead, and the sort of life they lead changes according to the way in which they get their living, according to the tools

From H. B. Acton, *The Illusion of the Epoch: Marxism-Leninism as a Philosophical Creed* (London: Cohen and West, 1955), pp. 125–31. Reprinted with the
permission of Routledge & Kegan Paul Ltd.

and organization of labour they employ to get food and shelter and to satisfy their other needs. As men have improved their tools, a division of labour has developed, so that some men live in towns, others on the land, some organize production and others carry out manual tasks under the supervision of masters. The division of labour leads to class divisions, and at different times different classes have dominated human societies in accordance with whatever was the predominant mode of production. For what the mode of production is and what sort of division of labour this requires determine which class shall dominate. There is also a division of labour between material and mental work. When this division has taken place within a dominant class, there will be a sub-class who specialize in the production of ideas. Since these ideas are produced from within the dominant class, they will be imposed upon the whole society. They will in fact be expressions of the needs and aspirations of the dominant class, though they will seem, both to those who frame them and to many others too, to be of universal significance. It is not only religious and metaphysical ideas, therefore, which reproduce a false consciousness of things, but other ideas, too, produced by specialists at the behest of a given class or within the framework of a given historical epoch. A given historical epoch is a period during which a given mode of production prevails. "If in all ideology men and their circumstances appear upside down as in a *camera obscura,* this phenomenon arises just as much from their historical life-process as the inversion of objects in the retina does from their physical life-process." [1] That is, it is in the nature of things that men should get distorted views of the world, just as it is in the nature of things that they should receive inverted images on the retina.

The following passages may serve to illustrate the notion of an "ideology" developed in *The German Ideology.* On page 14, Marx and Engels refer to "morality, religion, metaphysics, all the rest of ideology and their corresponding forms of consciousness"; on page 16, they say that the French and the English, though they have been "in the toils of political ideology, have nevertheless made the first attempts to give the writing of history a materialistic basis by being the first to write histories of civil society, of commerce and industry"; on page 20, they say that the division of mental from material labour leads "to the formation of 'pure' theory, theology, philoso-

---

[1] *The German Ideology* (London, 1942, reprint), p. 14.

phy, ethics, etc."; on page 23, they write that "all struggles within
the State, the struggle between democracy, aristocracy and monarchy, the struggle for the franchise, etc., are merely the illusory
forms in which the real struggles of the different classes are fought
out among one another . . ."; on page 30, they say that those who
endeavour to understand any epoch of history in terms of political
and religious issues "share the *illusion of the epoch*"; on page 40,
they refer to the "active, conceptive ideologists" of a class "who
make the perfecting of the illusion of the class about itself their
chief source of livelihood"; on page 43, they write of "the illusion
of ideologists in general, e.g. the illusions of the jurists, politicians
(of the practical statesmen among them, too)" and to "the dogmatic
dreamings and distortions of these fellows"; and on page 80, in criticizing the "true socialists," Marx and Engels say that those theorists
of socialism "have abandoned the realm of real history for the realm
of ideology."

The first feature that emerges from these passages is that Marx
and Engels regarded ideologies as systems of misleading or illusory
ideas. But no one can justifiably describe something as misleading
or illusory except by comparison with something he thinks is not
misleading and not illusory. What, then, according to Marx and
Engels, is it that is not misleading and not illusory? In *The German
Ideology* they state quite clearly what they think it is. "We set out,"
they say, "from real active men, and on the basis of their real life-
process we demonstrate the development of the ideological reflexes
and echoes of this life-process. The phantoms formed in the human
brain are also, necessarily, sublimates of their material life-process,
which is empirically verifiable and bound to material premises." On
the next page they say: "Where speculation ends—in real life—there
real, positive science begins: the representation of the practical process of development of men." [2] That is to say, there is, according to
Marx and Engels, a system of ideas ("the representation of the practical process of development") about man, his religions and his
societies, which is not illusory, which is not ideology. This system
of ideas is the positive science of man and society, a science based
on observation of men as they really are in their day-to-day concerns. Thus the positive science of man in society is *contrasted with*
"ideological reflexes." This is, of course, quite in accordance with
Feuerbach. In his opinion, the only way to discover what exists is

---

[2] *The German Ideology*, pp. 14–15.

by means of sense observation, and since this does not lead rationally to a revelation of God, heaven, or immortality, the religious
view of things needs to be explained in terms of what the senses
reveal. Marx and Engels accept this, but proceed to argue that an
empirical science of man must trace back all his other activities to
the ways in which he gains a living, and to the social organization
involved in this. This contrast between "ideologies" on the one
hand, and "real, positive science" on the other, is clearly based, as
was Comte's contrast between positive science and theologico-meta-
physical thinking, upon a distinction between what is held to be
unverifiable and what is believed to be verifiable. And lest it be
urged that *The German Ideology,* an early work, was later superseded in this respect, I refer also to the famous Preface to Marx's
A Contribution to a Critique of Political Economy (1859)—frequently cited by Marxists as fundamental for an understanding of
the Materialist Conception of History—where we find the view of
The German Ideology repeated as follows: "In considering such
revolutions the distinction should always be made between the material revolution of the economic conditions of production which
can be accurately substantiated in the manner of the natural sciences, and the legal, political, religious, artistic or philosophical—
in short ideological forms, in which we become conscious of this
conflict and fight it out." [3] It should be noticed that the phrase I
have translated by "accurately substantiated in the manner of the
natural sciences" is, in the German *naturwissenschaftlich treu zu
konstatierenden* and thus gives the idea of an accurate, honest *natural*-scientific procedure. "Ideology" was used in this sense right to
the end of Engels' life, since he wrote to Mehring on July 4, 1893:
"Ideology is a process accomplished by the so-called thinker consciously indeed, but with a false consciousness. The real motives
impelling him remain unknown to him, otherwise it would not be
an ideological process at all." [4] The fundamental idea is of a scientific procedure that enables its users to show what are the *real* aims
of men who are conscious only of their own apparent aims.

A second important feature of the Marxist theory is that the
"ideological" thinker is held to be not only theoretically, but also
practically, misleading and misled. Feuerbach, Marx and Engels ar-

---

[3] Second edition. Ed Kautsky (Stuttgart, 1907), pp. LV–VI. Also, translated by
N. I. Stone (New York, 1904), p. 12. I have modified Stone's translation to bring
out the force of "naturwissenschaftlich treu."

[4] *Selected Correspondence,* p. 511.

gued, was too sanguine about the results of unmasking the religious illusions. His books and lectures, they considered, opposed the religious false consciousness in a purely theoretical manner, whereas the only effective way of opposing it was to overthrow in deed as well as word the social conditions that give rise to it. [Marx held the] view that genuine science is a practical as well as a theoretical activity. Just as, on the Marxist view, the sciences of nature involve practice, in the form of experimentation and manufacture, so the science of society, properly understood, involves the transformation of human society, as well as understanding how it works. It should here be observed that one of the problems that caused the most puzzlement to nineteenth-century thinkers was how the methods and teachings of empirical science fitted into a society that had hitherto seemed to be based on religious belief and Christian morality. Some of the theories of the natural sciences—in geology, for example, and in biology—appeared to conflict with Christian dogmas, while the technological changes associated with scientific advance seemed to weaken the whole religious attitude, causing many people to adopt spontaneously the view that nature must be a self-regulating mechanism. Thus the question arose whether the science which was undermining the Christian view of things could also provide standards for human conduct. Comte and his followers thought that science itself was a moral enterprise; the qualities that led to successful scientific research were moral qualities of humility and disinterestedness that would also lead to the regeneration of human society. Marx and Engels did not share this view, but they did believe that, as a scientific understanding of physical processes was at the same time a mastery over them, so a scientific understanding of human society would involve the subjection of social forces to human control. On their view, pure theory is an abstraction, not something that could really exist and be true. Genuine theory, on the other hand, they held to be at the same time a practical mastery over events. Thus Feuerbach's exposure of religion and metaphysics was, they held, an abstract, merely contemplative exposure, and therefore not fully scientific in the way in which the Marxist theoretical-cum-practical exposure is. It is clear, of course, that this view involves morality with empirical science as Comtism does, though in a different way, but before I can discuss the matter further, there are some other features of the Marxist theory of ideologies that need to be brought out.

A third aspect of the Marxist theory of ideologies concerns what is to count as an ideology. We began this account of the theory of ideologies with an exposition of the religious-theological-metaphysical one. The passages I have quoted from the writings of Marx and Engels show that they also included as ideologies, that is, as forms of "false consciousness," "morality," "ethics," "political ideology," and "legal," "artistic," and "philosophical" ideologies. We may suppose that the philosophical ideology is the same as the metaphysical, and that no important distinction is being drawn between morality and ethics. We must then ask in what sense ethics or morality, art, law, and politics are forms of false consciousness. The language used would suggest that we are as deluded when we make moral, æsthetic, legal or political judgments as, on the Marxist view, we are when we make religious and metaphysical judgments, that, for example, the differences between right and wrong, beautiful and ugly, legal and illegal, constitutional and unconstitutional, are merely imaginary, and hide from us some real experienced need or desire. Feuerbach rejected God and heaven in favour, as he thought, of human love and justice, and for this was jibed at as "a pious atheist." [5] But Marx seems to have thought that moral ideas themselves were a sort of illusion the reality of which was something more fundamental in human life; and so too for art, law, and politics. People are only free from illusions, on this view, when their pronouncements on matters of morality, art, law, and politics are consciously related to the scientifically ascertainable realities which they reflect. . . .

[5] Karl Löwith, *Von Hegel zu Nietzche*, 2nd ed. (Zürich-Wien, 1941), p. 363.

EIGHT

IDEOLOGY AND THEORY
LESZEK KOLAKOWSKI

Let me attempt to establish in very general terms what I understand by the concept "ideology," and how ideology is distinguished in particular from science.

By ideology I understand the sum of conceptions which enables a social group (a social class, for example, but not only a class) to systematize the *values* in which the mystified consciousness and the activity of this group are expressed. This is not an exact definition but simply a preliminary characterization that helps us to describe the ways in which ideology is differentiated from scientific work. In other words: the social function of ideology is to consolidate belief in the values which are essential to the fruitful activity of the group. Thus, ideology is not, and cannot be, "pure" theory, for the knowledge of reality as such cannot incite anyone to activity. Ideology incorporates value judgments or descriptive judgments, which are either the mystified expression of belief in certain values, or else are subordinated to the affirmation of beliefs and values. Patriotism, for example, or nationalism (conceived not as a sentiment but as a conviction of the value of the "people" or the "nation"), is an ideology. The slogans of liberty and equality are ideological, as are those of fatherland, honor, and eternal bliss. Socialism, democracy, and liberalism are ideologies that incorporate political values.

The distinction betwen ideology and science is not a distinction between falsehood and truth. They are distinguished by their social function and not by their degree of veracity. I am using the concept of ideology, therefore, roughly in the sense in which Marx used it, but not in the sense in which it is employed in current Marxist literature. For Marx, the concept of ideology comprises a negative judgment; it always signifies a distorted consciousness. That does not mean, however, that an ideology must be simply an assemblage of false beliefs; it is determined by its function, which is the organization of values. Thus the acceptance of an ideology is not a

From Leszek Kolakowski, *Der Mensch ohne Alternative: Von der Möglichkeit und Unmöglichkeit, Marxist zu sein* (Munich: R. Piper & Co. Verlag, 1960), pp. 24–29. Translated by Tom Bottomore. Published with the permission of Geisenheyner & Crone, Stuttgart.

pure intellectual act, but is a practical affirmation, an embryonic activity. Since all political action needs an ideology, it is impossible to get rid of ideology as a social phenomenon.

A special instance of ideology is myth, which is characterized by the following qualities: a myth is the sum of stories concerning particular occurrences such as the history of the gods or of individual men. The mythic character of such a story is, however, independent of its accuracy, and is determined by the function which it fulfills. The mythic character of the Gospels is quite independent of the answer to the question whether Christ was a historical figure or not. There was also a myth about Napoleon, and about Stalin, even though they were evidently historical figures. Every people, and every political movement, creates its own myths, which are the *concrete systematization of values;* that is, an assemblage of values which are embodied not in abstractions, but in particular individuals and situations, and which serve to unify the social group which generated them. Myth is also the collective awareness of a common origin; legendary tales serve to elaborate a quasi-familial bond between those who believe in the myth, a bond between the members of a community who trace their physical or spiritual origins to the same figures that embody the appropriate values.

Another special instance of ideology is utopia (in the comprehensive sense of the word)—that is, a body of acknowledged values concerning social relations that are considered unrealizable but are formulated as a programme. (The legend of paradise or of the Golden Age is a myth, but the vision of the millennium is a utopia.) The utopian character of values, like the mythic character of particular legends, is independent of the knowledge as to whether they are realizable or not. In this sense, the idea of socialism is also a utopia—which does not mean that socialism is impossible. Whereas myth in its social-psychological function organizes the group around its existing values, utopia organizes the hope that values will be realized in social institutions. As yet, no social mass movement has appeared without a utopia, and none has been able to renounce myths.

With this introduction we can now turn to those particular features associated with the rise of Marxism and its development into an ideology. The specific and historically unique antinomy presented in the evolution of Marxism consists in the fact that this doctrine, which revealed how social consciousness is mystified through the pressure of political circumstances, and which proclaimed the complete liberation of consciousness from myth, has itself become a victim of such mystification.

The uniqueness of this situation is that we have here a case in which a genuinely scientific theory, which grew out of the rationalist tradition and was deeply rooted in the intellectual, not the religious, life of European culture, has become the ideal superstructure of an organized political mass movement. In this way, however, the Marxist idea that social consciousness reflects an inverted image of reality, as in a camera obscura, was subsequently reduced to the axiom that this mystification has its source only in class consciousness; that it is either the product of intellectual immaturity (as in the case of those oppressed classes which existed before the proletariat) or else simply a conscious deceit (in the case of the possessing class).

In both cases, the interpretation of the social consciousness was preeminently idealistic, since it attributed the distorted picture of the world which was formed in men's heads to a quality of these heads—to ignorance or the wish to deceive. In both cases, therefore, the essence of Marx's thought—the theory of alienation—was lost. Instead, there emerged the very optimistic conviction that the working class, which, as a "class for itself," is incarnated exclusively in the Party and automatically liberated from all mystifications, no longer has any reason to hanker after a distorted view of the world once it has created a political organization. This conception is understandable, since it then follows that the Party, which is the materialized spirit of the class, has already achieved a total emancipation, or quite simply, that it is never wrong. In practice, therefore, Marx's theory of alienation is replaced, as the result of a perfectly comprehensible tendency, by a dogma of infallibility.

In this situation the problem of the distorting influence that political organization itself exercises upon the theoretical consciousness could not emerge within Marxist thought. In earlier mass movements it did not emerge because they had only an ideology in Marx's sense, and this was not created from scientific ideas. At their inception they adopted a flexible ideology which was not regulated by any scientific laws. Now, however, it became necessary to make a scheme of thought that was originally scientific responsive to the pressure of the organization—that is, to remove all rational control.

The religious ideologies could never pass from a scientific to a religious stage, because they were never scientific; from the outset, therefore, they were easily capable of adaptation to every requirement of the social situation. But the development of Marxism has transformed a science into a mythology, into a soft and malleable material from which the backbone of reason has been eliminated. The development occurred in a typically ideological way, but because of the tradition in which it originated it was concealed behind a scientific facade. The outcome was a striving for a "total" culture which was thoroughly permeated by an ideology employing scientific slogans, although it had long since ceased to be founded upon scientific laws. (Nevertheless, there were still very valuable scientific by-products created in opposition to institutional Marxism. The methodological advances made by Marx were not wholly forgotten, and they provided, indeed, an inspiration for great scientific achievements. An example is to be found in the works of G. Lukács.)

The rise of institutional Marxism confirmed Marx's theory of alienation. It illustrated, in particular, the destructive effects of the political organization upon scientific thought when thought came into conflict with ideology. The association of thought and ideology, which should have formed a symbiosis, ended as the parasitic existence of ideology, the cells of which spread through scientific thought and endangered its life. This should not provoke either indignation or condemnation, since it is the natural tendency of a political organization. Once it has been created as a social fact, the organization has at least one interest of its own: to maintain an inner "belongingness" by opposing bitterly every attempt at disintegration. The organizational bond is in opposition to the class bond, for the existence of the class is given by the objective situation (Marx's "class in itself"). A disintegration of consciousness is fatal to the organization, and so its ideology has to be protected from rational control.

Science, on the other hand, promotes in the course of its development just this principle of social control, of the independence of its content from political pressure—the principle of objectivity, revisionism, permanent criticism, and continual confrontation of all possible viewpoints. Thus ideology and science are in perpetual conflict with each other, and this conflict cannot be eliminated by expressions of goodwill, for goodwill does not abolish social regularities. The transformation of Marxism into an institution was not a "lapse" which can be put aside by a "sincere repentance" like a sin in the confessional.

NINE

THE ECONOMIC AND SOCIAL FUNCTIONS OF THE LEGAL INSTITUTIONS

KARL RENNER

Our enquiry, then, is not concerned with positive legal analysis, the systematic exposition of legal institutions, a field which has been amply covered by others. Nor are we investigating the problems of the creation of law. We shall refrain from analysing the questions as to how the norms originate which make up the legal institutions, how a legal norm grows from its economic background, and what are the economic causes of the creation of legal norms. This field, it is true, has not been cultivated, but we shall keep away from it. We propose to examine only the economic and social effect of the valid norm as it exists, so long as the norm does not change.

Those acquainted with socialist literature will at once perceive that we have taken as our subject the mutual relations between law and economics. The traditional Marxist school conceives the economic relations as the substructure and the legal institutions as the superstructure. "Substructure" and "superstructure" are metaphors, borrowed from architecture; it is obvious that they serve only to illustrate the connection, not to define it in exact terms. This superstructure, according to Marx's well-known formula,[1] comprises not only law but also ethics and culture, in fact every ideology. This terminology must therefore apply to many facts other than those relevant to the law, whose structures are completely

From Karl Renner, *The Institutions of Private Law and Their Social Functions* (London: Routledge & Kegan Paul Ltd., 1949), pp. 55–60. Reprinted with the permission of Routledge & Kegan Paul Ltd.

[1] Preface to Marx's *Critique of Political Economics,* transl. by N. I. Stone, N.Y. London, 1904. "The sum total of these relations of production constitutes the economic structure of society—the real foundations on which rise legal and political superstructures."

Friedrich Engels, Preface to Marx's *Der achtzehnte Brumaire,* 3rd edition, Hamburg, 1885: "The law according to which all struggle, whether in the political, religious, philosophical or any other ideological field, is in fact only the more or less clear expression of struggles among social classes whose existence and hence collisions are again conditioned by the degree of development of their economic position, their methods of production and their manner of exchange dependent thereon." And many other passages. . . .

different and must be separately defined. The relation between the philosophy of an age and the economic substructure of that age is obviously determined by key concepts quite different from those of legal norm, exercise of a right, and the like. We must desist, therefore, from attempting to give a general exposition of the Marxist concept of superstructure. We must recognise that each of these social phenomena, which in their general aspects are quite aptly illustrated by Marx's metaphor, requires a specific investigation. We attempt this investigation in regard to law.

Our previous explanations have made it clear that the relation is not merely one of cause and effect. It would be no solution of our problem to say that the economic structure generates the norm. Such an assumption could apply only to one of the fields of learning, that concerned with the creation of laws. Yet the mechanism by which economy as the causal factor brings about the effect of law, is obscure and unexplored. It probably would not become intelligible by any ultimate abstraction, such as the application of the primitive categories of cause and effect, nor does Stammler's formula [Rudolf Stammler, *Wirtschaft und Recht nach der materialistischen Geschichtszauffassung* (Leipzig: 1896)] of the regulating form and the regulated substance make it any clearer. In the second province, that of positive legal analysis, the concepts of cause and effect generally mean little; the main concern here is obviously that of motive, means and ends, and the appropriate method of explanation is teleological, not causal. If we were to describe the superstructure of the law in the third field (that of the economic and social efficacy of the norms) as exclusively the effect of the social and economic substructure, our conclusions would be proved to be absurd by the very facts to which they refer.

It is mere platitude to say that laws can influence economy sufficiently to change it and can therefore be considered as causes of economic results. Marx, of course, was the last person to deny this. "The influence of laws upon the conservation of the relations of distribution and consequently their influence upon production must be specifically determined" (*Neue Zeit,* p. 744). [This quotation and the following one come from Marx's Introduction to the *Grundrisse.* The Introduction was first published by Karl Kautsky in the journal *Neue Zeit,* XXI (1), 1903, from which Renner quotes.—Ed.] Laws are made with the intention of producing economic results, and as a rule they achieve this effect. Social life is not so simple that we can grasp it, open it and reveal its kernel like a nut, by placing it between the two arms of a nutcracker called cause and effect. Although he was much occupied with legal problems, Marx never found time to "determine the influence of the laws" (as above); yet he saw the problem clearly as is proved in particular by the following methodological hint: "The really difficult point to be discussed here, however, is how the relations of production as relations of the law enter into a disparate development. An instance is Roman civil law in its relations to modern production" (ibid. p. 779). We make use of this hint in the formulation of our problem: (1) Law which continues unchanged in relation to changing economic conditions; (2) Changed economic conditions in relation to the new norms and the new law. Our study, however, will be concerned with the first part of the problem only.

We start with a definite legal system based upon a definite economic foundation as it appears at a given moment of history. All economic institutions are at the same time institutions of the law. All economic activities are either, like sale and purchase, acts-in-the-law, or, like farming one's own land, the mere exercise of a right; or if neither, like the work of a mill-hand at his loom, even though they are extra-legal activities, they are nevertheless performed within definite legal conditions. We see that the act-in-the-law and the economic action are not identical.

The process of eating has a physiological, an economic and a volitional aspect but it is not an act of will with the qualities of an act-in-the-law. Yet the conditions under which it takes place are determined to some extent by the law.

The circulation of goods in a capitalist society is mediated by sale and purchase and by ancillary contracts: these are transactions for which the law of obligations provides various forms. Production, however, is not in itself an act-in-the-law. It can be the mere exercise of the right of ownership, as in the case of the peasant. In the capitalist factory, however, the legal aspect of production is more complicated. For the capitalist, production is the exercise of his right of ownership, since factory and machines are his property. For the worker it is the fulfilment of a legal obligation which has been established by the contract of employment. In so far as it is the latter, it is an act-in-the-law; in so far as it is the former, it is the mere exercise of a right. Thus a simple economic category is equivalent to a combination of various legal categories, there is no point-to-point correspondence. A number of distinct legal institutions serves a single economic process. They play a part which I will call their economic function.

Yet every economic process which in theory is an isolated unit is only part of the whole process of social production and reproduction. If the economic function is related to this whole, it becomes the social function of the legal institution.

A comprehensive exposition of the functions fulfilled by the legal institutions at every stage of the economic process has been given in *Das Kapital*, Marx's principal work. No other investigator, either before or after him, was more aware of their importance for even the most minute details of this process. We shall see that no other economic theory gives so much insight into the connections between law and economics. Marx's predecessors and successors either refused to recognise the problem or could not do it full justice.

If we regard a social order as static and confine our attention to a certain moment of history, then the legal norms and the economic process merely appear as mutually conditioned and subservient to one another. Within the economic structure economic process and legal norm appear as the same thing: the former seen as an external, technico-natural event, the latter as an inherent relation of wills, seen from the point of view of individual will-formation. We call the external, technico-natural process the substratum of the norm. This sounds very plausible. But we can no more study the laws of gravity from a stone in a state of rest than we can learn the art of cooking from the cook who was pricked by the Sleeping Beauty's spindle. All that we can observe is that in a state of rest legal and economic institutions, though not identical, are but two aspects of the same thing, inextricably interwoven. We must define and describe this co-existence.

This observation, however, only stresses the fact that they are mutually determined. We must study the process in its historical sequence, the gradual transition of a social order from a given stage to the next. The inherent laws of development can only be revealed if the events are seen in motion, in the historic sequence of economic and legal systems. If we examine two consecutive periods, chosen at random, we may obtain results which, though they apply to these particular periods of transition, cannot claim to be generally valid. To decide the function of the law in general, we have to study inductively all social orders as they appear in the course of history, from the most primitive to the most highly developed. By this method we obtain the general categories of the social order and at the same time the general functions of the law.

This procedure is legitimate in spite of the fact that every individual stage of development has its specific nature and is subject to its peculiar laws. Marx frequently refers to general principles of this kind, declaring them to be justified. "All periods of production have certain characteristics in common . . . production in general is an abstract concept, but a reasonable one in that it really establishes and emphasizes what is common, and thus saves us repetition." ". . . a unity brought about by the fact that the subject, mankind, and the object, nature, are always the same" (*Neue Zeit,* vol. 21, p. 712). Yet Marx disparages these general abstractions in economics often enough to fortify our objections against them. One of his reasons was the tendency of economists, which still exists, to regard the categories of the capitalist order as eternal and sacrosanct. Another reason lies in the limitations of his own task, viz. to explore and describe one individual period only. "Yet it is the very difference from what is general and common which is the essential element of a particular development." If Marx had concentrated upon the definition of peculiar characteristics of one epoch as he found them, he might have given a description in the manner of a research student, but the laws of social development would have remained hidden from him. Marx, however, seeks to explain the specific historical phenomenon alongside with previous individual forms as being merely an individual manifestation of the general principle. In this way he discovers inherent connections within the development.

The following may serve as an example: "Surplus labour is a general social phenomenon as soon as the productivity of human labour power exceeds the immediate needs of life, but its appearance in the feudal epoch differs from that in the capitalist epoch—in the former it is villeinage, in the latter surplus value."

We cannot dispense in our enquiry with a general survey of the functions performed by the legal institutions. Every individual function which is historically determined is correlated to the whole and can only be clearly understood within its context. A diagrammatic exposition of the functions at least clears the field. A concrete detail cannot be demonstrated otherwise than by relating it to the general whole. "A phenomenon is concrete because it integrates various determining factors, because it is a unity of multiplicity. If it is thought out, it appears as the product and result of an integrating process."

TEN

MARX AND THE STATE

RALPH MILIBAND

I

As in the case of so many other aspects of Marx's work, what he thought about the state has more often than not come to be seen through the prism of later interpretations and adaptations. These have long congealed into *the* Marxist theory of the state, or into *the* Marxist-Leninist theory of the state, but they cannot be taken to constitute an adequate expression of Marx's own views. This is not because these theories bear *no* relation to Marx's views but rather that they emphasize some aspects of his thought to the detriment of others, and thus distort by over-simplification an extremely complex and by no means unambiguous body of ideas; and also that they altogether ignore certain strands in Marx's thought which are of considerable interest and importance. This does not, in itself, make later views better or worse than Marx's own: to decide this, what needs to be compared is not text with text, but text with historical or contemporary reality itself. This can hardly be done within the compass of an essay. But Marx is so inescapably bound up with contemporary politics, his thought is so deeply buried inside the shell of official Marxism and his name is so often invoked in ignorance by enemies and partisans alike, that it is worth asking again what he, rather than Engels, or Lenin or any other of his followers, disciples or critics, actually said and appeared to think about the state. This is the purpose of the present essay.

Marx himself never attempted to set out a comprehensive and systematic theory of the state. In the late 1850s he wrote that he intended, as part of a vast scheme of projected work, of which *Capital* was only to be the first part, to subject the state to systematic study.[1] But of this scheme, only one part of *Capital* was in fact completed. His ideas on the state must therefore be taken from such

---

From *The Socialist Register 1965*. Edited by Ralph Miliband and John Saville (London: The Merlin Press Ltd., 1965), pp. 278–96. Reprinted with the permission of Ralph Miliband and The Merlin Press Ltd.

[1] K. Marx to F. Lassalle, 22 February 1858, and K. Marx to F. Engels, 2 April 1858 (*Selected Correspondence*, Moscow, n.d.), pp. 125, 126.

historical *pièces de circonstance* as *The Class Struggles in France,*
the *18th Brumaire of Louis Bonaparte* and *The Civil War in
France,* and from his incidental remarks on the subject in his other
works. On the other hand, the crucial importance of the state in
his scheme of analysis is well shown by his constantly recurring
references to it in almost all of his writings; and the state was also a
central preoccupation of the "young Marx": his early work from
the late 1830s to 1844 was largely concerned with the nature of the
state and its relation to society. His most sustained piece of work
until the 1844 *Economic and Philosophical Manuscripts,* apart from
his doctoral dissertation, was his *Critique of the Hegelian Philosophy of Right,* of which only the *Introduction,* actually written after
the *Critique* itself, has so far appeared in English.[2] It is in fact
largely through his critique of Hegel's view of the state that Marx
completed his emancipation from the Hegelian system. This early
work of Marx on the state is of great interest; for, while he soon
moved beyond the views and positions he had set out there, some
of the questions he had encountered in his examination of Hegel's
philosophy recur again and again in his later writings.

II

Marx's earliest views on the state bear a clear Hegelian imprint. In
the articles which he wrote for the *Rheinische Zeitung* from May
1842 to March 1843, he repeatedly spoke of the state as the guardian
of the general interest of society and of law as the embodiment of
freedom. Modern philosophy, he writes in July 1842, "considers the
state as the great organism in which must be realized juridical,
moral and political freedom and where the individual citizen, in
obeying the laws of the state only obeys the natural laws of his own
reason, of human reason." [3]

On the other hand, he also shows himself well aware that this
exalted view of the state is in contradiction with the real state's
actual behaviour: "a state which is not the realization of rational
freedom is a bad state," he writes,[4] and in his article on the Rhine-

---

[2] For the *Critique,* see *Marx/Engels Gesamtausgabe* (MEGA) (Moscow, 1927),
I, 1/1, pp. 403–553; for the *Introduction,* first published in the *Franco-German
Annals* of 1844, *ibid.,* I, 1/1, pp. 607–21, and T. B. Bottomore, Ed., *K. Marx,
Early Writings* (London, 1963).

[3] MEGA, *ibid.,* p. 249.

[4] *Ibid.,* p. 248.

land Diet's repressive legislation against the pilfering of forest wood, he eloquently denounces the Diet's denial of the customary rights of the poor and condemns the assignation to the state of the rôle of servant of the rich against the poor. This, he holds, is a perversion of the state's true purpose and mission; private property may wish to degrade the state to its own level of concern, but any modern state, in so far as it remains true to its own meaning, must, confronted by such pretensions, cry out "your ways are not my ways, and your ideas are not my ideas." [5]

More and more, however, Marx found himself driven to emphasize the external pressures upon the state's actions. Writing in January 1843 on the plight of the wine growers of the Moselle, he remarks that "in the examination of the institutions of the state, one is too easily tempted to overlook the concrete nature of circumstances (*"die sachliche Natur der Verhältnisse"*) and to explain everything by the will of those empowered to act." [6]

It is this same insistence on the need to consider the "concrete nature of circumstances" which lies at the core of the *Critique of Hegel's Philosophy of Right,* which Marx wrote in the spring and summer of 1843, after the *Rheinische Zeitung* had been closed down. By then, his horizons had widened to the point where he spoke confidently of a "break" in the existing society, to which "the system of acquisition and commerce, of ownership and of exploitation of man is leading even more rapidly than the increase in population." [7] Hegel's "absurdity," he also writes in the *Critique,* is that he views the affairs and the activities of the state in an abstract fashion; he forgets that the activities of the state are human functions: "the affairs of the state, etc., are nothing but the modes of existence and activity of the social qualities of men." [8]

The burden of Marx's critique of Hegel's concept of the state is that Hegel, while rightly acknowledging the separation of civil society from the state, asserts their reconciliation in the state itself.

[5] *Ibid.,* p. 283.

[6] *Ibid.,* p. 360. Note also his contemptuous reference in an article of May 1842 on the freedom of the Press to "the inconsistent, nebulous and timorous reasoning of German liberals, who claim to honour freedom by setting it up in an imaginary firmament, rather than on the solid ground of reality" (*ibid.,* p. 220; A. Cornu, *Karl Marx et Friedrich Engels. Leur Vie et leur Oeuvre* (Paris, 1958), II, p. 17).

[7] K. Marx to A. Ruge, May 1843, MEGA, p. 565; see also K. Marx to A. Ruge, March 1843, *Sel. Cor., op. cit.,* p. 25.

[8] MEGA, *ibid.,* p. 424.

In his system, the "contradiction" between the state and society is resolved in the supposed representation in the state of society's true meaning and reality; the alienation of the individual from the state, the contradiction between man as a private member of society, concerned with his own private interests, and as a citizen of the state finds resolution in the state as the expression of society's ultimate reality.

But this, says Marx, is not a resolution but a mystification. The contradiction between the state and society is real enough. Indeed, the political alienation which it entails is the central fact of modern, bourgeois society, since man's political significance is detached from his real private condition, while it is in fact this condition which determines him as a social being, all other determinations appearing to him as external and inessential: "real man is the private man of the present constitution of the state." [9]

But the mediating elements which are supposed, in Hegel's system, to ensure the resolution of this contradiction—the sovereign, the bureaucracy, the middle classes, the legislature—are not in the least capable, says Marx, of doing so. Ultimately, Hegel's state, far from being above private interests and from representing the general interest, is in fact subordinate to private property. What, asks Marx, is the power of the state over private property? The state has only the illusion of being determinant, whereas it is in fact determined; it does, in time, subdue private and social wills, but only to give substance to the will of private property and to acknowledge its reality as the highest reality of the political state, as the highest moral reality.[10]

In the *Critique,* Marx's own resolution of political alienation and of the contradiction between the state and society is still envisaged in mainly political terms, i.e. in the framework of "true democracy." "Democracy is the solution to the riddle of all constitutions"; in it, "the constitution appears in its true reality, as the free product of man." "All other political systems are specific, definite, particular political forms. In democracy, the formal principle is also the material principle." It constitutes, therefore, the real unity of the universal and the particular.[11] Marx also writes: "In all states which

---

[9] *Ibid.,* pp. 498–99. See also J. Hyppolite, *Etudes sur Marx et Hegel* (Paris, 1955), pp. 123 ff., and M. Rubel, *K. Marx. Essai de Biographie Intellectuelle* (Paris, 1957), pp. 58 ff.

[10] MEGA, *ibid.,* p. 519.

[11] *Ibid.,* pp. 434–35.

differ from democracy, the state, the law, the constitution are sovereign without being properly dominant, that is to say without materially affecting the other non-political spheres. In democracy, the constitution, the law, the state itself are only the people's self-determination, a specific aspect of it, in so far as that aspect has a political constitution." [12]

Democracy is here intended to mean more than a specific political form, but Marx does not yet define what else it entails. The struggle between monarchy and republic, he notes, is still a struggle within the framework of what he calls the "abstract state," i.e. the state alienated from society; the abstract political form of democracy is the republic. "Property and all that makes up the content of law and the state is, with some modifications, the same in the United States as in Prussia; the republic in America is thus only a purely political form as is the monarchy in Prussia." [13] In a real democracy, however, the constitution ceases to be purely political; indeed Marx quotes the opinion of "some modern Frenchmen" to the effect that "in a real democracy the political state disappears." [14] But the concrete content of "true democracy" remains here undefined.

The *Critique* already suggests the belief that political emancipation is not synonymous with human emancipation. The point, which is, of course, central to Marx's whole system, was made explicit in the two articles which he wrote for the *Franco-German Annals*, namely the *Jewish Question,* and the *Introduction* to a *Contribution to the Critique of Hegel's Philosophy of Right.*

In the first essay, Marx criticizes Bruno Bauer for confusing political and human emancipation, and notes that "the limit of political emancipation is immediately apparent in the fact that the *state* may well free itself from some constraint, without man himself being *really* freed from it, and that the state may be a *free state,* without *man* being free." [15] Even so, political emancipation is a great advance; it is not the last form of human emancipation, but it is the last form of human emancipation within the framework of the existing social order.[16] Human emancipation, on the other hand, can only be realized by transcending bourgeois society, "which has torn up all genuine bonds between men and replaced them by self-

[12] *Ibid.,* p. 435.
[13] *Ibid.,* p. 436.
[14] *Ibid.,* p. 435.
[15] *Ibid.,* p. 582. Italics in original.
[16] *Ibid.,* p. 585.

ishness, selfish need, and dissolved the world of men into a world
of atomized individuals, hostile towards each other." [17] The more
specific meaning of that emancipation is defined in the *Jewish Question,* in Marx's strictures against "Judaism," here deemed synonymous with trade, money and the commercial spirit which has come
to affect all human relations. On this view, the political emancipation of the Jews, which Marx defends,[18] does not produce their
social emancipation; this is only possible in a new society, in which
practical need has been humanized and the commercial spirit
abolished.[19]

In the *Introduction,* which he wrote in Paris at the end of 1843
and the beginning of 1844, Marx now spoke of "the doctrine, that
man is for man the supreme being" and of the "categorical impera-
tive" which required the overthrow of all conditions in which "man
is a degraded, enslaved, abandoned and contemptible being." [20]
But he also added another element to the system he was constructing, namely the proletariat as the agent of the dissolution of the
existing social order;[21] as we shall see, this view of the proletariat is
not only crucial for Marx's concept of revolution but also for his
view of the state.

By this time, Marx had already made an assessment of the relative
importance of the political realm from which he was never to de-
part and which also had some major consequence for his later
thought. On the one hand, he does not wish to underestimate the
importance of "political emancipation," i.e. of political reforms
tending to make politics and the state more liberal and democratic.
Thus, in *The Holy Family,* which he wrote in 1844 in collaboration
with Engels, Marx describes the "democratic representative state"
as "the perfect modern state," [22] meaning the perfect modern *bourgeois* state, its perfection arising from the fact that "the public
system is *not* faced with any privileged exclusivity," [23] i.e. economic
and political life are free from feudal encumbrances and con-
straints.

But there is also, on the other hand, a clear view that political

---

[17] *Ibid.,* p. 605.
[18] See S. Avineri, "Marx and Jewish Emancipation" in *Journal of the History of
Ideas,* vol. XXV (July–September 1964), pp. 445–50.
[19] MEGA, *op. cit.,* p. 606.
[20] *Ibid.,* p. 615.
[21] *Ibid.,* pp. 619 ff.
[22] K. Marx and F. Engels, *The Holy Family* (Moscow, 1956), p. 154.
[23] *Ibid.,* p. 157. Italics in original.

emancipation is not enough, and that society can only be made truly human by the abolition of private property. "It is natural necessity, *essential human properties,* however alienated they may seem to be, and *interest* that holds the members of civil society together; *civil,* not *political* life is their *real* tie. It is therefore not the state that holds the *atoms* of civil society together . . . only *political super-stition* today imagines that social life must be held together by the state, whereas in reality the state is held together by civil life." [24] The modern democratic state "is based on emancipated slavery, on bourgeois society . . . the society of industry, of universal compe-tition, of private interest freely following its aims, of anarchy, of the self-alienated natural and spiritual individuality . . .";[25] the "es-sence" of the modern state is that "it is based on the unhampered development of bourgeois society, on the free movement of private interest." [26]

A year later, in *The German Ideology,* Marx and Engels defined further the relation of the state to bourgeois society. "By the mere fact that it is a *class* and no longer an *estate,*" they wrote, "the bour-geoisie is forced to organize itself no longer locally but nationally, and to give a general form to its mean average interest"; this "gen-eral form" is the state, defined as "nothing more than the form of organization which the bourgeois necessarily adopt both for internal and external purposes, for the mutual guarantee of their property and interest." [27] This same view is confirmed in the *Poverty of Philosophy* of 1847, where Marx again states that "political condi-tions are only the official expression of civil society" and goes on: "It is the sovereigns who in all ages have been subject to economic conditions, but it is never they who have dictated laws to them. Legislation, whether political or civil, never does more than pro-claim, express in words, the will of economic relations." [28]

This whole trend of thought on the subject of the state finds its most explicit expression in the famous formulation of the *Com-munist Manifesto*: "The executive of the modern state is but a committee for managing the common affairs of the whole bour-

[24] *Ibid.,* p. 163. Italics in original.
[25] *Ibid.,* p. 164.
[26] *Ibid.,* p. 166.
[27] K. Marx and F. Engels, *The German Ideology* (New York, 1939), p. 59. Italics in original.
[28] K. Marx, *The Poverty of Philosophy* (London, 1936), p. 70.

geoisie";[29] and political power is "merely the organized power of one class for oppressing another." [30] This is the classical Marxist view on the subject of the state, and it is the only one which is to be found in Marxism-Leninism. In regard to Marx himself, however, and this is also true to a certain extent of Engels as well, it only constitutes what might be called a primary view of the state. For, as has occasionally been noted in discussions of Marx and the state,[31] there is to be found another view of the state in his work, which it is inaccurate to hold up as of similar status with the first,[32] but which is none the less of great interest, not least because it serves to illuminate, and indeed provides an essential context for, certain major elements in Marx's system, notably the concept of the dictatorship of the proletariat. This secondary view is that of the state as independent from and superior to all social classes, as being the dominant force in society rather than the instrument of a dominant class.

III

It may be useful, for a start, to note some qualifications which Marx made even to his primary view of the state. For in relation to the two most advanced capitalist countries of the day, England and France, he often makes the point that, at one time or another, it is not the ruling class as a whole, but a fraction of it, which controls the state;[33] and that those who actually run the state may well belong to a class which is not the economically dominant class.[34] Marx

---

[29] K. Marx and F. Engels, *Selected Works*, hereafter noted as *S.W.* (Moscow, 1950), I, p. 35.

[30] *Ibid.*, p. 51.

[31] See, e.g. J. Plamenatz, *German Marxism and Russian Communism* (London, 1954), pp. 144 ff.; J. Sanderson, "Marx and Engels on the State" in the *Western Political Quarterly*, vol. XVI, no. 4 (December 1963), pp. 946–55.

[32] As is suggested by the two authors cited above.

[33] See, e.g. *The Class Struggles in France, passim, The 18th Brumaire of Louis Bonaparte, passim.*

[34] See, e.g. "The Elections in Britain" in K. Marx and F. Engels, *On Britain* (Moscow, 1953), pp. 353 ff. "The Whigs are the *aristocratic representatives* of the bourgeoisie, of the industrial and commercial middle class. Under the condition that the bourgeoisie should abandon to them, to an oligarchy of aristocratic families, the monopoly of government and the exclusive possession of office, they make to the middle class, and assist it in conquering, all those concessions, which in the course of social and political developments have shown themselves to have become *unavoidable* and *undelayable.*" (Ibid., p. 353. Italics in original.)

does not suggest that this *fundamentally* affects the state's class character and its rôle of guardian and defender of the interests of property; but it obviously does introduce an element of flexibility in his view of the operation of the state's bias, not least because the competition between different factions of the ruling class may well make easier the passage of measures favourable to labour, such as the Ten Hours Bill.[35]

The extreme manifestation of the state's independent rôle is, however, to be found in authoritarian personal rule, Bonapartism. Marx's most extensive discussion of this phenomenon occurs in *The 18th Brumaire of Louis Bonaparte,* which was written between December 1851 and March 1852. In this historical study, Marx sought very hard to pin down the precise nature of the rule which Louis Bonaparte's *coup d'état* had established.

The *coup d'état,* he wrote, was "the victory of Bonaparte over parliament, of the executive power over the legislative power"; in parliament, "the nation made its general will the law, that is, made the law of the ruling class its general will"; in contrast, "before the executive power it renounces all will of its own and submits to the superior command of an alien will, to authority"; "France, therefore, seems to have escaped the despotism of a class only to fall back beneath the despotism of an individual and, what is more, beneath the authority of an individual without authority. The struggle seems to be settled in such a way that all classes, equally impotent and equally mute, fall on their knees before the rifle butt." [36]

Marx then goes on to speak of "this executive power with its enormous bureaucratic and military organization, with its ingenious state machinery, embracing wide strata, with a host of officials numbering half a million, besides an army of another half million, this appalling parasitic body which enmeshes the body of French society like a net and chokes all its pores." [37] This bureaucratic power, which sprang up in the days of the absolute monarchy, had, he wrote, first been "the means of preparing the class rule of the bourgeoisie," while "under the Restoration, under Louis Phillipe, under the parliamentary Republic, it was the instrument of the ruling class, however much it strove for power of its own." [38] But the *coup d'état* had seemingly changed its rôle: "only under the second

[35] *Ibid.,* p. 368.
[36] *S.W.,* I, p. 300.
[37] *Ibid.,* p. 301.
[38] *Ibid.,* p. 302.

Bonaparte does the state seem to have made itself completely independent"; "as against civil society, the state machine has consolidated its position so thoroughly that the chief of the Society of December 10 [i.e. Louis Bonaparte] suffices for its head. . . ." [39]

This appears to commit Marx to the view of the Bonapartist state as independent of any specific class and as superior to society. But he then goes on to say, in an often quoted phrase: "And yet the state power is not suspended in mid-air. Bonaparte represents a class, and the most numerous class of French society at that, *the small-holding peasants*." [40] However, lack of cohesion makes these "incapable of enforcing their class interests in their own name whether through a parilament or a convention";[41] they therefore require a representative who "must at the same time appear as their master, as an authority over them, as an unlimited governmental power that protects them against the other classes and sends them rain and sunshine from above. The political influence of the small-holding peasants, therefore, finds its final expression in the executive power subordinating society to itself." [42]

"Represent" is here a confusing word. In the context, the only meaning that may be attached to it is that the small-holding peasants *hoped* to have their interests represented by Louis Bonaparte. But this does not turn Louis Bonaparte or the state into the mere instrument of their will; at the most, it may limit the executive's freedom of action somewhat. Marx also writes that "as the executive authority which has made itself an independent power, Bonaparte feels it his mission to safeguard 'bourgeois order.' But the strength of this bourgeois order lies in the middle class. He looks on himself, therefore, as the representative of the middle class and issues decrees in this sense. Nevertheless, he is somebody solely due to the fact that he has broken the political power of this middle class and daily breaks it anew"; and again, "as against the bourgeoisie, Bonaparte looks on himself, at the same time, as the representative of the peasants and of the people in general, who wants to make the lower classes of the people happy within the frame of bourgeois so-

---

[39] *Ibid.*, p. 302.

[40] *Ibid.*, p. 302. Italics in original.

[41] Marx also notes that the identity of interest of the smallholding peasants "begets no community, no national bond and no political organization among them," so that "they do not form a class" (*ibid.*, p. 302). For an interesting discussion of Marx's concept of class, see S. Ossowski, *Class Structure in the Social Consciousness* (London, 1963), ch. V.

[42] *S.W.*, I, p. 303.

ciety. . . . But, above all, Bonaparte looks on himself as the chief of the Society of 10 December, as the representative of the *lumpen-proletariat* to which he himself, his *entourage,* his government and his army belong. . . ." [43]

On this basis, Louis Napoleon may "represent" this or that class (and Marx stresses the "contradictory task" of the man and the "contradictions of his government, the confused groping about which seeks now to win, now to humiliate first one class and then another and arrays all of them uniformly against him . . ." [44]); but his power of initiative remains very largely unimpaired by the specific wishes and demands of any one class or fraction of a class.

On the other hand, this does *not* mean that Bonapartism, for Marx, is in any sense neutral as between contending classes. It may *claim* to represent all classes and to be the embodiment of the whole of society. But it does in fact exist, and has been called into being, for the purpose of maintaining and strengthening the existing social order and the domination of capital over labour. Bonapartism and the Empire, Marx wrote much later in *The Civil War in France,* had succeeded the bourgeois Republic precisely because "it was the only form of government possible at a time when the bourgeoisie had already lost, and the working class had not yet acquired, the faculty of ruling the nation." [45] It was precisely under its sway that "bourgeois society, freed from political cares, attained a development unexpected even by itself." [46] Finally, Marx then characterizes what he calls "imperialism," by which he means Napoleon's imperial régime, as "at the same time, the most prostitute and the ultimate form of the State power which nascent middle-class society had commenced to elaborate as a means of its own emancipation from feudalism, and which full-grown bourgeois society had finally transformed into a means for the enslavement of labour by capital." [47]

In *The Origin of the Family, Private Property and the State,* written a year after Marx's death, Engels also notes: "By way of exception, however, periods occur in which the warring classes balance each other so nearly that the state power, as ostensible media-

[43] *Ibid.,* pp. 308–9.
[44] *Ibid.,* p. 309.
[45] K. Marx, *The Civil War in France, S.W.,* I, p. 470.
[46] *Ibid.,* p. 470.
[47] *Ibid.,* p. 470.

tor, acquires, for the moment, a certain degree of independence of both." [48] But the independence of which he speaks would seem to go much further than anything Marx had in mind; thus Engels refers to the Second Empire, "which played off the proletariat against the bourgeoisie and the bourgeoisie against the proletariat" and to Bismarck's German Empire, where "capitalists and workers are balanced against each other and equally cheated for the benefit of the impoverished Prussian cabbage junkers." [49]

For Marx, the Bonapartist state, however independent it may have been *politically* from any given class, remains, and cannot in a class society but remain, the protector of an economically and socially dominant class.

                                                                            IV

In the *Critique of Hegel's Philosophy of Right,* Marx had devoted a long and involved passage to the bureaucratic element in the state, and to its attempt "to transform the purpose of the state into the purpose of the bureaucracy and the purpose of the bureaucracy into the purpose of the state." [50] But it was only in the early 'fifties that he began to look closely at a type of society where the state appeared to be genuinely "above society," namely societies based on the "Asiatic mode of production," whose place in Marx's thought has recently attracted much attention.[51] What had, in the *Critique,* been a passing reference to the "despotic states of Asia, where the political realm is nothing but the arbitrary will of a particular individual, where the political realm, like the material, is enslaved," [52] had, by 1859, become one of Marx's four main stages of history: "In broad outlines," he wrote in the famous Preface to *A Contribution to the Critique of Political Economy,* "Asiatic, ancient, feudal and modern

---

[48] F. Engels, *The Origin of the Family, Private Property and the State, S.W.* II, p. 290.

[49] *Ibid.,* pp. 290–91. For further comments on the subject from Engels, see also his letter to C. Schmidt, 27 October 1890, in *S.W.,* II, pp. 446–47.

[50] MEGA, *op. cit.,* I, 1/1, p. 456.

[51] See, e.g. K. Wittfogel, *Oriental Despotism* (Yale, 1957), ch. IX; G. Lichtheim, "Marx and the 'Asiatic Mode of Production'" in *St. Antony's Papers,* no. 14, Far Eastern Affairs (London, 1963). [Part is reprinted in this volume, pp. 151–71.] Also K. Marx, *Pre-Capitalist Economic Formations,* with an introduction by E. J. Hobsbawm (London, 1964). This is a translation of a section of Marx's *Grundrisse Der Kritik der Politischen Okonomie (Rohentwurf)* (Berlin, 1953).

[52] MEGA, I, 1/1, p. 438.

bourgeois modes of production can be designated as progressive epochs in the economic formation of society." [53]

The countries Marx was mainly concerned with in this connection were India and China, and also Russia as a "semi-Asiatic" or "semi-Eastern" state. The Asiatic mode of production, for Marx and Engels, has one outstanding characteristic, namely the absence of private property in land: "this," Marx wrote to Engels in 1853, "is the real key, even to the Oriental heaven. . . ." [54] In the Asiatic form (or at least predominantly so)," he noted, "there is no property, but individual possession; the community is properly speaking the real proprietor";[55] in Asiatic production, he also remarked, it is the state which is the "real landlord." [56] In this system, he also wrote later, the direct producers are not "confronted by a private land-owner but rather, as in Asia, [are] under direct subordination to a state which stands over them as their landlord and simultaneously as sovereign"; "the state," he went on, "is then the supreme lord. Sovereignty here consists in the ownership of land concentrated on a national scale. But, on the other hand, no private ownership of land exists, although there is both private and common possession and use of land." [57]

A prime necessity of the Asiatic mode of production, imposed by climate and territorial conditions, was artificial irrigation by canals and waterworks; indeed, Marx wrote, this was "the basis of Oriental agriculture." In countries like Flanders and Italy the need of an economical and common use of water drove private enterprise into voluntary association; but it required "in the Orient, where civilization was too low and the territorial extent too vast to call into life voluntary associations, the interference of the centralized power of Government. Hence an economical function devolved upon all Asiatic governments, the functions of providing public works." [58]

---

[53] *S.W.,* I, p. 329.

[54] K. Marx to F. Engels, 2 June 1853, *Sel. Cor.,* p. 99.

[55] K. Marx, *Pre-Capitalist Formations, op. cit.,* p. 79.

[56] *New York Daily Tribune,* 5 August 1853, in Lichtheim, *op. cit.,* p. 94.

[57] K. Marx, *Capital* (Moscow, 1962), III, pp. 771–72.

[58] K. Marx and F. Engels, *The First Indian War of Independence* (1857–59) (Moscow, n.d.), p. 16. In *Capital* (Moscow, 1959), I, p. 514, ft. 2, Marx also notes that "one of the material bases of the power of the State over the small disconnected producing organisms in India, was the regulation of the water supply"; also, "the necessity for predicting the rise and fall of the Nile created Egyptian astronomy, and with it the dominion of the priests, as directors of agriculture" (*ibid.,* p. 514, ft. 1); for some further elaborations on the same theme, see also F. Engels, *Anti-Dühring* (Moscow, 1962), p. 248.

Finally, in the *Grundrisse,* Marx speaks of "the despotic government which is poised above the lesser communities," [59] and describes that government as the "*all-embracing unity* which stands above all these small common bodies . . . since the *unity* is the real owner, and the real pre-condition of common ownership, it is perfectly possible for it to appear as something separate and superior to the numerous real, particular communities . . . the despot here appears as the father of all the numerous lesser communities, thus realizing the common unity of all." [60]

It is therefore evident that Marx does view the state, in the conditions of Asiatic despotism, as the dominant force in society, independent of and superior to all its members, and that those who control its administration are society's authentic rulers. Karl Wittfogel has noted that Marx did not pursue this theme after the 1850s and that "in the writings of the later period he emphasized the technical side of large-scale waterworks, where previously he had emphasized their political setting." [61] The reason for this, Professor Wittfogel suggests, is that "obviously the concept of Oriental despotism contained elements that paralysed his search for truth";[62] hence his "retrogressions" on the subject. But the explanation for Marx's lack of concern for the topic would seem much simpler and much less sinister; it is that he was, in the 'sixties and the early 'seventies, primarily concerned with Western capitalism. Furthermore, the notion of bureaucratic despotism can hardly have held any great terror for him since he had, in fact, worked through its nearest equivalent in capitalist society, namely Bonapartism, and had analysed it as an altogether different phenomenon from the despotism encountered in Asiatic society. Nor is it accurate to suggest, as does Mr. Lichtheim, that "Marx for some reason shirked the problem of the bureaucracy" in post-capitalist society.[63] On the contrary, this may be said to be a crucial element in Marx's thought in the late 'sixties and in the early 'seventies. His concern with the question, and with the state, finds expression in this period in his discussion of the nature of political power in post-capitalist societies, and particularly in his view of the dictatorship of the proletariat. This theme had last occupied Marx in 1851–52; after almost twenty years it was

[59] K. Marx, *Pre-Capitalist Economic Formations, op. cit.,* p. 71.
[60] *Ibid.,* p. 69. Italics in original.
[61] K. Wittfogel, *Oriental Despotism, op. cit.,* p. 381.
[62] *Ibid.,* p. 387.
[63] Lichtheim, *op. cit.,* p. 110.

again brought to the fore by the Paris Commune, by his struggles
with anarchism in the First International and by the programmatic
pronouncement of German Social Democracy. It is to this, one of the
most important and the most misunderstood aspects of Marx's work
on the state, that we must now turn.

v

It is first of all necessary to go back to the democratic and representative republic, which must be clearly distinguished from the
dictatorship of the proletariat: for Marx, the two concepts have
nothing in common. An element of confusion arises from the fact
that Marx bitterly denounced the class character of the democratic
republic, yet supported its coming into being. The contradiction is
only apparent; Marx saw the democratic republic as the most advanced type of political régime in *bourgeois society,* and wished to
see it prevail over more backward and "feudal" political systems.
But it remained for him a system of class rule, indeed the system
in which the bourgeoisie rules most directly.

The limitations of the democratic republic, from Marx's point of
view, are made particularly clear in the *Address of the Central
Committee of the Communist League* which he and Engels wrote
in March 1850. "Far from desiring to revolutionize all society for
the revolutionary proletarians," they wrote, "the democratic petty
bourgeois strive for a change in social conditions by means of which
existing society will be made as tolerable and comfortable as possible for them." They would therefore demand such measures as
"the diminution of state expenditure by a curtailment of the bureaucracy and shifting the chief taxes on to the big landowners and
bourgeois . . . the abolition of the pressure of big capital on small,
through public credit institutions and laws against usury . . . the
establishment of bourgeois property relations in the countryside by
the complete abolition of feudalism." But in order to achieve their
purpose they would need "a democratic state structure, either constitutional or republican, that will give them and their allies, the
peasants, a majority; also a democratic communal structure that
will give them direct control over communal property and over a
series of functions now performed by the bureaucrats." [64] However,

---

[64] K. Marx and F. Engels, *Address of the Central Committee to the Communist
League, S.W.,* I, p. 101.

they added, "as far as the workers are concerned, it remains certain that they are to remain wage workers as before; the democratic petty-bourgeois only desire better wages and a more secure existence for the workers . . . they hope to bribe the workers by more or less concealed alms and to break their revolutionary potency by making their position tolerable for the moment." [65]

But, Marx and Engels go on, "these demands can in no wise suffice for the party of the proletariat"; while the petty-bourgeois democrats would seek to bring the revolution to a conclusion as quickly as possible, "it is our interest and our task to make the revolution permanent, until all more or less possessing classes have been forced out of their position of dominance, until the proletariat has conquered state power, and the association of proletarians, not only in one country but in all the dominant countries of the world, has advanced so far that competition among the proletarians of these countries has ceased and that at least the decisive productive forces are concentrated in the hands of the proletarians. For us the issue cannot be the alteration of private property but only its annihilation, not the smoothing over of class antagonisms but the abolition of classes, not the improvement of existing society but the foundation of a new one." [66]

At the same time, while the demands and aims of the proletarian party went far beyond anything which even the most advanced and radical petty-bourgeois democrats would accept, the revolutionaries must give them qualified support and seek to push the democratic movement into even more radical directions.[67] It was, incidentally, precisely the same strategy which dictated Marx's later attitude to all movements of radical reform, and which led him, as in the *Inaugural Address* of the First International in 1864, to acclaim the Ten Hours Act or the advances of the co-operative movement as the victories of "the political economy of labour over the political economy of property." [68]

In 1850, Marx and Engels had also suggested that one essential task of the proletarian revolutionaries would be to oppose the decentralizing tendencies of the petty-bourgeois revolutionaries. On the contrary, "the workers must not only strive for a single and indivisible German republic, but also within this republic for the

[65] *Ibid.*, p. 101.
[66] *Ibid.*, p. 102.
[67] *Ibid.*, p. 101.
[68] *Ibid.*, pp. 307-9.

most determined centralization of power in the hands of the state authority. . . ." [69]

This is not only the most extreme "statist" prescription in Marx's (and Engels's) work—it is the only one of its kind, leaving aside Marx's first "Hegelian" pronouncements on the subject. More important is the fact that the prescription is intended *not* for the proletarian but for the bourgeois democratic revolution.[70] In 1850, Marx and Engels believed, and said in the *Address,* that the German workers would not be able "to attain power and achieve their own class interest without completely going through a lengthy revolutionary development." [71] The proletarian revolution would see the coming into being of an altogether different form of rule than the democratic republic, namely the dictatorship of the proletariat.

In a famous letter to J. Weydemeyer in March 1852, Marx had revealed the cardinal importance he attached to this concept by saying that, while no credit was due to him for discovering the existence of classes in modern society or the struggles between them, "what I did that was new was to prove (1) that the *existence of classes* is only bound up with *particular historical phases in the development of production,* (2) that the class struggle necessarily leads to the *dictatorship of the proletariat,* (3) that this dictatorship itself only constitutes the transition to *abolition of all classes* and to a *classless society*." [72]

Unfortunately, Marx did not define in any specific way *what* the dictatorship of the proletariat actually entailed, and more particularly what was its relation to the state. It has been argued by Mr. Hal Draper in an extremely well documented article that it is a "*social description,* a statement of the class character of the political power. It is not a statement about the forms of the government machinery." [73] My own view, on the contrary, is that, for Marx, the dictatorship of the proletariat is *both* a statement of the class character of the political power *and* a description of the political power

[69] *Ibid.,* p. 106.

[70] It is, in this connection, of some interest that Engels should have thought it necessary to add a Note to the 1885 edition of the Address, explaining that this passage was based on a "misunderstanding" of French revolutionary experience and that "local and provincial self-government" were not in contradiction with "national centralization." (*Ibid.,* p. 107.)

[71] *Ibid.,* p. 108.

[72] K. Marx to J. Weydemeyer, 5 March 1852, *Sel. Cor.,* p. 86. Italics in original.

[73] H. Draper, "Marx and the Dictatorship of the Proletariat" in *New Politics,* vol. I, no. 4, p. 102. Italics in original.

itself; and that it is in fact the nature of the political power which it described which guarantees its class character.

In the *18th Brumaire*, Marx had made a point which constitutes a main theme of his thought, namely that all previous revolutions had "perfected this [state] machine instead of smashing it. The parties that contended in turn for domination regarded the possession of this huge state edifice as the principal spoils of the victors." [74] Nearly twenty years later, in *The Civil War in France*, he again stressed how every previous revolution had consolidated "the centralized State power, with its ubiquitous organs of standing army, police, bureaucracy, clergy and judicature"; and he also stressed how the political character of the state had changed "simultaneously with the economic changes of society. At the same pace at which the progress of modern history developed, widened, intensified the class antagonism between capital and labour, the State power assumed more and more the character of the national power of capital over labour, of a public force organized for social enslavement, of an engine of class despotism. After every revolution marking a progressive phase in the class struggle, the purely repressive character of the State power stands out in bolder and bolder relief." [75]

As Mr. Draper notes, Marx had made no reference to the dictatorship of the proletariat in all the intervening years. Nor indeed did he so describe the Paris Commune. But what he acclaims above all in the Commune is that, in contrast to previous social convulsions, it sought not the further consolidation of the state power but its destruction. What it wanted, he said, was to have "restored to the social body all the forces hitherto absorbed by the State parasite feeding upon, and clogging the free movement of, society." [76] Marx also lays stress on the Commune's popular, democratic and egalitarian character, and on the manner in which "not only municipal administration but the whole initiative hitherto exercised by the State was laid into the hands of the Commune." [77] Moreover, while the communal form of government was to apply even to the "smallest country hamlet," "the unity of the nation was not to be broken, but, on the contrary, to be organized by the Communal Constitution, and to become a reality by the destruction of the State power which claimed to be the embodiment of that unity independent of,

[74] *S.W.*, I, p. 301.
[75] *Ibid.*, pp. 468–69.
[76] *Ibid.*, p. 473.
[77] *Ibid.*, p. 471.

and superior to, the nation itself, from which it was but a parasitic excrescence." [78]

In notes which he wrote for *The Civil War in France*, Marx makes even clearer than in the published text the significance which he attached to the Commune's dismantling of the state power. As contributing evidence of his approach to the whole question, the following passage from the Notes is extremely revealing: "This [i.e. the Commune] was," he wrote, "a Revolution not against this or that, legitimate, constitutional, republican or Imperialist form of State power. It was a Revolution against the *State* itself, of this supernaturalist abortion of society, a resumption by the people for the people of its own social life. It was not a revolution to transfer it from one fraction of the ruling class to the other but a Revolution to break down this horrid machinery of Classdomination [*sic*] itself . . . the Second Empire was the final form(?) [*sic*] of this State usurpation. The Commune was its definite negation, and, therefore, the initiation of the social Revolution of the nineteenth century." [79] It is in the light of such views that Marx's verdict on the Commune takes on its full meaning: this "essentially working-class government," he wrote, was "the political form at last discovered under which to work out the economic emancipation of labour." [80]

It is of course true that, while Engels, long after Marx's death, did describe the Paris Commune as the dictatorship of the proletariat,[81] Marx himself did not do so. The reason for this would seem fairly

[78] *Ibid.*, p. 472.

[79] *Marx-Engels Archives* (Moscow, 1934), vol. III (VIII). p. 324. Italics in original. I am grateful to Mr. M. Johnstone for drawing my attention to these Notes. Note also, e.g., the following: "Only the Proletarians, fired by a new social task to accomplish by them for all society, to do away with all classes and class rule, were the men to break the instrument of that class rule—the State, the centralized and organized governmental power usurping to be the master instead of the servant of society. . . . It had sprung into life against them. By them it was broken, not as a peculiar form of governmental (centralized) power, but as its most powerful, elaborated into seeming independence from society expression and, therefore, also its most prostitute reality, covered by infamy from top to bottom, having centred in absolute corruption at home and absolute powerlessness abroad" (*ibid.*, p. 326). The peculiar English syntax of such passages is obviously due to the fact that they are only notes, not intended for publication.

[80] *S.W.*, I, p. 473.

[81] "Of late," Engels wrote in an Introduction to the 1891 edition of *The Civil War in France*, "the Social-Democratic philistine has once more been filled with wholesome terror at the words: Dictatorship of the Proletariat. Well and good, gentlemen, do you want to know what this dictatorship looks like? Look at the Paris Commune. That was the Dictatorship of the Proletariat." (*S.W.*, I, p. 440.)

obvious, namely that, for Marx, the dictatorship of the proletariat would be the outcome of a socialist revolution on a national scale; the Commune, as he wrote in 1881, was "merely the rising of a city under exceptional conditions," while "the majority of the Commune was in no wise socialist, nor could it be." [82] Even so, it may justifiably be thought that the Commune, in its de-institutionalization of political power, did embody, for Marx, the essential elements of his concept of the dictatorship of the proletariat.

Precisely the opposite view has very generally come to be taken for granted; the following statement in Mr. Lichtheim's *Marxism* is a typical example of a wide consensus: "His (Marx's) hostility to the state was held in check by a decidedly authoritarian doctrine of political rule during the transition period: prior to being consigned to the dustbin of history, the state was to assume dictatorial powers. In different terms, authority would inaugurate freedom—a typically Hegelian paradox which did not worry Marx though it alarmed Proudhon and Bakunin. . . ." [83]

The trouble with the view that Marx had a "decidedly authoritarian doctrine" is that it is unsupported by any convincing evidence from Marx himself; and that there is so much evidence which directly runs counter to it.

Marx was undoubtedly the chief opponent of the anarchists in the International. But it is worth remembering that his central quarrel with them concerned above all the manner in which the struggle for a socialist revolution ought to be prosecuted, with Marx insisting on the need for political involvement within the existing political framework, against the anarchists' all or nothing rejection of mere politics; and the quarrel also concerned the question of the type of organization required by the international workers' movement, with Marx insisting on a *degree* of control by the General Council of the International over its affiliated organizations.

As for the rôle of the state in the period of transition, there is the well-known passage in the "private circular" against the anarchists issued by the General Council in 1872, *Les Prétendues Scissions dans l'Internationale,* and most probably written by Marx: "What all socialists understand by anarchism is this: as soon as the goal of the proletarian movement, the abolition of class, shall have been

[82] K. Marx to F. Domela-Nienwenhuis, 22 February 1881, in *Sel. Cor.,* p. 410.
[83] G. Lichtheim, *Marxism* (London, 1961), p. 374.

reached, the power of the state, whose function it is to keep the
great majority of the producers beneath the yoke of a small minority
of exploiters, will disappear, and governmental functions will be
transformed into simple administrative functions. The Alliance
[i.e. Bakunin's Alliance of Socialist Democracy] turns the thing
upside down. It declares anarchism in the ranks of the workers to
be an infallible means for disrupting the powerful concentration of
social and political forms in the hands of the exploiters. Under this
pretext, it asks the International, when the old world is endeavour-
ing to crush our organization, to replace organization by anarchism.
The international police could ask for nothing better. . . ." [84]

This can hardly be construed as an authoritarian text; nor certainly is Marx's plaintive remark in January 1873 quoted by Lenin
in *State and Revolution* that "if the political struggle of the working
class assumes violent forms, if the workers set up this revolutionary
dictatorship in place of the dictatorship of the bourgeoisie, they
commit the terrible crime of violating principles, for in order to
satisfy their wretched, vulgar, everyday needs, in order to crush the
resistance of the bourgeoisie, instead of laying down their arms and
abolishing the state, they give the state a revolutionary and transitory form. . . ." [85]

Nor is there much evidence of Marx's "decidedly authoritarian
doctrine" in his marginal notes of 1875 on the Gotha Programme
of the German Social-Democratic Party. In these notes, Marx bitterly attacked the programme's references to "the free state" ("free
state—what is this?") and this is well in line with his belief that
the "free state" is a contradiction in terms; and he then asked:
"What transformation will the state undergo in communist society?
In other words, what social functions will remain in existence there
that are analogous to present functions of the state?" Marx, however, did not answer the question but merely said that it could only
be answered "scientifically" and that "one does not get a flea-hop
nearer to the problem by a thousandfold combination of the word
people with the word state." [86] He then goes on: "Between capitalist
and communist society lies the period of the revolutionary transformation of the one into the other. There corresponds to this also

---

[84] G. M. Stekloff, *History of the First International* (London, 1928), pp. 179–80,
and J. Freymond, ed., *La Première Internationale* (Geneva, 1962), II, p. 295.

[85] V. I. Lenin, *State and Revolution* (London, 1933), p. 54.

[86] K. Marx, *Critique of the Gotha Programme, S.W.*, II, p. 30.

a political transition period in which the state can be nothing but *the revolutionary dictatorship of the proletariat.*" [87]

This does not advance matters much, but neither does it suggest the slightest "authoritarian" impulse. In the *Critique of the Gotha Programme,* Marx as always before, made a sharp distinction between the democratic republic and the dictatorship of the proletariat, and Engels was clearly mistaken when he wrote in 1891 that the democratic republic was "even the specific form of the dictatorship of the proletariat." [88] On the contrary, Marx's critical attitude towards the democratic republic in the *Critique of the Gotha Programme* shows that he continued to think of the dictatorship of the proletariat as an altogether different and immeasurably freer form of political power. "Freedom," he wrote in the *Critique of the Gotha Programme,* "consists in converting the state from an organ superimposed upon society into one completely subordinated to it. . . ." [89] This would seem a good description of Marx's view of the state in the period of the dictatorship of the proletariat. No doubt, he would have endorsed Engels's view, expressed a few weeks after Marx's death, that "the proletarian class will first have to possess itself of the organized political force of the state and with this aid stamp out the resistance of the capitalist class and reorganize society." [90] But it is of some significance that, with the possible exception of his remark of January 1873, referred to earlier, Marx himself always chose to emphasize the liberating rather than the repressive aspects of post-capitalist political power; and it is also of some interest that, in the notes he made for *The Civil War in France,* and which were not of course intended for publication, he should have warned the working class that the "work of regeneration" would be "again and again relented [*sic*] and impeded by the resistance of vested interests and class egotisms," but that he should have failed to make any reference to the State as an agent of repression. What he did say was that "great strides may be [made] at once

[87] *Ibid.,* p. 30. Italics in original.

[88] Quoted in Lenin, *The State and Revolution,* p. 54. Lenin's own comment is also misleading: "Engels," he writes, "repeats here in a particularly striking manner the fundamental idea which runs like a red thread through all of Marx's works, namely, that the democratic republic is the nearest approach to the dictatorship of the proletariat" (*ibid.,* p. 54). Engels's phrase does not bear this interpretation; and whatever may be said for the view that the democratic republic *is* the nearest approach to the dictatorship of the proletariat, it is not so in Marx.

[89] *S.W.,* II, p. 29.

[90] F. Engels to P. Van Patten, 18 April 1883, *Sel. Cor., op. cit.,* p. 437.

through the communal form of political organization" and that "the time has come to begin that movement for themselves and mankind." [91]

The fact is that, far from bearing any authoritarian imprint, the whole of Marx's work on the state is pervaded by a powerful anti-authoritarian and anti-bureaucratic bias, not only in relation to a distant communist society but also to the period of transition which is to precede it. True, the state is necessary in this period. But the only thing which, for Marx, makes it tolerable is popular participation and popular rule. If Marx is to be faulted, it is not for any authoritarian bias, but for greatly understating the difficulties of the libertarian position. However, in the light of the experience of socialist movements since Marx wrote, this may perhaps be judged a rather less serious fault than its bureaucratic obverse.

[91] *Marx-Engels Archives, op. cit.,* p. 334.

ELEVEN

MARX AND THE "ASIATIC MODE OF PRODUCTION"

GEORGE LICHTHEIM

III

In January 1859, when writing the *Preface* to the *Critique of Political Economy*, Marx for the first (and last) time gave a summary of his method that indicates the exact relationship in which the economic process ("the mode of production of material life") stands to the historical process generally; and it is here, towards the close of the now classic formulation of the "materialist conception of history," that he introduces his four historical stages: "In broad outlines, Asiatic, ancient, feudal, and modern bourgeois modes of production can be designated as progressive epochs in the economic formation of society." [1] He was never again to display a similar degree of certainty in assigning their relative place to those forms of society which had embodied their characteristic features in definite stages of recorded history. Yet the general standpoint laid down in the *Preface* was not superseded or even substantially modified. (The qualifications introduced by Engels in the *Anti-Dühring* and the *Origins of the Family* are not, in my opinion, of basic importance.)[2] There are four, and only four, major historical epochs, the Asiatic being the first, and each corresponds to a definite social order which in turn lays the foundation for the succeeding one. These two aspects are

From George Lichtheim, "Marx and the 'Asiatic Mode of Production,' " *St. Antony's Papers*, No. 14: *Far Eastern Affairs*. © George Lichtheim, 1963. Reprinted by permission of George Lichtheim, Chatto & Windus Ltd., and Southern Illinois University Press.

[1] *Selected Works*, vol. I, p. 363. The translation fails to convey the Hegelian ring of the original. Since an exact rendering of Hegel's observations on world history into English is a stylistic impossibility, one is left with the bare statement that Marx echoes Hegel not only in distinguishing four major epochs of world history but also in the confident Europeanocentrism with which he pronounces sentence upon the three preceding ones.

[2] For a different view cf. Wittfogel, pp. 382 ff. [Karl A. Wittfogel, *Oriental Despotism: A Comparative Study of Total Power* (New Haven: Yale University Press, 1957)].

internally related, but must nonetheless for analytical purposes be considered separately.[3]

To start, then, with the "Asiatic mode" taken by itself, we have already seen what features can be said to distinguish it. [These features, mentioned earlier in the essay, are those outlined by Marx in a series of articles on India in the *New York Daily Tribune* during 1853: dispersion of population, provision of irrigation by central government, absence of private property in land. These articles, and others by Marx on non-European societies, have been reprinted in Shlomo Avineri (ed.), *Karl Marx on Colonialism and Modernization* (New York: Doubleday & Co., Inc. 1968).] In his unsystematic fashion, Engels had suggested two: climatic conditions and the pervasive habits of an Oriental government. Marx expanded these hints into a system by tracing the peculiar character of Oriental society to the absence of private ownership in land.[4] He related this to the overriding role of the central government by suggesting that under the "Asiatic system" the State was the "real landlord." [5] So far as private property in land is concerned we are left in no doubt what Marx thought of its role in dissolving the "Asiatic mode," since in the second and concluding of his important *Tribune* articles on British rule in India he expressly describes it as "the great *desideratum* of Asiatic society," [6] for the sake of which the infamies practised by the Indian *zamindar* and *ryotwar* systems, "abominable as they are," should nonetheless be regarded as a step towards the emancipation of Indian society. Now what of the role played by the State? That in Asia it was the "real landlord" Marx never doubted. For proof we have the passage in *Capital,* vol. III, where he refers to the situa-

---

[3] It seems to me to be a decided weakness of Wittfogel's treatment of the subject that he fails to do this.

[4] Engels's notion that the failure of Oriental society to develop private landed ownership was "mainly due to the climate" is a trifle naïve, and looks back to Hegel, or even Montesquieu: one of the many instances of his tendency to relapse into ordinary cause-and-effect explanation, in the manner of the Enlightenment. The point cannot be pursued here; the reader of Hegel's *Vorlesungen,* vol. I, pp. 178 ff., can easily discover where Engels obtained his basic notions about Oriental history. Marx, though equally inclined to take a Hegelian view of the historical process, relied for his factual information upon the classical economists, down to and including J. S. Mill, and upon British Blue Books and other official or semi-official sources.

[5] NYDT [*New York Daily Tribune;* see editor's note above], August 5, 1853; cf. *Gesammelte Werke,* vol. 9, p. 218; this article has for some reason not been included in any English-language collection known to the writer.

[6] NYDT, August 8, 1853; cf. *Selected Works,* vol. I, p. 353.

tion of the producers being confronted not by a private landowner, "but rather, as in Asia, under direct subordination to a state which stands over them as their landlord and simultaneously as sovereign." [7] These characteristics of "Asiatic society"—state control over the producer, and absence of private property in land—are presumably related to the strategic role of the central government in administering the irrigation system, but how does this complex interrelationship come about *historically?* Engels never bothered about such difficult questions, but from Marx we are entitled to expect an answer. Let us see how far he has provided one.

An indirect clue is afforded by his observation that where the small peasants "form among themselves a more or less natural production community, as they do in India . . . the surplus labour for the nominal owner of the land can only be extorted from them by other than economic pressure, whatever the form assumed may be." [8] This is followed by the remark about the state-sovereign doubling as landlord, so that taxes and ground-rents coincide. Marx then continues: "Under such circumstances there need exist no harder political or economic dependence than that common to all subjection to that state. The state is here the supreme landlord. Sovereignty here consists in the ownership of land concentrated on a national scale. Conversely, no private ownership of land exists, although there is both private and common possession and use of land." [9]

Does this point in the direction of a theory of conquest or some other form of political usurpation which blocks the emergence of true "private ownership" of land, leaving the subject peasant population only with "possession and use"? The puzzling thing is that the immediately following sentence states: "The specific economic form in which unpaid surplus labour is pumped out of (the) direct producers determines the relationship of rulers and ruled, as it grows directly out of production itself and in turn reacts upon it as a determining element. Upon this, however, is founded the entire formation of the economic community which grows up out of the produc-

[7] Quoted after the Moscow, 1960, English-language edition, p. 771.

[8] *Capital,* vol. III, p. 771. Marx here appends a footnote which adds: "Following the conquest of a country, the immediate aim of the conqueror was also to convert its people to his own use. Cf. Linguet (*Théorie des lois civiles, etc.,* London, 1767). See also Möser." It is not quite clear whether this refers to Indian conditions or whether it is meant to stand indifferently for all cases where peasant proprietors fall under some form of non-economic exploitation.

[9] *Ibid.,* pp. 771–72 (cited after the German text).

tion relations themselves, (and) therewith simultaneously its specific political form." [10] Other parts of the same lengthy passage refer to serfdom and similar forms of socio-economic bondage. It must be borne in mind that vol. III of *Capital* was pieced together by Engels from unfinished drafts. Even so it remains uncertain how Marx envisaged the historical genesis of a relationship which counterposes the State as supreme landlord to the peasant-producer. He makes it quite clear, however, that it is the dominance of the State which excludes genuine private ownership of land, i.e. the precondition of feudalism. If anything defines "the Orient" according to Marx (and Engels) it is this supremacy of the State, which reduces the landowners to the role of merely "nominal landlords" as Marx calls them.[11] There cannot then have been any genuine Oriental feudalism, at any rate not in India and China, the two Asian countries to which Marx had given some systematic attention. That he regarded their problems as broadly similar appears from a passage in *Capital*, vol. III, where he refers to the impact of European commerce upon Eastern societies:

> The obstacles presented by the internal solidity and organization of precapitalistic, national modes of production to the corrosive influence of commerce are strikingly illustrated in the intercourse of the English with India and China. The broad basis of the mode of production here is formed by the unity of small-scale agriculture and home industry, to which in India we should add the form of village communities built upon the common ownership of land, which incidentally was the original form in China as well. In India the English lost no time in exercising their direct political and economic power, as rulers and landlords, to disrupt these small economic communities. English commerce exerted a revolutionary influence on these communities and tore them apart only insofar as the low prices of its goods served to destroy the spinning and weaving industries which were an ancient integrating element of this unity of industrial and agricultural production. Even so this work of dissolution proceeds very gradually. And still more slowly in China, where it is not reinforced by direct political power. The substantial economy and saving in time afforded by the association of agriculture with manufacture put up a

[10] *Capital*, vol. III, p. 772; for the original text cf. *Das Kapital*, Berlin, 1949, vol. III, 841–82. The authorized English translation published in Moscow is both wooden and inaccurate.

[11] The above passage makes it clear that this refers to the original pre-conquest Indian landowners, and not only to the *zamindars*, as might be supposed from Marx's characterization of the latter as tax-gatherers imposed by the British Government upon the wretched Bengali peasants (cf. NYDT, August 5, 1853).

stubborn resistance to the products of the big industries whose prices include the *faux frais* of the circulation process which pervades them. Unlike the English, Russian commerce, on the other hand, leaves the economic ground-work of Asiatic production untouched.[12]

The interest of this passage is that it shows Marx, in the 1860's and while at work on *Capital,* reverting to the theme of his early newspaper articles. He does so also in a footnote in which the "absurd (in practice infamous) economic experiments" conducted by the British in India are duly condemned, with special reference to the creation of "a caricature of large-scale English estates" in Bengal.[13] Yet we have seen that in 1853 he had described private property in land as "the great *desideratum* of Asiatic society," and expressly mentioned the *zamindars.* There is of course no contradiction if one bears in mind that for Marx the rupture of India's ancient stagnation involved the payment of a terrible price in exploitation and dislocation. But the new stress in *Capital* on the futility and absurdity of these "economic experiments," together with the reference to the solidity of the ancient social structure built upon the union of farming and handicrafts, does strike rather a different note. When he remarks that "in the north-west they (sc. the English) did all they could to transform the Indian economic community with common ownership of the soil into a caricature of itself." [14] he seems to be saying, or at least hinting, that but for this outside interference the village community might have evolved in a sounder direction. Then there is the passing reference to the economic savings inherent in small-scale enterprise, as against the *faux frais* of modern large-scale industry—this last a familiar theme in socialist literature since Fourier, but one to which Marx normally did not give a great deal of attention. Altogether the tone of this passage seems to anticipate his well-known observations upon the prospects of the Russian vil-

---

[12] Cited after the Moscow edition, pp. 328–29; Engels's qualifying footnote (appended in 1894, i.e. almost thirty years after Marx had written these lines), about Russian commerce having in the meantime become genuinely capitalistic, does not affect the substance of the argument. Incidentally, the Soviet translation is not merely scandalously bad but in parts positively misleading; e.g. the key sentence really ought to run as follows: "Insofar as their commerce here revolutionizes the mode of production, it does so only as through the low price of their merchandise they destroy the spinning and weaving which constitutes an ancient and integrating part of this union of industrial-agricultural production and thus disrupt the communities."

[13] L.c., p. 328, note.

[14] *Ibid.*

lage community in the 1880's: there is a hint of "Narodism" about it.[15]

It is, I think, a fair inference from these passages that while in the 1850's Marx was inclined to emphasize the progressive role of Western capitalism in disrupting Oriental stagnation, by the time he came to draft his major economic work he was less certain that traditional society embodied no positive factors. At any rate, it may be said that by the 1860's his attitude had become ambivalent. We now find him remarking upon the stability of the ancient village communities, in a manner suggesting that he saw some genuine virtue in their peculiar mode of life. At the same time his hostility to capitalism had deepened. This is worth stressing as a qualification of the familiar statement that he had by the 1860's lost some of his early revolutionary ardour. If one has in mind his early attachment to a rather Jacobinical view of the coming European revolution, it is true to say that he grew more moderate in the measure that he became the theorist of a genuine labour movement with democratic aims. But at the same time he sharpened his critique of bourgeois society and the operation of capitalism as an economic system. The *Manifesto*, rather paradoxically, had celebrated the triumphant march of capitalism at the same time that it proclaimed the proletariat's coming victory. By the time Marx wrote *Capital* he was more concerned with factory legislation than with the proletarian revolution, but this did not make him more tolerant of "the system"; rather less so. The note of indulgence has vanished, and the tone has become one of unqualified hostility and contempt. In 1847 the bourgeoisie still gained some plaudits for battering down the Chinese walls of barbarism; by 1867 even the "Asiatic mode" comes in for favourable comment, at any rate so far as the village community is concerned: it is valued as a bulwark against social disintegration.

IV

Here, then, is something like a hiatus in the argument. To some extent the difficulty arises from the fact that the more strictly his-

---

[15] For Lenin's view on this issue, which of course was central to the gradual emergence of Russian Marxism from its Populist chrysalis, see his rather agitated defence of the "real" Marx against the Narodniks (who naturally quoted *Capital*, vol. III, when it suited them) in *The Development of Capitalism in Russia* (1900; new edn., Moscow, 1956, pp. 340 ff.); cf. Lichtheim, *Marxism: An Historical and Critical Study*, London, 1961, pp. 325 ff.

torical part of Marx's theory of Oriental society is to be found in the posthumously published draft for *Das Kapital*, the so-called *Grundrisse*.[16] Before turning to this theme it may be as well to note where he departs from his predecessors. There was an 18th century and early 19th century view of Asian society with which Marx was thoroughly familiar. It is briefly but succinctly set out in the *Wealth of Nations*, and it is amusing to find that Smith, like Marx, refers to Bernier's travels as a source.[17] Chinese isolationism and indifference to foreign trade attracted the unfavourable attention of Smith who thought that "upon their present plan they have little opportunity of improving themselves by the example of any other nation; except that of the Japanese":[18] a nice example of historical foresight. China is classed with "ancient Egypt and Indostan," and Smith makes the pertinent point that in both these countries the government paid much attention to the canal system.[19] He also observes that "the sovereigns of China, of ancient Egypt, and of the different kingdoms into which Indostan has at different times been divided, have always derived the whole, or by far the most considerable part, of their revenue from some sort of land-tax or rent. . . . It was natural, therefore, that the sovereigns of those countries should be particularly attentive to the interests of agriculture, upon the prosperity or declension of which immediately depended the yearly increase or diminution of their own revenue." [20] Later he remarks that "the sovereigns of China, those of Bengal while under the Mahometan government, and those of ancient Egypt, are said accordingly to have been extremely attentive to the making and maintaining of good roads and navigable canals, in order to increase, as much as possible, both the quantity and value of every part of the produce of the land. . . ." [21] He then goes on to discuss "the loss of the sovereign from the abuse and depredation of his tax-gatherers" and the interest of "the Mandarins and other tax-gatherers" in maintaining a

---

[16] Cf. *Grundrisse der Kritik der politischen Ökonomie (Rohentwurf) 1857–1858*, Berlin, 1953; originally published in two volumes (Moscow, 1939–41); part of this draft (over 1,000 pages in print) was revised and published by Marx in 1859 under the title *Zur Kritik der politischen Ökonomie*; the bulk was reworked from 1863 onwards into what is now called *Das Kapital*.

[17] Cf. *Wealth of Nations* (Modern Library edn., New York, 1937), p. 688, where the title of Bernier's *Voyages contenant la description des états du Grand Mogol*, etc. (Amsterdam, 1710), is given as *Voyages de François Bernier*.

[18] *Ibid.*, p. 64.

[19] P. 646.

[20] *Op. cit.*, p. 647.

[21] P. 789.

system of payment in kind that enabled them to fleece the peasants and defraud the central government.[22] There are the elements here of a theory of Oriental society, but it cannot be said that Smith makes much of them. He is content to register various features of Indian or Chinese administration, without inquiring to what extent they constitute a whole. In the following generation, we find James Mill, in his *History of British India* (1820), referring to an "Asiatic model of government" (vol. I, pp. 175 ff.), while John Stuart Mill (*Principles of Political Economy*, 1848) already employs the term "Oriental society" as distinct from European.[23] Marx was familiar with these writers. Where does he diverge from them?

Principally, it seems to me, in expanding their hints into a theory that is both historical and sociological.[24] Unfortunately the theory was never formulated in systematic fashion, but has to be pieced together from his published and unpublished writings, notably the *Grundrisse* of 1857–58, where it is, however, chiefly employed to bring out the contrast between Oriental society and Graeco-Roman antiquity. By drawing upon all these scattered sources (including a very early work, the *German Ideology* of 1845–46, which throws out some interesting hints about slavery and feudalism), we arrive at something like the following:

The various stages in the development of the social division of labour correspond to different forms of property.[25] The "first form" is communal and proper to "the undeveloped stage of production where a people sustains itself by hunting and fishing, by cattle-raising or at most by farming." [26] At this stage, the division of labour is rudimentary and consists for the most part in a further development of the primitive division of functions inherent in the family. "The social order therefore limits itself to an extension of the family: patriarchal tribal chiefs, below them the members of the tribe, finally slaves. The slavery latent in the family develops gradually with the growth of population and needs, and with the extension of

---

[22] P. 790.

[23] Op. cit. (1909 edn.), p. 20; Marx on the whole prefers the term "Asiatic society," perhaps first used by Richard Jones in *An Essay on the Distribution of Wealth* (1831); cf. Wittfogel, p. 373.

[24] I am obliged here to refer the reader to the chapter on Historical Materialism in *Marxism*, pp. 141 ff., for a discussion of Marx's methodology. (The originality of his approach, and the basic difference between his theory and the unsystematic hints thrown out by his predecessors, seems to me to have been understressed by Wittfogel.)

[25] Cf. *Die deutsche Ideologie, MEGA,* Section One, Vol. V, pp. 11 ff.

[26] *Ibid.*

external intercourse, both of war and barter trade." [27] This primitive tribal or communal organization is succeeded historically by a "second form" which in the 1845–46 sketch is equated with "the communal and state property of antiquity." This is said to arise particularly "from the union of several tribes to a city through contact or conquest, and while retaining slavery. Side by side with communal property, mobile and subsequently immobile private property develops, but as an abnormal form subordinated to communal property. The citizens of the state possess power over their labouring slaves only collectively, and for this reason alone they are tied to the form of communal ownership. It is the joint private property (*das gemeinschaftliche Privateigentum*) of the active citizens who are compelled *vis-à-vis* the slaves to remain in this primitive (*naturwüchsige*) manner of association. Hence the entire organization of society based thereupon, and therewith the power of the people, decays in the same degree in which especially immobile private property develops. The division of labour is more highly developed. We already find the contrast of town and country. . . .[28] The class relationship as between citizens and slaves is fully developed." [28] Marx notes as a possible objection that "the fact of conquest appears to contradict this whole conception of history," and goes on to demonstrate that "for the conquering barbarian people, war itself is . . . a regular form of intercourse, which is exploited all the more energetically the more the growth of population together with the traditional . . . primitive mode of production arouses the demand for new means of production." [29] This organization finds its ultimate development in Roman society, where "slavery remains the basis of the entire production" and the plebeians "stationed between free citizens and slaves never got beyond a *Lumpenproletariat*." It is succeeded by the "third form" of property, namely, "feudal or estate ownership." [30] In other words, by the European middle ages.

In 1845–46 Marx had not yet discovered Oriental society and the "Asiatic mode"; consequently he mentions only three pre-modern stages: tribal society is succeeded by classical antiquity founded on slavery, and the latter by European feudalism. By 1859 the *Preface* to the *Critique of Political Economy* presents four stages corresponding to different forms of property: Asiatic society, antiquity, feudal-

---

[27] *Ibid.*, p. 12.
[28] DI., *op. cit.*, p. 12.
[29] *Ibid.*, pp. 12–13.
[30] P. 13.

ism, and modern bourgeois society. Tribal society has disappeared, to be subsequently resurrected by Engels.[31] Now the 1859 work is based on the unpublished *Grundrisse* of 1857–58, and when we turn to this much-neglected source we obtain some light on how Marx had in the meantime come to regard the relationship of the Orient and the "Asiatic mode" to primitive tribal society on the one hand, and to classical antiquity and European feudalism on the other. His economic studies had acquainted him with the researches of the British school, and what we now get is a picture in which the skeleton of the "materialist conception of history" is fleshed out with economics.

True to his method, the approach remains historical. Marx begins by asking what are the "forms which precede capitalist production," [32] and he replies that the historical presupposition of the latter is the "separation of free labour from the objective preconditions of its realization. . . . Hence above all separation of the toiler from the soil as his natural laboratory: thus dissolution of small free landed property, as well as of the joint (*gemeinschaftlichen*) landed property resting upon the Oriental commune." [33] "In the first form of this landed property there appears a primitive (*naturwüchsige*) commonwealth as the precondition: (the) family and its extension to the tribe . . . or a combination of tribes. . . ." "Tribal community (*die Stammgemeinschaft*), the natural community, appears not as the result but as the precondition of joint appropriation . . . and utilization of the soil." "The earth is the great laboratory, the arsenal, which provides the means as well as the materials of work, and likewise the location, the basis, of the community." [34] The individual participates in ownership of the soil and the instruments of production only insofar as he is a member of this primitive commonwealth held together by the ties of consanguinity. "The real appropriation through the process of labour occurs under these presuppositions which are themselves not the product of labour, but appear as its natural or divine preconditions. This form, based on the same primitive relationship, can realize itself in many different ways. Thus

[31] Cf. the latter's *Origin of the Family* (1884). In passing it may be observed that Marx's sketch of 1845–46 supplies a very realistic hint at the emergence of slavery from within the tribal organization. Compare this with Engels's account of how and why "the old classless gentile society" with its "simple moral grandeur" succumbs to "civilized" pressure from outside; cf. *Selected Works*, vol. II, p. 231.

[32] *Grundrisse*, p. 375.

[33] *Ibid.*

[34] *Ibid.*, pp. 375–76.

it is not contradicted by the fact that in most of the Asiatic patterns (Grundformen) the encompassing unity, which stands above all these small communities, appears as the superior or as the sole proprietor, (and) the real communities only as hereditary possessors. Since the unity is the true owner and the real precondition of common ownership, it can appear as a particular something (als ein Besonderes) above the many real particular communities, where the individual is then in fact without property, or property . . . appears as though mediated for him through a grant by the total unity (der Gesamteinheit)—which is realized in the despot as the father of the many communities—to the individual through the intermediacy of the particular community. The surplus product . . . thus belongs inherently to this supreme unity. In the midst of Oriental despotism, and of the absence of ownership (Eigentumslosigkeit) which juridically seems to obtain therein, there thus exists in fact as the basis this tribal or communal ownership, generally produced by a combination of manufacture and agriculture within the small community, which thus becomes entirely self-sustaining and contains within itself all the conditions of reproduction and surplus production. Part of its surplus labour belongs to the higher unity which at last exists as a person, and this surplus labour makes its appearance both in tribute, etc., and in common labours for the glorification of the unity: in part the real despot, in part the imaginary tribal being, the god." [35]

This kind of common ownership, held together at the top by the "higher unity which at last exists as a person," appears under different historical variants: either the small communities maintain a separate existence and the individual works his plot independently, together with the members of his family; or again, "the unity may extend to communalism at work itself, which may be a formalized system, as in Mexico, notably in Peru, among the ancient Celts, (and) some Indian tribes. Further, the communal form (die Gemeinschaftlichkeit) within the tribal organization may appear realized in a head of the tribal family, or rather as the mutual interrelationship of the heads of families. Thence either a more despotic or more democratic form of this commonwealth. The common preconditions of genuine appropriation through labour, waterworks (underlined by Marx), very important among the Asiatic people, means of communication, etc., thus appear as a work of the superior unity, the des-

[35] Ibid., pp. 376–77.

potic government suspended above the small communities. Towns
come into existence here only where there is a particularly favourable location for foreign trade; or where the head of state and his
satraps exchange their revenue (surplus product) against labour,
expend it as labour-funds." [36]

As against this centralized system—historically typified above all
by the various Oriental despotisms—Graeco-Roman antiquity, with
its development of private property in land, represents what Marx
describes as "the second form" wherein the original communal
(tribal) organization raises itself to a higher socio-historical level.
The lengthy process whereby the urban patriciate of independent
landowners, which here monopolizes political power, builds up its
peculiar institutions (ultimately resting upon slave labour, and constant war to acquire more slaves) and eventually brings about its
own downfall, is described with many fascinating details, and—quite
in accordance with Hegel, but also with Niebuhr and nineteenth-
century historiography generally—the decline and fall of antiquity
leads straight on to the Germanic middle ages:

"An (other) form of ownership by the labouring individuals, self-
sustaining members of the community, of the natural conditions of
their work, is the *German*. Unlike the specifically Oriental form, the
member of the community is not as such a co-owner of the communal property . . . nor, unlike the Roman or Greek form . . . is
the soil occupied by the community. . . ." (follows a brief analysis
of the *ager publicus* as the specifically Roman institution, whereby
the individual Roman citizen exercises his sovereign private ownership over a particular area of Roman soil).[37] As against these earlier
forms, "the German community"—which is treated by Marx as the
original cell of the medieval body politic—represents something
new: "Ancient classical history is a history of cities, but of cities
founded upon landed property and agriculture; Asiatic history is a
kind of indifferent union of town and country (the great cities are
to be regarded merely as princely camps, as superfetations above the
economic construction proper); the middle ages (German age) starts
from the countryside as the seat of history, whose further development then proceeds through the antagonism of town and country;
modern (history) is urbanization of the land, not as in antiquity
ruralization of the town." [38] Among the Germans, the coming-

[36] P. 377.
[37] *Grundrisse*, pp. 380–81.
[38] P. 382.

together of the clan chiefs does not subvert their original independence: "The community appears as union, not as unity (*als Vereinigung, nicht als Verein*)," the (originally tribal, later feudal) landowners constituting themselves as "independent subjects." [39] "The community does not therefore in fact exist as a *state* . . . as in antiquity, because it does not exist as a *city*. For the community to come into real existence, the free landed proprietors must come together in a meeting, whereas, e.g., in Rome it existed apart from these meetings, in the being of the city itself and the officials standing at its head." [40] True, the medieval Germans also had their *ager publicus*, their commons, but it did not, as in Rome, appear "as the peculiar economic existence of the state, side by side with the private owners." It merely served as a "supplement to individual ownership" and thus represents the sharpest possible contrast to the "Asiatic form" where the individual has "no ownership, only possession";[41] but it also contrasts sharply with the Graeco-Roman system, where the city has a life of its own, being the collective organization and quasi-ideal representation of the citizens in their public capacity, as distinct from their private existence. Thus, in the European middle ages, private property predominates from the start. "The community exists only in the mutual relation of these individual landowners." [42] Our modern liberties (Marx might have added, but did not) have their roots in the Germanic forests.

What he does add is an extremely interesting and subtle analysis of tribal and communal ownership in antiquity, interlarded with polemical excursions against Proudhon[43] which need not concern us here. When he returns to his original theme—tribal organization as the source of the subsequent threefold differentiation into Oriental, Graeco-Roman, and German-medieval forms of private and common ownership—it is to emphasize once more that the tribal system, "wherein the community originally dissolves itself," recognizes no property save that held by members of the tribe, so that conquered tribes are automatically deprived of it. "Slavery and serfdom are thus only further developments of the property rooted in the tribal system. They necessarily modify all its forms," though least of all in the "Asiatic form," with its "self-sustaining union of manufacture

[39] P. 383.
[40] P. 383.
[41] *Ibid.*
[42] P. 384.
[43] Pp. 384–92.

and agriculture on which this form rests." [44] What Marx describes as "the general slavery of the Orient" (as distinct from the personal slavery of classical antiquity) appears as a special case of the institution of property. The latter—"in its Asiatic, Slav, antique, German, form" [45]—originally signifies "the relation of the labouring (producing) . . . subject to the conditions of his production or reproduction." [46] Historically this relationship takes different forms, depending upon the existence of the individual "as a member of a tribe or community (whose property he is up to a certain point)": an interesting hint which hardly squares with the rather more idyllic picture subsequently painted by Engels. Man originally makes his appearance on earth as part of a primitive collective: "a generic being, tribal being, herd animal—though by no means a *zoon politikon* in the political sense." [47] He individualizes himself through the historical process, which is primarily a process of evolving various forms of communal and private property, i.e., various ways of organizing his social intercourse with nature and the—natural or artificial—preconditions of work. The different forms of this metabolism correspond to different stages of society, among which Oriental society is historically closer to man's primitive origins, having conserved some elements of primitive communism "in the midst of Oriental despotism." Hence the succession of stages—Asiatic, antique, feudal, modern—mirrors the gradual dissolution of the "primitive unity," and the evolution of private ownership properly so called. The forcible disruption of the Indian or Chinese village community by European capital completes the process by rendering it truly global.

V

With this historical sketch in mind we can now return to our starting-point and try to establish whether Marx's and Engels's utterances on the subject of Oriental society are reducible to a consistent pattern.[48]

[44] Pp.392.
[45] P. 395.
[46] *Ibid.*
[47] Pp. 395–96.
[48] I express a mere personal opinion when I say that the argument outlined in pp. 375–96 of the *Grundrisse* seems to me to be among the most brilliant and incisive of Marx's writings. Unfortunately it remained a mere sketch and, what is worse, it did not see the light until 1939–41. Had it been published around 1900, instead of remaining unknown until our days, one may suppose that Max

The picture in some ways is a puzzling one. Reference has already been made to the gradual change in Marx's attitude towards the Asian village community and its resistance to the battering-rams of Western capitalism. Now when one turns to the other structural element of the "Asiatic mode of production," the centralized governmental despotism, it would seem as though Marx and Engels gradually deepened their hostility to this form of rule, to the point of discovering some positive virtues not only in private property but even in European feudalism and the Germanic middle ages. How else account for Marx's 1859 statement about "Asiatic, ancient, feudal, and modern bourgeois modes of production" being "progressive epochs in the economic formation of society"? It must be remembered that these words were written shortly after he had composed his unpublished draft of 1857–58, with its quasi-Hegelian stress on the element of personal freedom inherent in the rude institutions of the European middle ages. It must also be recalled that for Marx "progressive" does not signify "whatever happens to be going on," as it later did for his more thoughtless followers. "Progress" in his sense stands for the unfolding of man's dormant powers. European feudalism is "progressive" compared with Asiatic or Graeco-Roman society because thanks to its relatively healthy starting-point it embodies new potentialities of growth and human development; in Hegel's terminology, it represents "a new principle." These potentialities clearly have to do with a circumstance to which Marx alludes in passing in the *Grundrisse*: the fact that among the Germans political power did not at first exist separately from the individuals, but was simply the result of joint decisions taken in public. Engels was subsequently to go further by implying that the German barbarians rejuvenated Europe by infusing the remnants of their clan organization into the decaying fabric of the Roman Empire.[49] Sound Teutonic orthodoxy, one might say, as well as containing an indubitable amount of truth.[50] But exactly how does it relate to the more strictly theoretical concepts formulated by Marx and Engels?

There is no question that both men maintained and even accentuated their original aversion to Oriental rule considered as a politi-

---

Weber and his school would have found even better reason for relating themselves to Marx's researches. Marx in fact anticipates a good deal of what Weber had to say about Oriental society.

[49] *Origin of the Family;* cf. *Sel. Works*, vol. II, p. 277.
[50] Cf. Marc Bloch, *Feudal Society*, London, 1961, pp. 145 ff.

cal system. As we have seen, their first tentative utterances go back to the 1850's, when Marx was still inclined on occasion to play off the moral superiority of the decaying Confucian empire against the crude materialist aims of the encroaching Europeans. These polemical sideswipes are, however, scarcely to be taken seriously. They relate back to the familiar eighteenth-century habit of contrasting the virtuous Chinese with the hypocritical Europeans: an amiable fantasy which Marx commonly ranked with other childish naïveties of the Rousseauist age. When he speaks as a theorist, the term "semi-Asiatic" carries connotations which are both precise and unflattering. Moreover, it was gradually extended to Russia and became the standard reproach addressed to the Government of that country. In this respect Engels took the lead [51] but Marx followed suit in contrasting "Russia" with "Europe," [52] and thereafter consistently referred to the Tsarist Government as a despotism suspended above an unfree peasantry. The references are too numerous and familiar to need citing. Later in 1875 we find Engels classing Russia with the "Asiatic mode" in an article where incidentally he comments on the village community.[53] The same point is briefly made in a better-known work, the *Anti-Dühring*: "Where the ancient communes have continued to exist, they have for thousands of years formed the basis of the most barbarous form of state, Oriental despotism, from India to Russia." [54] Lastly, there are Engels's writings of the 1890's, in which it is indeed suggested that Tsarist despotism is crumbling (and even that "the young Russian bourgeoisie has the State entirely in its power"), but here too the surviving "despotic autocracy of the Tsar" is related to "the old communistic village community" —now in process of breaking up.[55]

In between, he and Marx had, however, given qualified support to the notion that the village community might become the starting-

[51] The article in the *New York Tribune* of April 19, 1853, in which Russia is first described as "semi-Asiatic," was signed by Marx, but actually written by Engels; cf. *Gesammelte Werke,* vol. 9, p. 23.

[52] NYDT, August 5, 1853; cf. *Gesammelte Werke,* vol. 9, p. 215.

[53] "Such a complete isolation of the individual (village) communities from each other . . . is the natural foundation of Oriental despotism, and from India to Russia this societal form, wherever it prevailed, has always produced despotism and has always found therein its supplement." Cf. *Internationales aus dem Volksstaat (1871–75),* Berlin, 1894, p. 56.

[54] *Anti-Dühring* (German edn.), Moscow, 1935, p. 165; cf. Foreign Languages Publishing House edn., Moscow, 1954, p. 251.

[55] Cf. *Volksstaat,* l.c., pp. 61–72.

point of a socialist development. How was this to be accomplished? We have two statements by Marx, both regrettably brief. In his letter to Vera Zasulich of March 8, 1881, we find him ready to go some distance in accepting the Populist idea that the resistance of the village community to private capitalism might offer the emerging socialist movement a unique opportunity; though after stating that "this community is the *point d'appui* of social regeneration in Russia," he is at pains to add that "the pernicious influences which attack it from all sides" must be eliminated, so as "to assure it of normal conditions for a spontaneous development." [56] Then there is the preface to the Russian edition of the *Communist Manifesto*, dated January 21, 1882, with the quasi-Trotskyist suggestion that "if the Russian Revolution becomes the signal for a proletarian revolution in the West, so that both complement each other, the present Russian common ownership of land may serve as the starting-point for a communist development." [57] These hints point in the direction of a controversy which was destined to convulse the Russian socialist movement for decades, but they do not contribute much to the strictly theoretical concept of the "Asiatic mode." At most they imply that for Marx socialism offered a way out of the uncomfortable dilemma suggested by his researches into Oriental society: the element of personal freedom, so plainly lacking in that society and equally so plainly at the roots of West European feudalism (and capitalism), might enter the system after the collapse of its "political superstructure." In different terms, the approaching fall of Tsarism presented an opportunity to develop the healthy core of the ancient communal organization, instead of disrupting it completely in the interest of capitalism.

It is noteworthy that Marx—and to some extent Engels—saw such an opportunity latent in Russia, but not in India or China: presumably because Russia was only "semi-Asiatic." It was not a genuinely European country, but it nonetheless possessed the germ of development, whereas "the East" proper was stagnant. For the same reason, unfortunately, Russia was a permanent menace to Europe, and even its internal progress tended to make it more dangerous, because

---

[56] Full text in *Marx-Engels Archiv*, vol. I, Frankfurt, 1926, pp. 309–42; cf. Blackstock and Hoselitz, *The Russian Menace to Europe*, London, 1953, pp. 275 ff.

[57] *Sel. Works*, vol. I, p. 24. In his 1894 gloss on this text, Engels pours a good deal of water into this heady wine; cf. "Russia and the Social Revolution Reconsidered," in Blackstock and Hoselitz, *op. cit.*, pp. 229 ff.

more aggressive and powerful.[58] The way out lay in a form of Europeanization which did away with the autocracy without—as the liberals would have it—simultaneously introducing Western capitalism. The commune—or what was left of it—was to be preserved as the future basis of a socialist society, or at any rate as an element of such a society. With this analysis the Populists were in agreement, and those among them who in the 1880's and 1890's gradually transformed themselves into Marxists could feel that they had not renounced the ideals and values which had originally brought them to socialism. Conversely, Marx for his part might think that by relating socialism back to pre-individualist, communal, forms of ownership, he had closed the circle of his argument: bourgeois society, so far from being "natural" and permanent, was revealed to be simply one socio-economic formation among others.

The unsolved, or half-solved, problem lay in the genesis of the Oriental State. In his writings of the early 1850's Marx had stressed both its centralized character and its independence from the vast mass of scattered village communes. In the 1857–58 draft the roots of despotism in general are traced back to the tribal organization, with its tendency to "realize" its internal unity in a personal ruler. Subsequently we find references to "the state" as "the supreme landlord," but no analysis of the means whereby the despotic sovereign builds up his power by surrounding himself with an administrative apparatus. From all this it is not difficult to conclude that Marx for some reason shirked the problem of the bureaucracy. Yet the latter's role is frequently alluded to in his other writings, notably in his diatribes against Bonapartism. His failure to make more of it in connection with the "Asiatic mode" remains an oddity. Perhaps the fact that he thought of it as a "caste" as distinct from a "class" of society lessened his interest in the subject; but though a possible explanation this is hardly an adequate defence.[59]

    [58] Cf. Marx, *Herr Vogt* (1859), in *Gesammelte Werke,* vol. 14, especially pp. 497–98: "Incidentally, the emancipation of the serfs *in the sense of the Russian government* would multiply the aggressiveness of Russia a hundredfold. Its aim is simply the completion of the autocracy through the elimination of the barriers hitherto opposed to the great autocrat by the many little autocrats of the serf-based Russian gentry; as well as by the self-governing peasant communes whose material basis, the common ownership, is to be destroyed by the so-called emancipation."
    [59] For a critique of Marx's and Engels's views on the subject of Oriental despotism see Wittfogel, pp. 380 ff.; it seems to me, though, that W. overdoes the theme of Marx's alleged theoretical backsliding in his later writings. The most one can say is that the earlier suggestions were not systematically developed.

In his *Theories of Surplus Value* (1861–63) Marx quotes Richard Jones to the effect that "the surplus revenue from the soil, the only revenues except those of the peasants of any considerable amount, were (in Asia, and more especially in India) distributed by the state and its officers." [60] Taken together with his own previous observations on the importance of centrally controlled irrigation in Asia, and with Engels's subsequent remarks (mainly in the *Anti-Dühring*) about the emergence of a ruling class from within primitive society, the elements of a complete theory of Oriental despotism appear to be present. Why were they not fully exploited? Perhaps an indirect answer is afforded by a somewhat lengthy passage from Engels which demonstrates at once the enormous advance in understanding he and Marx had actually effected in relation to earlier writers, and the point where their investigations tailed off into an uncritical acceptance of the prevalent Victorian attitude in regard to state and society:

> It is not necessary for us to examine here how this independence of social functions in relation to society increased with time until it developed into domination over society; how he who was originally the servant, where conditions were favourable changed gradually into the lord; how this lord, depending on the conditions, emerged as an Oriental despot or satrap, the dynast of a Greek tribe, chieftain of a Celtic clan, and so on; to what extent he subsequently had recourse to force in the course of this transformation; and how finally the individual rulers united into a ruling class. Here we are only concerned with establishing the fact that the exercise of a social function was everywhere the basis of political supremacy; and further, that political supremacy has existed for any length of time only when it discharged its social functions. However great the number of despotisms which rose and fell in Persia and India, each was fully aware that above all it was the entrepreneur responsible for the collective maintenance of irrigation throughout the river valleys, without which no agriculture was possible there. It was reserved for the enlightened English to lose sight of this in India; they let the irrigation canals and sluices fall into decay, and are now at last discovering, through the regularly recurring famines, that they have neglected the one activity which might have made their rule in India at least as legitimate as that of their predecessors.[61]

Setting aside the polemical glance at the British Government in India, what does this passage suggest, if not that Engels—and by

[60] R. Jones, *Literary Remains, Consisting of Lectures and Tracts on Political Economy*, London, 1859, pp. 448 ff.; cf. Marx, *Theorien über den Mehrwert*, Stuttgart, 1921, vol. III, p. 501.

[61] *Herr Eugen Dühring's Revolution in Science*, Moscow, 1954, p. 249.

implication Marx, since he had seen the text before publication—thought of the "ruling class" in political terms, as the governing caste responsible for the exercise of those superior functions without which social life must come to a stop? The *Anti-Dühring* admittedly is a semi-popular tract primarily addressed to a working-class audience, but if Engels on this occasion expresses himself rather loosely, he does not contradict his or Marx's previous utterances. Political power arises from the exercise of a necessary social function: it then becomes independent of society (and of its own origins), but retains its roots in a collective need which it serves, *tant bien que mal*, until the social organism itself changes its character so as to require a different kind of "superstructure." The state, in short, is an epiphenomenon. Although it does have a life of its own, it is subservient to the real basic needs of society; consequently the long-run process can be analysed in terms of the latter.

In passing, it may be observed that Engels in the above passage identifies the "ruling class" so completely with the governing caste as to provoke the rejoinder that on his assumptions Bismarck might have claimed to be a more legitimate representative of German society than the elected *Reichstag*. It is not at all clear how Engels would have met the argument that the political *élite* of a given society is, and must always remain, something different from, and superior to, the socially dominant class. It is true that in nineteenth-century Germany—and to some extent in Victorian England—the two coincided, inasmuch as the landed aristocracy had retained its political and social role, while steadily yielding economic power to the bourgeoisie. But this symbiosis was a peculiarity of European history, and its roots—as Marx observed in his 1857–58 sketch—lay in the relatively free and autonomous development of public life during the early middle ages. The Orient had never experienced anything of the kind, and since Engels had put his finger on the crucial role of the state—i.e. the bureacracy—in administering the central economic functions, it was really incumbent upon him to explain in what sense the governing caste was a "ruling class." Failure to clarify this matter was bound to obscure the entire problem of political power and the state in general.

At this point, however, we are on the threshold of the modern age, and for the same reason at the end of our brief investigation into the manner in which Marx and Engels, at the peak of the Victorian era, saw the problem of political power in an Eastern setting. It can hardly surprise a contemporary reader to find that they did not seriously examine the possibility of despotic rule in an industrial society: in other words, the problem of what we have learned to call totalitarianism. To have done so would have meant to overstep the presuppositions they shared with their contemporaries: chief among them the confident belief that in Europe, anyhow, the despotic reorganization of society from the top was excluded by the very nature of that society. If we have in recent years begun to doubt this certainty, we may nevertheless extract what comfort we can from Marx's belief that the inner principle of Western historical development has from the start been quite different from that of the East or of Graeco-Roman antiquity. For my own part I am inclined to think that—in this as in most other matters—he was right, and that we are entitled to look upon European history as an evolution propelled by a dialectic of its own, to which there is no parallel in Oriental history. Needless to say, this Hegelian-Marxist view is incompatible with the notion that European, or Western, society is subject to a general law of growth and decay (or "challenge and response" to employ the currently fashionable jargon) applicable to *all* major civilizations. On the contrary, it insists upon the West's uniqueness; and to that extent the present writer has no hesitation in calling himself a Hegelian.

TWELVE

KARL MARX'S
"ENQUÊTE OUVRIÈRE

HILDE WEISS

It appears from Marx's letter of November 5, 1880, addressed to Sorge that the "Enquête Ouvrière" published in the *Revue Socialiste* on April 20, 1880, was the work of Marx himself. He writes: "I have prepared for him [Benoît Malon, the editor of the *Revue Socialiste*] the 'Questionneur' [*sic*] which was first published in the *Revue Socialiste* and afterwards distributed in a large number of copies throughout France." [1] Only the detailed questionnaire, containing a hundred questions, and the accompanying text seem to have survived. A note in a later issue of the *Revue Socialiste,* the style of which suggests that it may have been written by Marx, indicates that some replies had been received, and that when a sufficient number had come in they would be published.[2] The journal *Egalité,* which was published during this period, and which Marx described in the same letter to Sorge as the first "workers' paper" in France, repeatedly urged its readers to take part in the survey and included copies of the questionnaire.[3]

From Hilde Weiss, "Die 'Enquête Ouvrière' von Karl Marx," *Zeitschrift für Sozialforschung,* V (Paris: Félix Alcan, 1936), 76, 83–88, 91–97. Translated by Tom Bottomore. Published with the permission of Presses Universitaires de France.

[1] "Twenty-five thousand copies of this appeal were printed and were sent to all labor organizations, socialist and democratic groups, French newspapers and individuals who requested copies." (Note on the "Enquête Ouvrière" in *Revue Socialiste,* April 20, 1880).

[2] "Concerning the 'Enquête Ouvrière': A number of our friends have already responded to our questionnaire, and we are grateful to them. We urge those of our friends and readers who have not yet replied to do so quickly. In order to make the survey as complete as possible we shall defer our own work until a large number of questionnaires has been returned. We ask our proletarian friends to reflect that the completion of these 'cahiers du travail' is of the greatest importance, and that by participating in our difficult task they are working directly for their own liberation." *Revue Socialiste,* July 5, 1880.

[3] "In its last issue the *Revue Socialiste* has taken the initiative in an excellent project. . . . The significance of an investigation of working-class conditions as they have been created by bourgeois rule is to place the possessing caste on trial, to assemble the materials for a passionate protest against modern society, to display before the eyes of all the oppressed, all wage-slaves, the injustices of which they are the constant victims, and thereby to arouse in them the will to end such conditions." *L'Egalité,* April 28, 1880.

* * *

Marx's "Enquête Ouvrière" differs in three respects from previous investigations of social conditions. First, as is clear from the statement of its purpose, and from the questions themselves, it aimed to provide an exact description of actual social conditions. Secondly, it proposed to collect information only from the workers themselves. Thirdly, it had a didactic aim; it was meant to develop the consciousness of the workers in the sense expounded in Marx's social theory.

Marx also intended that his "Enquête Ouvrière" should diffuse among the general public a knowledge of the working and living conditions of the workers, and he had, therefore, some ulterior motives in undertaking his study. At the same time, however, his socialist views imposed upon him the obligation to depict as faithfully as possible the existing social misery. He assigns to social investigation the task of aiding the workers themselves to gain an understanding of their situation. For philanthropists the workers, as the most miserable stratum of society, were the object of welfare measures; but Marx saw in them an oppressed class which would become master of its own fate when once it had become aware of its situation. With the development of industrial capitalism, not only the misery of the proletariat, but also its will to emancipation increased. In his preface to the questionnaire Marx describes the "Enquête Ouvrière" as a basis for "preparing a reconstruction of society."

However, it is not only in its aims that Marx's "Enquête Ouvrière" differs from the private and official investigations that had preceded it, but also in the manner in which it was carried out. Earlier surveys, even if they had the intention, could not discover the real character of social evils, because they employed inadequate means to collect their information. They were addressed almost exclusively to factory owners and their representatives, to factory inspectors where there were such people, or to government officials (as in the case of Villeneuve-Bargement's inquiry).[4] Even where doctors or philanthropists who made such surveys went directly to working-class families, they were usually accompanied by factory owners or their representatives. Le Play, for example, recommends

---

[4] [Villeneuve-Bargement, *Economie politique chrétienne ou Recherches sur la nature et les causes du paupérisme en France et en Europe et sur les moyens de le soulager et de le prévenir,* 3 vols. (Paris: Paulin, 1834)—Ed.]

visits to working class families ". . . with an introduction from
some carefully selected authority"; and he advises extremely diplo-
matic behavior towards the family members, including the payment
of small sums of money, or the distribution of presents, as a recom-
pense. The investigator should ". . . praise with discrimination the
cleverness of the men, the charm of the women, the good behavior
of the children, and discreetly hand out small presents to all of
them." [5] In the course of a thorough critical examination of survey
methods that appears in Audiganne's account of the discussions in
his circle of workers, it is said of Le Play: "Never was a more misleading course embarked upon, in spite of the very best intentions.
It is simply a question of the approach. A false viewpoint and a false
method of observation give rise to a completely arbitrary series of
suppositions, which bear no relation whatsoever to social reality, and
in which there is apparent an invincible partiality for despotism
and constraint." [6] Audiganne indicates as one of the common mis-
takes in the conduct of surveys the pomp and ceremony which is
adopted by investigators when they visit working-class families. "If
there is not a single tangible result produced by any survey carried
out under the Second Empire, the blame must be assigned, in large
measure, to the pompous manner in which they were conducted." [7]
Marx and Engels also described the methods by which workers were
induced to give testimony through social research of this kind, even
to the extent of presenting petitions against the reduction of their
working hours.

Marx's questionnaire, which was addressed directly to the workers,
was something unique. The article on social surveys in the *Dictionary of Political Economy* observes bluntly: "Those who are to
be questioned should not be allowed to participate in the inquiry." [8]
This justified Audiganne's criticism that ". . . people judge us without knowing us." [9]

Marx asks the workers alone for information about their social
conditions, on the grounds that only they and not any "providential
savior" know the causes of their misery, and they alone can discover
effective means to eliminate them. In the preface to the question-

[5] *Les Ouvriers Européens*, Vol. I, p. 223.

[6] Audiganne, *Mémoires d'un ouvrier de Paris, 1871–1872* (Paris, 1873), p. 61.

[7] Audiganne, *op. cit.*, p. 93.

[8] *Dictionnaire de l'économie politique* (Paris, 1854), p. 706.

[9] Audiganne, *op. cit.*, p. 1.

naire he asks the socialists for their support, since they need, for their social reforms, exact knowledge of the conditions of life and work of the oppressed class, and this can only be brought to light by the workers themselves. He points out to them the historical role which the working class is called upon to play and for which no socialist utopia can provide a substitute.

This method of collecting information, by asking the workers themselves, represents a considerable progress over the earlier inquiries. It is, of course, understandable that Marx had to restrict himself to this method. Apart from the political and educational purposes which he wanted to combine with his investigation, his method of obtaining information directly from the workers was intended to open the eyes of the public and of the state. From the point of view of modern social research in this field, the restriction of such an inquiry into working conditions to the responses of workers themselves would be considered inadequate. This method of inquiry is still vitally important in modern social surveys; but the monographs that were to have resulted from the "Enquête Ouvrière" would need to be complemented, and their findings checked, by statistical materials, and by the data available from other surveys. . . .

The didactic purpose of the "Enquête Ouvrière" arises, as will be shown later, from the arrangement and formulation of the questions; but it is apparent also in the preface, and especially in the title that Marx gives to the monographs which it is proposed to write on the basis of the replies to the questionnaire; he calls them "cahiers du travail" ("labor-lists") in contrast to the "cahiers de doléances" ("grievance-lists") of 1789. The specific character of his survey is shown by his coining of this new term, which is connected with a living tradition of the French workers, the petitions of the Third Estate. But while the "cahiers de doléances" put forward trivial demands in a servile manner, the "cahiers du travail" were meant to contain a true and exact description of the condition of the working class and of the path to its liberation. Moreover, the accomplishment of this program is not to be left to the goodwill of a king; the workers are to struggle forthrightly and consciously for their human rights. It is not by chance that Marx also refers in this context to the "socialist democracy," whose first task is to prepare the "cahiers du travail." The workers, who have to wage a class struggle and to accomplish a renewal of society, must first of all become capable of recognizing their own situation and of seeing the readiness of individuals to work together in a common cause.

The "cahiers du travail," as I have noted, were not only to provide a better knowledge of working-class conditions, but were also to educate the workers in socialism. By merely reading the hundred questions, the worker would be led to see the obvious and commonplace facts that were mentioned there as elements in a general picture of his situation. By attempting seriously to answer the questions, he would become aware of the social determination of his conditions of life; he would gain an insight into the nature of the capitalist economy and the state, and would learn the means of abolishing wage labor and attaining his freedom. The questionnaire thus provides the outline of a socialist manual, which the worker can fill with a living content by absorbing its results.

Several of the questions are formulated in such a way—for instance, by the introduction of valuations—that the worker is led at once to the answer which the didactic purpose of the survey requires. Thus, Marx refers to the misuse of public power when it is a matter of defending the privileges of entrepreneurs; and a subsequent question asks whether the state protects the workers "against the exactions and the illegal combinations of the employers." The contrast is intended to make the worker aware of the class character of the state. Another example is provided by the case where workers share in the profits of the enterprise. The respondent is asked to consider whether business concerns with this apparently social orientation differ from other capitalist enterprises, and whether the legal position of the workers in them is superior. "Can they go on strike? Or are they only permitted to be the humble servants of their masters?" (Question 99). It should be said, however, that only a relatively small proportion of the questions seek to influence opinion so directly.

It is far more significant, in relation to the two aspects of the survey, that Marx was successful in setting out the questions in a clear and practical manner. They are easily intelligible and deal with matters of direct concern to the worker. The simplicity and exactness of the questions in the "Enquête Ouvrière" represent an advance over earlier surveys. Audiganne had observed quite rightly that these surveys asked questions that were far too comprehensive, abstract, and complicated, and compromised the answers on important issues by introducing irrelevant questions.[10] For the same reasons, the various private investigations could provide no better picture of the real social conditions and attitudes of the workers.

The content of the questions posed in the earlier surveys, as well as their aims and techniques of inquiry, corresponded very closely with the interests of employers. For example, the question whether workers were paid wholly in cash, or whether a part of their wages were given in the form of goods or rent allowances, was asked both in the government survey of 1872 and in the "Enquête Ouvrière"; but in the former case it was asked from the point of view of the employers, in the latter from the point of view of the workers. In the official survey, payments in the form of goods are treated as a "supplement" to wages, but Marx regards every form of wage payment other than in cash as a method of reducing wages.

Since Marx's survey does represent an advance over earlier attempts, it is all the more surprising that very few replies to the questionnaire were apparently received.[11] Two reasons may explain this failure: first, the scope of the questionnaire, and second, the circumstances of the time. Even today, it is not easy for the average worker, in his spare time, to answer a questionnaire containing a hundred questions; and it was all the more difficult in a period when workers were being asked to do this for the first time. Their ability to write and to express themselves was still limited; they read very little, and their newspapers were published in small editions, as well as being hampered by the censorship. Second, the French labor movement was still in the period of depression that followed the Paris Commune. Had there been at that time an independent labor movement, the survey could have been carried out much more effectively. It was, indeed, because of the backwardness of the labor movement and of the working class generally,[12] that Marx gave his survey the didactic purpose of awakening the workers

[10] For one example among many, see Ducarre, *Rapport sur les conditions du travail en France* (Versailles, 1875), p. 195: "What is the physical condition of the working population in your district, from the point of view of sanitary conditions, population increase, and expectation of life?" It is easy to imagine the prolixity of the replies.

[11] It has proved impossible to find even the few replies that did arrive, in spite of an active search for them.

[12] The reports compiled by workers on the occasion of the Vienna Exhibition (1873) show clearly how far the workers at that time were influenced by utopian ideas and by the views of employers.

to a realization of their condition. Thus Marx's survey had at the same time to create the circumstances in which an inquiry could be carried out.

THE TEXT OF THE QUESTIONNAIRE [13]

No government—whether monarchical or bourgeois-republican—has dared to undertake a serious investigation of the condition of the French working class, although there have been many studies of agricultural, financial, commercial and political crises.

The odious acts of capitalist exploitation which the official surveys by the English government have revealed, and the legislative consequences of these revelations (limitation of the legal working day to ten hours, legislation concerning the labour of women and children, etc.), have inspired in the French bourgeoisie a still greater terror of the dangers which might result from an impartial and systematic inquiry.

While awaiting the time when the republican government can be induced to follow the example of the English monarchical government and inaugurate a comprehensive survey of the deeds and misdeeds of capitalist exploitation, we shall attempt a preliminary investigation with the modest resources at our disposal. We hope that our undertaking will be supported by all those workers in town and country who realize that only they can describe with full knowledge the evils which they endure, and that only they—not any providential saviours—can remedy the social ills from which they suffer. We count also upon the socialists of all schools, who, desiring social reform, must also desire *exact* and *positive* knowledge of the conditions in which the working class, the class to which the future belongs, lives and works.

These "labour-lists" ("cahiers du travail") represent the first task which socialist democracy must undertake in preparation for the regeneration of society.

The following hundred questions are the most important ones. The replies should follow the order of the questions. It is not necessary to answer all the questions, but respondents are asked to make their answers as comprehensive and detailed as possible. The name of the respondent will not be published unless specifically authorized, but it should be given together with the address, so that we can establish contact with him.

From T. B. Bottomore and Maximilien Rubel (editors), *Karl Marx: Selected Writings in Sociology and Social Philosophy* (London: C. A. Watts & Company Ltd., 1956), pp. 203–12. Copyright © 1956 C. A. Watts & Company Ltd. Reprinted with the permission of C. A. Watts & Company Ltd., and McGraw-Hill Book Company.

[13] [Hilde Weiss notes that this was, to her knowledge, the first German translation of the "Enquête Ouvrière." The first English translation of the questionnaire and of some passages from the prefatory statement was published in T. B. Bottomore and Maximilien Rubel, editors, *Karl Marx: Selected Writings in Sociology and Social Philosophy.*—Ed.]

The replies should be sent to the director of the *Revue Socialiste* (Monsieur Lécluse, 28 rue Royale, Saint-Cloud, near Paris).

The replies will be classified and will provide the material for monographs to be published in the *Revue Socialiste* and subsequently collected in a volume.

I

1. What is your occupation?
2. Does the workshop in which you are employed belong to a capitalist or to a joint-stock company? Give the names of the capitalist employers or of the directors of the company.
3. State the number of persons employed.
4. State their ages and sex.
5. What is the minimum age at which children (boys or girls) are employed?
6. State the number of supervisors and other employees who are not ordinary wage earners.
7. Are there any apprentices? How many?
8. Are there, in addition to the workers usually and regularly employed, others who are employed at certain periods?
9. Does your employer's industry work exclusively or primarily for the local market, for the national market, or for export?
10. Is the workshop in the country or in the town? Give the name of the place where it is situated.
11. If your workshop is in the country, does your industrial work enable you to live, or do you combine it with agricultural work?
12. Is your work done by hand or with the aid of machinery?
13. Give details of the division of labour in your industry.
14. Is steam used as motive power?
15. State the number of workshops in which the different branches of the industry are carried on. Describe the special branch in which you are employed, giving information not only about the technical aspects, but also about the muscular and nervous strain involved, and the general effects of the work on the health of the workers.
16. Describe the sanitary conditions in the workshop; size of the rooms, space assigned to each worker; ventilation, temperature, whitewashing of the walls, lavatories, general cleanliness; noise of machines, metallic dust, humidity, etc.
17. Is there any municipal or governmental supervision of the sanitary conditions in the workshops?
18. In your industry, are there any harmful fumes which cause specific illnesses among the workers?
19. Is the workshop overcrowded with machines?

20. Are the machines, the transmission system, and the engines supplying power, protected so as to avoid any accidents?

21. Enumerate the accidents which have occurred in your personal experience.

22. If you work in a mine enumerate the preventive measures taken by your employer to ensure adequate ventilation and to prevent explosions and other dangerous accidents.

23. If you are employed in a chemical works, in a factory, in the metal-working industry, or in any other industry which is particularly dangerous, enumerate the safety measures introduced by your employer.

24. How is your factory lighted (by gas, paraffin, etc.)?

25. In case of fire, are there enough emergency exits?

26. In case of accidents, is the employer obliged *by law* to pay compensation to the worker or his family?

27. If not, has he ever paid compensation to those who have met with an accident while working to enrich him?

28. Is there a medical service in your workshop?

29. If you work at home, describe the condition of your work-room. Do you use only tools, or do you use small machines? Are you helped by your children or by any other people (adults or children, male or female)? Do you work for individual clients or for a contractor? Do you deal directly with the latter, or do you deal with a middleman?

II

30. State your daily hours of work, and working days in the week.

31. State the holidays during the year.

32. What are the breaks in the working day?

33. Are meals taken at regular intervals or irregularly? Are they taken in the workshop or elsewhere?

34. Do you work during the meal breaks?

35. If steam power is used, when is the power turned on, and when is it turned off?

36. Is there any night work?

37. State the hours of work of children and of young persons below the age of 16.

38. Are there shifts of children and young persons which replace each other during the hours of work?

39. Are the laws concerning the employment of children enforced by the government or the municipality? Are they respected by the employer?

40. Are there any schools for the children and young persons em-

ployed in your trade? If there are, what are the school hours? Who runs the schools? What is taught in them?

41. When work continues day and night how are the shifts organized?

42. What is the normal increase in hours of work during periods of great industrial activity?

43. Are the machines cleaned by workers specially employed for this work, or are they cleaned gratuitously by the workers who are employed on them during the working day?

44. What are the regulations and the penalties for lateness? At what time does the working day begin, and at what time does it begin again after meals?

45. How much time do you spend in getting to work and in returning home?

III

46. What kind of work contract do you have with your employer? Are you engaged by the day, by the week, by the month, etc.?

47. What are the conditions laid down for giving or receiving notice?

48. In the event of the contract being broken, what penalty is imposed on the employer if it is his fault?

49. What penalty is imposed on the worker if it is his fault?

50. If there are apprentices, what are the terms of their contract?

51. Is your work regular or irregular?

52. In your trade, is the work seasonal, or is it, in normal times, spread more or less evenly over the year? If your work is seasonal, how do you live in the periods between working?

53. Are you paid time rates or piece rates?

54. If you are paid time rates, are you paid by the hour or by the day?

55. Is there additional pay for overtime work? What is it?

56. If you are paid piece rates, how are the rates fixed? If you are employed in an industry in which the work performed is measured by quantity or weight, as is the case in the mines, does your employer or his representatives resort to trickery in order to defraud you of a part of your earnings?

57. If you are paid piece rates, is the quality of the article made a pretext for fraudulent deductions from your wages?

58. Whether you are paid piece rates or time rates, when are you paid, or in other words how long is the credit which you extend to your master before receiving the price of the work carried out? Are you paid at the end of a week, a month, etc.?

59. Have you noticed that the delay in paying your wages makes it necessary for you to resort frequently to the pawnbroker, paying a high rate of interest, and depriving yourself of things which

you need; or to fall into debt to shopkeepers, becoming their
victim because you are their debtor? Do you know any instances
in which workers have lost their wages through the bankruptcy
of their employers?

60. Are wages paid directly by the employer, or by middlemen (sub-
contractors, etc.)?

61. If wages are paid by sub-contractors, or other middlemen, what
are the terms of your contract?

62. What is your daily and weekly wage rate in money?

63. What are the wages of women and children working with you in
the same workshop?

64. What was the highest daily wage in your workshop during the
past month?

65. What was the highest piece-rate wage . . . ?

66. What was your wage during the same period, and if you have a
family what were the wages of your wife and children?

67. Are wages paid entirely in money, or in some other way?

68. If you rent your dwelling from your employer, what are the conditions? Does he deduct the rent from your wages?

69. What are the prices of necessities such as:
    (a) rent of dwelling; conditions of letting; number of rooms,
    number of inhabitants, repairs and insurance: purchase and
    maintenance of furniture, heating, lighting, water;
    (b) food: bread, meat, vegetables, potatoes, etc., milk, eggs, fish,
    butter, oil, lard, sugar, salt, spices, coffee, chicory, beer, cider,
    wine, etc., tobacco;
    (c) clothing for parents and children, laundry, personal toilet,
    baths, soap, etc.;
    (d) various expenses: postage, loans and pawnbrokers' charges,
    children's school or apprenticeship fees, papers and books,
    contributions to friendly societies, or for strikes, co-operatives
    and defence societies;
    (e) expenses, if any, caused by your work;
    (f) taxes.

70. Try to draw up a budget of the weekly and annual income and
expenditure of yourself and your family.

71. Have you noticed, in your personal experience, a greater rise in the
price of the necessities of life, such as food and shelter, than in
wages?

72. State the fluctuations in wage rates which are known to you.

73. State the wage reductions in periods of stagnation and industrial
crisis.

74. State the wage increases in so-called periods of prosperity.

75. Note the interruptions of work resulting from changes of fashion
and from particular and general crises. Give an account of your
own experiences of involuntary unemployment.

76. Compare *the price of the article you produce*, or of the services you provide, with the price of your labour.

77. Quote any instance you know of workers being displaced by the introduction of machinery or by other improvements.

78. With the development of machinery and the productivity of labour, has the intensity and duration of work increased or diminished?

79. Do you know of any instance of an increase of wages in consequence of the progress of production?

80. Have you ever known any ordinary workers who were able to retire at the age of 50 and to live on the money acquired in their capacity as wage earners?

81. For how many years, in your trade, can a worker of average health continue to work?

IV

82. Are there any defence organizations in your trade, and how are they conducted? Send their statutes and rules.

83. How many strikes have occurred in your trade, in the course of your career?

84. How long did these strikes last?

85. Were they general or partial?

86. Was their aim an increase in wages, or were they organized to resist a wage reduction? Or were they concerned with the length of the working day, or caused by other factors?

87. What results did they achieve?

88. Say what you think of the actions of the *Prud'hommes* (arbitrators).[14]

89. Has your trade supported strikes by workers of other trades?

90. Give an account of the rules and penalties instituted by your employer for the government of his wage earners.

91. Have there been any combinations of employers for the purpose of imposing wage reductions, increasing working hours, or preventing strikes, or, in general, for getting their own way?

92. Do you know any instances in which the Government has misused the forces of the State, in order to place them at the disposal of employers against their employees?

93. Do you know any instances in which the Government has intervened to protect the workers against the exactions of the employers and their illegal combinations?

94. Does the Government apply against the employers the existing labour laws? Do its inspectors carry out their duties conscientiously?

[14] [The *conseil des prud'hommes* is a committee of arbitration in disputes between workers and employers—ED.]

95. Are there, in your workshop or trade, any friendly societies for cases of accident, illness, death, temporary incapacity for work, old age, etc.? Send their statutes and rules.

96. Is membership of these societies voluntary or obligatory? Are their funds controlled exclusively by the workers?

97. If the contributions are obligatory and under the control of the employers, are they deducted from wages? Is interest paid on these contributions? Are they returned to the worker when he leaves or is dismissed? Do you know any instances in which workers have benefited from so-called retirement funds controlled by the employers, but whose capital is derived from the workers' wages?

98. Are there any co-operative societies in your trade? How are they managed? Do they employ workers from outside in the same way as the capitalists do? Send their statutes and rules.

99. Are there any workshops in your trade, in which the workers are remunerated partly by wages and partly by a so-called participation in the profits? Compare the sums received by these workers with those received by workers where there is no so-called participation in profits. State the obligations of workers living under this system. Can they go on strike? Or are they only permitted to be the humble servants of their masters?

100. What is the general physical, intellectual, and moral condition of men and women workers employed in your trade?

101. General comments.

SELECTED BIBLIOGRAPHY

WORKS BY KARL MARX

The most comprehensive bibliography of Marx is that published by Maximilien Rubel, *Bibliographie des oeuvres de Karl Marx* (Paris: Marcel Rivière, 1956), and *Supplément à la bibliographie des oeuvres de Karl Marx* (Paris: Marcel Rivière, 1960), which includes information about the various editions and major translations of Marx's writings. In the following bibliography, I have listed in Section A those manuscripts and published works of Marx which are most important for the understanding of his sociology, in the language in which they were originally written or published; and in Section B, the principal English translations. Titles enclosed in brackets refer to manuscripts; in some cases the titles were given by subsequent editors.

SECTION A. MARX'S WRITINGS

1843   [*Kritik des Hegelschen Staatsrechts.*]

1844 a. "Zur Judenfrage," in *Deutsch-Französische Jahrbücher* (Paris: published by the editors, Arnold Ruge and Karl Marx, 1844).

      b. "Zur Kritik der Hegelschen Rechtsphilosophie: Einleitung," in *Deutsch-Französische Jahrbücher.*

      c. [*Zur Kritik der Nationalökonomie, mit einem Schlusskapitel uber die Hegelsche Philosophie*]. Now generally known as the *Economic and Philosophical Manuscripts.*

1845   [*Thesen über Feuerbach*].

1845–46 [*Die deutsche Ideologie*]. Written jointly with Friedrich Engels.

1847   *Misère de la philosophie* (Paris: A. Franck, 1847).

1848   *Manifest der Kommunistischen Partei.* Written jointly with Friedrich Engels. First published anonymously in 1848 with the name of the printer, J. E. Burghard, London. The names of the authors first appeared in the edition of 1872, published by the *Volksstaat*, Leipzig.

1852   *Der Achtzehnte Brumaire des Louis Bonaparte.* Published in the review *Die Revolution*, ed. by J. Weydemeyer, New York, 1852.

1857–58 [*Grundrisse der Kritik der politischen Oekonomie*].

1859   *Zur Kritik der politischen Oekonomie* (Berlin: Franz Duncker, 1859).

1867   *Das Kapital: Kritik der politischen Oekonomie*, Vol. I (Hamburg: Otto Meissner, 1867).

1861–79 Manuscripts of Vols. II, III, and IV of *Das Kapital*, subsequently published as follows:

      1885 *Das Kapital*, Vol. II, ed. Friedrich Engels (Hamburg: Otto Meissner, 1885).

      1894 *Das Kapital*, Vol. III, ed. by Friedrich Engels (Hamburg: Otto Meissner, 1894).

      1905– *Theorien über den Mehrwert*, 3 vols., ed. Karl Kautsky
      1910 (Stuttgart: J. H. W. Dietz Nachf., 1905, 1910).

185

1871   *Address of the General Council of the International Working Men's Association on the Civil War in France, 1871.* First published, without the name of the author, London, Edward Truelove, 1871.

SECTION B. ENGLISH TRANSLATIONS

A complete English translation of the writings of Marx and Engels is now in progress, to be published by Lawrence and Wishart, but this will not be available for several years. Among the existing English translations of Marx's principal writings, the following may be consulted:

"On the Jewish Question," "Contribution to the Critique of Hegel's Philosophy of Right: Introduction," "Economic and Philosophical Manuscripts," in T. B. Bottomore, ed., *Karl Marx: Early Writings* (London: Watts and Co., 1963; New York: McGraw-Hill Book Company, Inc., 1964).

Critique of Hegel's Philosophy of Right, ed. Joseph O'Malley (Cambridge: Cambridge University Press, 1971).

There are further selections from Marx's early writings in David McLellan, ed., *Karl Marx: Early Texts* (Oxford: Blackwell, 1971); and in Lloyd Easton and Kurt Guddat, eds., *Writings of the Young Marx on Philosophy and Society* (New York: Anchor Books, 1967).

The German Ideology, Part I, with selections from Parts II and III; edited with an introduction by C. J. Arthur (London: Lawrence and Wishart, 1970).

The Poverty of Philosophy (New York: International Publishers, 1963).

The Communist Manifesto, Centenary edition of the English translation of 1888, together with the prefaces written by Marx and Engels for various editions, and an Introduction by Harold J. Laski (London: George Allen & Unwin, 1948; New York: Pantheon Books, 1967).

The 18 Brumaire of Louis Bonaparte (London, George Allen & Unwin, 1926).

Marx's Grundrisse, ed. David McLellan (London: Macmillan & Co., Ltd., 1971). See also the translation of one long section of the *Grundrisse* in Eric Hobsbawm, ed., *Karl Marx: Pre-Capitalist Economic Formations* (London: Lawrence and Wishart, 1964).

A Contribution to the Critique of Political Economy, Introduction by Maurice Dobb (London: Lawrence and Wishart, 1971).

Capital, Vols. I–III (London: Lawrence and Wishart, 1970).

The Civil War in France (Peking: Foreign Languages Press, 1966).

Theories of Surplus Value (London: Lawrence and Wishart, 1969–72).

There is a selection from the whole of Marx's writings, considered in their relation to sociology, in T. B. Bottomore and Maximilien Rubel, eds., *Karl Marx: Selected Writings in Sociology and Social Philosophy* (London: Watts and Co., 1956; New York: McGraw-Hill Book Company, Inc., 1964).

CONTRIBUTORS

TOM BOTTOMORE taught for a number of years at the London School of Economics and Political Science, was Head of the Department of Political Science, Sociology, and Anthropology at Simon Fraser University in British Columbia, 1965–67, and is now Professor of Sociology in the University of Sussex. His writings include *Sociology: A Guide to Problems and Literature*, *Elites and Society*, *Classes in Modern Society*, and *Critics of Society: Radical Thought in North America*.

H. B. ACTON was Professor of Philosophy in the University of London, and is now Professor of Moral Philosophy, University of Edinburgh. His writings include *The Illusion of the Epoch: Marxism-Leninism as a Philosophical Creed*, *What Marx Really Said*, and *Kant's Moral Philosophy*.

SHLOMO AVINERI has taught for many years at the Hebrew University of Jerusalem where he is now Professor of Political Theory. His works include *The Social and Political Thought of Karl Marx* and *Hegel's Theory of the Modern State*.

ISAIAH BERLIN was Chichele Professor of Social and Political Theory, University of Oxford, and is now President of Wolfson College, Oxford. He has been Visiting Professor in the University of Chicago, Harvard University, and Princeton University, and Schweitzer Professor of the Humanities at the City University of New York. His writings include *Karl Marx*, *Historical Inevitability*, and *Four Essays on Liberty*.

BENEDETTO CROCE (1866–1952) was the most influential Italian philosopher of his time, an interpreter of Vico and Hegel who devoted his attention especially to the philosophy of history and to aesthetics. His major writings include the four volumes of *Philosophy of Spirit*, *History as the Story of Liberty*, and his early essays on Marxism, collected in the volume *Historical Materialism and the Economics of Karl Marx*.

LESZEK KOLAKOWSKI taught philosophy in the University of Warsaw. He played a prominent part in the Polish revolt against Stalinism in October 1956, and became widely known as an original and critical Marxist thinker. In 1966 he was expelled from the Polish Communist Party and was subsequently dismissed from his teaching post in Warsaw. He is now at All Souls College, Oxford. His writings include *Philosophy and Everyday Life*, *Religious Consciousness and the Church Affiliation*, and *Marxism and Beyond*.

GEORGE LICHTHEIM is well known as a writer on Marxism and on current politics. His works include *Marxism: An Historical and Critical Study*, *Marxism in Modern France*, *The Origins of Socialism*, and *Imperialism*.

GEORG LUKÁCS (1885–1971) was one of the outstanding Marxist philosophers of this century. Minister for Education in the short-lived Hungarian Soviet of 1919, then in exile in Vienna and Moscow, he returned to Hungary in 1945 and became Professor of Aesthetics and Philosophy of Culture at Budapest University, but had to go into exile again for a brief period after taking part in the Hungarian revolt of 1956. His principal writings are *The Theory of the Novel, History and Class Consciousness, The Young Hegel,* and *The Historical Novel.*

RALPH MILIBAND taught for many years at the London School of Economics and Political Science and is now Professor of Politics in the University of Leeds. He is coeditor of the annual *Socialist Register,* and his books include *Parliamentary Socialism* and *The State in Capitalist Society.*

STANISLAW OSSOWSKI (1897–1963) was Professor of the Theory of Culture at the University of Lodz, and afterwards at the University of Warsaw. During the German occupation of Poland and the following Stalinist period, he continued to teach sociology clandestinely. His best-known work (the only one available in English) is *Class Structure in the Social Consciousness.*

KARL RENNER (1870–1950) was a leader of the Austrian Social Democratic Party and a prominent member of the group of Marxist thinkers who became known as the "Austro-Marxists." He became Chancellor of the first Austrian Republic in 1918, and again in 1945 was appointed Chancellor (later President) of the second Republic. His principal writings are *The Institutions of Private Law and their Social Functions, Marxism, War and the International,* and *Man and Society.*

JOSEPH A. SCHUMPETER (1883–1950) was one of the leading economists of his generation. Professor at the Universities of Graz and Bonn, he was subsequently Professor of Economics at Harvard University. His major works are *The Theory of Economic Development, Imperialism and Social Classes, Business Cycles, Capitalism, Socialism and Democracy,* and *History of Economic Analysis.*

HILDE WEISS attended the universities of Berlin, Jena, Frankfurt, and Paris, and published in 1936 *Les Enquêtes Ouvrières en France entre 1830 et 1848.* She now teaches sociology at Brooklyn College, New York.